Personal Values
and Consumer
Psychology

Personal Values and Consumer Psychology

Edited by
Robert E. Pitts, Jr.
University of Mississippi
Arch G. Woodside
University of South Carolina

LexingtonBooks
D.C. Heath and Company
Lexington, Massachusetts
Toronto

Library of Congress Cataloging in Publication Data

Main entry under title:
  Personal values and consumer psychology.

  Includes index.
  1. Consumers—Addresses, essays, lectures. 2. Values—Addresses,
essays, lectures. I. Pitts, Robert E. II. Woodside, Arch G.
HF5415.3.P45   1984   658.8′342   83–48123
ISBN 0–669–06937–X
ISBN 0-669-09807-8 (pbk.)

Second printing, November 1984

Published simultaneously in Canada

Printed in the United States of America on acid-free paper

International Standard Book Number: 0-669-06937-x Casebound

International Standard Book Number: 0-669-09807-8 Paperbound

Library of Congress Catalog Card Number: 82-48123

Contents

Contents

Contents

Preface

Historically, the value systems which individuals hold have been thought to be a major influence on human behavior. Generally defined as relatively abstract life-shaping standards and goals, personal and group values have been examined as an important link to understanding human behavior in anthropological, sociological, and psychological contexts.

In recent years, personal values have become generally accepted as elemental influences in consumer psychology. Values have been related both theoretically and empirically to motives, economic values, beliefs, and attitudes, as well as purchases for product categories and brands. In fact, such well-respected authorities as John Howard of Columbia University contend that if we know a consumer's value structure, we possess knowledge of the basic linkage leading to purchase. In light of this interest in personal values, value monitors have been included in many firms' environmental scanning programs as indicants of potential changes in consumers' marketplace behaviors. Personal values also are becoming recognized as important additions to lifestyle and psychographic segmentation studies.

It is because values are so abstract and so central, however, that application of value concepts is complicated. A single value may be linked to several elements of the decision process in a very complex manner. Further, the same belief, attitude, or behavior may in fact be an outgrowth of different values in different individuals. Thus, personal values must be viewed as somewhat abstract, complex constructs capable of providing underlying continuity to beliefs and behavior.

The specific impetus for this volume grew out of a workshop on personal values and consumer psychology held in the early summer of 1983 on the campus of the University of Mississippi. Jointly sponsored by the American Psychological Association's Division 23 and the American Marketing Association, the workshop brought together interested academicians from marketing and social science, as well as practitioners with value application experience or interests. Papers from the workshop and contributions from other leading authorities in consumer psychology are presented in this book to provide a broad view of personal values and consumer psychology. The papers provide a view of the impact of personal values on the consumer, the mechanisms through which value research may be conducted, and some of the applications of values currently being used. Attention is also given to ethnic, racial, and other subcultural related value differences as they pertain to the consumptive process.

A book such as this requires the efforts of a large number of people. The authors represent a wide cross section of disciplines. They were drawn from the leading authorities in the use and theory of personal values in their respective fields. Their cooperation and encouragement has made them friends, as well as respected colleagues.

We are especially indebted to Dr. Leon Schiffman for his assistance in coordinating the VALS and AT&T based contributions.

The conference and much of the work on this book was done by the School of Business Administration, University of Mississippi. The early editorial and assembly work was performed superbly by Ann Canty, with the later assistance of John Tsalikis. Ms. Judy Johnson served as the project secretary.

Part I
Personal Values and
Consumer Psychology

Part I presents an introduction and review of the use of personal values in consumer psychology. Each chapter examines personal values from a distinctively different viewpoint.

In chapter 1, Howard and Woodside position personal values as an integral component in the consumer decision process. The concept of relevant values and that of linking specific values to the evaluation of certain product attributes in the purchase decision is discussed. In the model presented, values are shown to influence problem recognition, the search for information, and beliefs.

Munson explores measurement and application issues in chapter 2. The chapter offers an overview across psychology, sociology, and organizational and consumer behavior. A value paradigm distinguishing between values, attitudes, and behavior is also presented. Munson raises several important issues in measurement and application.

Chapter 3 presents an integration of values and lifestyles as operationalized through the VALS methodology. Holman introduces the nine value and corresponding lifestyle profiles commercially supplied through SRI International. In-depth interviews by researchers at Young and Rubicam, Inc. are used to provide insight into each value type.

In the closing chapter of this section, Pitts and Woodside present a study of values as explanatory variables in market segmentation. In the first part of the study, values are used to identify benefit segments for two specific product decisions. Next, Howard's hypothesized terminal value to product class and instrumental value to brand-within-class relationships are explored. Using a range of frequently applied segmentation criteria, values are shown to be externally effective variables in segmentation.

1 Personal Values Affecting Consumer Psychology

John A. Howard and
Arch G. Woodside

The complexity of consumer psychological problems depends in large part on the consumer's level of learning about the problem. Economists, psychologists, and marketing scholars tend to think of the buyer's process of learning about products and solving buying problems as occurring in three stages: extensive problem solving (EPS), limited problem solving (LPS), and routinized response behavior (RRB). A consumer learns about buying problems and what actions to take through experience and knowledge of information about the problem. When a consumer recognizes a buying problem and has had little or no experience or knowledge of product information, an *extensive problem solving* stage of learning exists. The consumer is buying an unfamiliar brand in an unfamiliar product class. If the consumer is buying an unfamiliar brand in a familiar product class, this is the stage of *limited problem solving*. When a consumer recognizes a buying problem as one with which there is prior experience buying and using the brands in a product class, a *routinized response behavior* stage of learning exists. This is buying a familiar brand in a familiar product class.

These three learning stages are related to three different buying problems.

Learning Stage	Buying Problem
EPS	Is this product for me?
LPS	Is this brand for me?
RRB	Is this the situation for me to buy?

Is This Product for Me?

In the EPS learning stage, a buyer recognizes a buying problem for the first time or the buyer is made aware of a new product class. Similarly, the buyer may be considering buying a brand in a product class which he purchased some time ago and has forgotten much of his prior knowledge and experience in buying the brand. Thus, three situations are likely to produce an EPS learning stage for buyers.

Buying Problem Situation	Example
Recognizing a buying problem for the first time	Teenager buying his first pack of cigarettes
New product class awareness	First learning about pocket calculators in the late 1960s
Buying a product again after forgetting much about the previous purchase experience	An older couple shopping for living room furniture to replace the furniture bought ten years ago

In EPS learning stages, buyers are first likely to ask themselves a very basic question before searching for information and forming their beliefs toward a product and purchasing the product. Buyers ask themselves, "Is this product for me?" "Am I the type of person that wants to buy and use this product?" is another way of phrasing this question.

Asking "Is this product for me?" is the person's attempt to relate the buying problem to his own value system. A *value* is an enduring belief about how good a particular broad class of activities and things are for you. For example, having an exciting life may be a very important value for one person while having a comfortable life may be a more important value for another person.

Certain products and activities may fit a person placing an exciting life high in importance (e.g., motorcycles, participating in outdoor sports, hunting), while other products and activities may fit another person placing a comfortable life high in importance (e.g., a home in the country, reading fiction, watching outdoor sports).

Thus, values affect a buyer's recognition of a problem. Values are the broad functions common to all personalities. A value is either consciously or unconsciously a standard or criterion for guiding behavior (Rokeach 1969).

The generally accepted definition of value has two parts: (1) an enduring belief that a specific mode of conduct is personally or socially preferable and (2) an enduring belief that a specific end-stage of existence is personally or socially preferable. Preferable modes of conduct are called *instrumental* or *doing values*, while *terminal* or *being values* are preferable end-states of existence. Instrumental values are more stable than attitudes, but less stable than terminal values. An individual's ranking (hierarchical organization) of the values represents his or her personal *value system*.

People can be grouped according to the degree of similarity of their value systems. Persons within groups having similar value systems are likely to have similar answers to the question "Is this product for me?" The answers to this question are more likely to be different between groups of people having different value systems. Also, persons in one group with similar value systems are likely to have different socioeconomic characteristics than a second group of persons with different value systems. For example, in one study, persons who ranked a sense of accomplishment, self-respect, and freedom as particularly high terminal values were more likely to be college graduates, earning income above $40,000, and professionally or manageri-ally employed (Pitts 1977).

In order for values to perform their role in guiding choices of products, a buyer must ask, "What are the important characteristics of the product and of using the product?" "How do these characteristics relate to my value system?" Thus, a person attempts to learn basic information about products in EPS learning stages to answer the question "Is this product for me?"

The characteristics about a product which the buyer finds to be impor-tant are called *choice criteria*. These are criteria for choosing among the brands of a particular product class. Choice criteria for three product classes are provided in table 1-1. Consumers are not likely to use many choice cri-teria to evaluate brands in a product class. In fact, consumers are likely to select five plus or minus two criteria for evaluating a product (Campbell 1969; Jarvis and Wilcox 1974; Simon 1974). Usually consumers consider only a few product characteristics to be important enough to be their choice criteria.

The key point is that different consumers form different choice criteria according to their value systems. Two value systems related to the product class of deodorants are shown in figure 1-1. The relationships shown were found from one research study using the 18 terminal and 18 instrumental values developed by Rokeach (1969). Consumers grouped into value system 1 had a specific subset of values related to a specific set of choice criteria, as shown in figure 1-2. For these customers, the relevant choice criteria for

Table 1-1
Lists of Choice Criteria for Three Product Classes

Automobiles	Deodorants	Recreation Travel
Price	Prevents odor	Cost
Economy of operation	Prevents wetness	Accessibility
Exciting to drive	Fragrance or scent	Activities for a group
Style	Long lasting	Good food
Luxurious or plush interior	Does not stain	Relaxation
Dependability	Not sticky	Physical exercise
Interior space	Easy to use	Educational benefits
Prestige	Does not irritate	Comfortable accommodations
Performance	A familiar type	Good for the whole family
Friends own same type	Price	Excitement

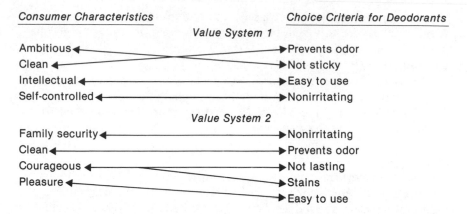

Source: Developed from Robert E. Pitts, "The Influence of Personal Value Systems on Product Class and Brand Preferences—A Segmentation Approach," unpublished doctoral dissertation, University of South Carolina, 1977, p. 131 and Robert E. Pitts and Arch G. Woodside, "Personal Value Influences on Consumer Product Class and Brand Preferences," *Journal of Social Psychology,* 119 (1983), pp. 37–53.

Figure 1–1. Value Systems Related to Choice Criteria for Deodorants

deodorants are prevents odor, not sticky, easy to use, and nonirritating. Consumers with value system 2 use a somewhat different set of choice criteria for the deodorant product class, although some overlap in choice criteria between the two groups is shown in figure 1–2. Notice in both parts of figure 1–2 that the instrumental value of clean is related to the same choice criteria (prevents odor) for both groups.

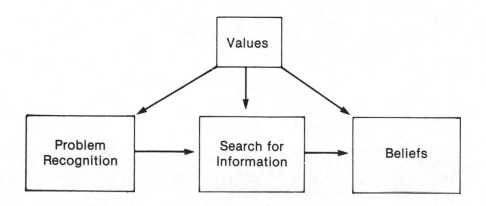

Figure 1–2. Values and Solving Buying Behavior Problems

Two-headed connecting arrows are used to indicate: (1) having particular values causes the consumer to use particular choice criteria in judging the product class because (2) these choice criteria serve these particular values.

Relevant values are those that consumers believe apply when solving problems. If a product class is not found to relate to a consumer's value system, the product class will be ignored by consumers in solving their buying problems. Values, then, affect a consumer's problem recognition, search for information, and beliefs, as shown in figure 1–2.

Values affect beliefs in the sense that values give rise to particular choice criteria for a product class. Beliefs are the buyer's positioning of a brand in that class based on those choice criteria. Consumers do not think about and form beliefs toward all the attributes related to a product. Consumers form beliefs concerning a product and brands for a limited number of attributes, usually three or four attributes. Thus, values affect beliefs by helping the consumer determine the choice criteria for evaluating brands in a product class. The consumer's beliefs are evaluations of where a brand is located on choice criteria.

Do values affect attitudes, intentions, and purchase behavior directly? No, according to figure 1–2 and the research evidence available, values have only an indirect affect on attitudes, intentions, and purchase behavior (Howard 1977).

The study of values is useful for marketing management in designing products which conform to specific sets of choice criteria. For example, a spray-powdered deodorant with a high price can be developed for a segment of consumers with similar value systems. A low-priced roll-on antiperspirant can be developed for consumers with value systems different from the first group of consumers. Value systems can be used in writing advertisements. Values have been related to consumers' beliefs about the stores in which they choose to shop (Stone 1954).

The following commercial claim shown on television reflects one marketing attempt to relate consumer values to an automobile brand.

"Are you the sporty type or a bit conservative? It doesn't matter.
Toyota has the car to fit your style" (values) (WIS-TV 1978).

Brand identification should be considered when communicating with buyers. In order to think about purchasing a car, a buyer must have some way of identifying it. He often uses the brand name, such as Chevrolet Nova, but he needs more than this to recognize it when he sees it. He uses the physical characteristics. In addition, he needs these physical characteristics to think about the brand. For example, the consumer has difficulty forming an attitude toward a brand unless he knows some of its physical characteristics.

Just as with choice criteria, however, he doesn't need many physical characteristics, just a few. Typically, two or three are adequate for the consumer to make a brand identification.

Instant Breakfast	*Vegetable Bacon*
Powdered	Picture on package
Comes in a box	Kind of package
Comes in many flavors	Size of package
You drink it	Whether refrigeration required
Package in individual portions	

Thus, something labeled instant breakfast that is powdered, comes in a box with several flavors packaged in individual portions, and that you drink is to the buyer instant breakfast.

Just as with attitude, which results from beliefs about where the brand is located in choice criteria, *brand identification* results from beliefs about where the brand is located in physical criteria. To complete the picture, beliefs and brand identification are shown in figure 1–3. Search for information causes these identifying beliefs, the beliefs cause brand identification, and brand identification causes attitude, as shown in figure 1–3 (Laroche and Howard 1980).

Having discussed attitude and brand identification in general terms, let us turn now to the specifics of how beliefs about choice criteria are converted to attitude. "Is this brand for me?" includes two parts: "What does this brand offer that is relevant for me?" and "Do I prefer what this brand offers?" The first part refers to forming beliefs about the brand for a set of choice criteria. The second part refers to evaluating the beliefs in order to form an attitude. For example:

Forming the Belief	*Evaluating the Belief*
Is the Chevette a low-priced automobile?	Do I want a low-priced, medium-priced, or high-priced automobile?
Is the Chevette economical to operate?	Do I want an automobile that is economical to operate?
Is the Chevette a prestige automobile?	Do I want a prestige automobile?

If a buyer answers yes to these six questions, then the buyer will be likely to buy a Chevette, assuming the attributes of price, economy of operation, and prestige form the buyer's entire set of choice criteria. Even if all the answers are yes, the buyer may decide not to buy if another brand is believed to have the preferred levels of attributes to a greater extent than Chevette.

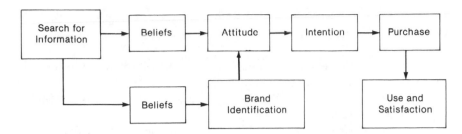

Figure 1-3. Eight Events in Solving Buyer Behavior Problems

Note also that the buyer would be likely to buy a Chevette if the answers to all the questions were no, assuming the three attributes were the entire choice criteria. For example, the consumer does not believe the Chevette is a low-priced automobile and he does not want a low-priced automobile, he would therefore evaluate Chevette positively on the price attribute.

When the belief is that the brand has a particular level of an attribute and the consumer does not prefer that level, then the brand is evaluated negatively for that attribute. For example, if you believe that Chevette is a low-priced automobile and you do not prefer a low-priced automobile, you would evaluate Chevette negatively on price. (The opposite would also produce a negative evaluation. Here, the brand does not have a specific level of a product attribute and this level is preferred.)

A buyer forms his attitude toward buying a brand by answering the question "Is this brand for me?" Attitude is the overall positive or negative feeling toward the brand and toward buying the brand.

Is This Brand for Me?

Buyers in the EPS learning stage develop choice criteria for evaluating a product class. If the buyer decides that the choice criteria related to a product also relates significantly to his value system and he has a need to buy the product, a second question needs to be answered—"Is this the brand for me?"

For most product classes, buyers are offered several alternative brands to evaluate. Buyers use their choice criteria formed in the EPS learning stage to decide whether or not to buy the brand. For example, if price, prestige, and economy of operation are a part of a buyer's choice criteria for automobiles, the buyer will judge a brand by asking

1. What is the brand's price? Is the price high, medium, or low compared to other brands?

2. Does the brand offer me low, medium, or high prestige?
3. Does the brand provide economy of operation?

The consumer's answers to these questions are his beliefs toward the brand. Forming beliefs toward a brand in a product class is a step toward forming an attitude toward the brand. By this we mean an attitude toward buying or not buying the brand.

Forming beliefs toward a brand also occurs in the limited problem solving (LPS) learning stage. Buyers in LPS have a much simpler task than those in EPS because they use existing choice criteria to form beliefs about a new brand in a familiar product class. This is also true for a brand which has existed for some time, but the buyers have just learned about it recently. This is the key point in LPS—the buyer does not need to develop new choice criteria in forming his beliefs, but instead he uses the choice criteria that he developed earlier for other brands in that product class.

Notice in the example of three choice criteria for automobiles that each criterion had two or more levels: low, medium, and high for price and prestige, and economical versus noneconomical operation. This is an important point. Each choice criterion has two or more levels. A belief is the buyer's perception of the level of the choice criterion for the brand. For example, the belief that the Chevette is a low-priced automobile is the perception of a low level for the choice criterion of price for the brand Chevette. The attitude toward the act of buying a Chevette is produced from the beliefs about the consequences of buying a Chevette and whether or not these consequences are preferred (evaluating the beliefs).

Thus, the LPS learning stage includes only forming beliefs, evaluating these beliefs, and forming the attitudes toward brands. It does not include forming the choice criteria, which is done in EPS. Forming positive attitudes toward buying a brand usually leads to forming an intention to purchase greater than zero.

Is This the Situation for Me to Buy?

Consumers in routinized response behavior (RRB) have already acquired a great deal of knowledge and experience with brands in a product class related to solving a particular buying problem. They have been buying some of the brands in the product class and are familiar with others in it. Choice criteria, beliefs, and attitude have been learned before consumers behave in a RRB manner. Whether or not the buyer is in a buying situation for the brand is the dominant issue in RRB.

When a cigarette smoker runs out of cigarettes, he is likely to follow a routinized response behavior and purchase a preferred brand. Running out of cigarettes is a situational variable, and this variable plays an important role in RRB.

A housewife may buy a certain brand of cereal at the supermarket on Saturday with little prior thought. "I always shop on Saturday at this supermarket, and I always buy this brand of cereal when I shop" may be her routinized decision rules.

Similar RRB may be observed for purchasing managers buying supplies in industrial firms. Each month a standard order of the same size will be placed with the same suppliers for the same supplies as the order placed the month before.

RRB is likely to include different choices of behavior by the consumer depending on situational conditions. Consider a housewife asking if her favorite brand of coffee was within 5 cents a pound of other preferred brands: if yes, she purchased her favorite brand; if no, she purchased the cheapest brand in her preferred set. RRB is the most common behavior for frequently purchased, low-priced items, such as those found in supermarkets or among purchases of industrial supplies.

Heavy users of frequently purchased, low-priced products often use the product in the same situations. These situational-product-use scenarios can be studied to differentiate heavy users from light users or one segment of heavy users from other heavy user segments.

One researcher recommends using observational studies to discover whether different usage situations exist and whether they are determinant, in the sense that they appear to affect the importance of various product characteristics (Dickson 1983). Standardized questions also have been used to measure the impact of situations on product usage and brand choice. For example, in one study, agreement by adult males to the following statement was found to be related to heavy beer drinking: One of the greatest pleasures of life is sitting down in front of the TV at night (Bearden, Woodside, Ronkainen 1977). This study indicated that one brand, Budweiser, was associated with drinking beer in social situations while another, Schlitz, was associated with drinking beer while watching television.

Summary

Solving buying behavior problems includes answering three basic questions:

1. Is this product for me?
2. Is this brand for me?
3. Is this the situation for me to buy?

These three questions relate to three learning stages in buying behavior: extensive problem solving (EPS), limited problem solving (LPS), and routinized response behavior (RRB). The use of the concepts of values and choice criteria are central to answering the first question. Forming and evaluating beliefs and attitudes about brands are used to answer the second question. You will recall there is some overlap in that in both EPS and LPS beliefs about brands must be formed in order for the buyer to actually purchase a brand. Situational variables, such as local price and availability, are used to answer the third question.

References

Bearden, William O., Arch G. Woodside, and Ilkka Ronkainen. "Contributions of Demographics, Psychographics, and Consumer Beliefs in Buyer Behavior Research." *Proceedings of the 4th International Research Seminar in Marketing*. Aix-en-Provence, France: Universite d'Aix-Marseille, 1977. Pp. 16–30.

Campbell, P.M. "The Existence of Evoked Set and Determinants of Its Magnitude in Brand Choice Behavior." Unpublished doctoral dissertation, Columbia University, 1969.

Dickson, Peter R. "Person-Situation: Segmentation's Missing Link." *Journal of Marketing* 46 (Fall 1983):61.

Howard, John A. *Consumer Behavior: Application of Theory*. New York: McGraw-Hill, 1977.

Jarvis, L.P. and J.B. Wilcox. "Evoked Set Size—Some Theoretical Foundations and Empirical Evidence." *1973 Combined Proceedings*. American Marketing Association, Chicago: 1974.

Laroche, Michael and John A. Howard. "Nonlinear Relations in a Complex Model of Buyer Behavior." *Journal of Consumer Research* 6 (March 1980):377–388.

Pitts, Robert E. "The Influence of Personal Value Systems on Product Class and Brand Preferences: A Segmentation Approach." Unpublished Dissertation, University of South Carolina, 1977.

Pitts, Robert E. and Arch G. Woodside. "Personal Value Influences on Consumer Product Class and Brand Preferences." *The Journal of Social Psychology* 119, (1983):37–53.

Rokeach, Milton. *Beliefs, Attitudes and Values*. San Francisco: Jossey-Bass, 1969.

Simon, "How Big is a Chunk?" *Science* 183 (1974):482–488.

Stone, Gregory P. "City Shoppers and Urban Identification: Observations on the Social Psychology of City Life." *American Journal of Sociology* 60 (1954):36–45.

Wind, Yoram, John F. Grashof, and Joel D. Goldhar. "Market-Based Guidelines for Design of Industrial Products." *Journal of Marketing* 42 (July 1978):27–37.

WIS-TV, Columbia, South Carolina. November 1, 1978.

2 Personal Values: Considerations on Their Measurement and Application to Five Areas of Research Inquiry

J. Michael Munson

Personal values research in the area of marketing and consumer behavior appears to be enjoying a modest rekindling of interest and enthusiasm. This is evidenced primarily by two factors: (1) the increase in the number of studies investigating values for their relationships to a slowly expanding list of consumer behavior-related dimensions (e.g., brand and generic product choice, charitable donations, media usage, leisure versus work choices, cross-cultural and subcultural applications, and values measurement issues); and (2) the enthusiastic participation and interest shown by marketing academics and practitioners in a recent conference held at the University of Mississippi which focused exclusively on personal values research in consumer behavior. Whether or not this renewed interest in values among marketers portends a true rebirth or simply reflects a temporary infatuation must, of course, remain unanswered until some future date. Nonetheless, a growing number of consumer behavior researchers share in the opinion that such a "values renaissance" is amply deserved and long overdue.

The current study has three purposes. The first is to provide the reader with an appreciation of the richness inherent within the construct of values by offering a brief overview of values research across four disciplines: psychology, sociology, organizational behavior, and consumer behavior. The second purpose is to clarify the distinction between values, attitudes, and behaviors, especially as viewed within the Rokeach (1973) value paradigm. The third purpose, and perhaps the most important one for consumer behaviorists and other social scientists concerned with values research, is to raise several questions regarding three aspects of values research: (1) issues regarding how values should be measured; (2) issues relating to using values as dependent variables; and (3) issues regarding the application of values to cross-cultural and subcultural settings, career and educational counseling, and sales force management research.

Values Research Across Four Disciplines

Throughout recorded history there has been an interest in understanding human values and their role in motivating and explaining behavior. References to values were made by philosophers such as Aristotle and Kant as they discussed aesthetics; Plato, Hobbes, and Rousseau as they deliberated over the problems of government and citizen responsibility; and military, industrial, and political leaders such as Alexander the Great, Eisenhower, Sloan, Ford, Rockefeller, and Morgan as they considered various strategies for motivating and leading their subordinates (Posner and Munson 1979).

The view that values play an important role in human behavior has been widely accepted. Literature from psychology, sociology, and organizational behavior has suggested that personal values may underlie and explain a variety of individual and organizational behaviors. A rather continuous and broad body of research has emerged within each of these three fields over the past twenty-plus years; it serves as impressive testimony to the utility of the values construct in explaining many diverse forms of human behavior. A few brief examples drawn from each of these various disciplines illustrate the point.

In the field of psychology, values have been found to be related to various personality types (Allport and Vernon 1931); dogmatism (Troldahl and Powell 1965); authoritarianism, ethnocentrism, Machiavellianism (Feather 1971; Rim 1970); interpersonal conflict among university students (Sikula 1970); n Achievement, n Affiliation, n Power (Rokeach and Berman 1971); religious background and political identification (Rokeach 1968–69).

Sociologists have found values to be useful in describing society's collective consciousness (Durkheim 1960); differentiating between Gemeinschaft and Gesellschaft social structures (Tonnies 1957); as determinants of social conduct (Blau 1964) and various aspects of social behavior (Rokeach 1968–69).

In the field of organizational behavior, research has shown that values influence corporate decisions on strategy (Guth and Tagiuri 1965); cause many of the "people problems" within organizations (McMurray 1963); differentiate between organizations (Clare and Sanford 1979) and between managers and nonmanagers (Munson and Posner 1980); are directly related to indices of managerial success (England and Lee 1974); and affect satisfaction with a group (Drake 1973).

In comparison with the extensive tradition of values research in the other social sciences, the fields of marketing and consumer behavior have been slow to embrace values research. Aside from the earlier studies of a few researchers (e.g., Rosenberg 1956; Yankelovich 1964; Levy 1981, Kassarjian and Kassarjian 1966), consumer-behavior-related values research did not begin to appear with any degree of regularity until the 1970s. Since then, the bulk of these studies have focused on the relationship between values and either product or brand choice behavior. Most of these studies have utilized the Rokeach Value Survey (RVS) (Rokeach 1973) or some variation thereof. For example, several researchers have found personal values to be related to preferences for particular automobile attributes (Scott and Lamont 1973; Vinson and Munson 1976; Munson 1977; Vinson, Scott, and Lamont 1977). Henry (1976) found values, as measured by the Kluckhohn-Strodtbeck (1961) paradigm, to be related to car ownership.

Along other lines, values have been found to be related to attitudes and behaviors toward charitable donations (Manzer and Miller 1978), and levels of consumer discontent (Vinson and Gutman 1978). A few studies have focused on cross-cultural and/or subcultural differences in values. Vinson and Munson (1976) found significant differences between the values of parents and their college-aged children and their preferences for product attributes. Munson and McIntyre (1978) found that Rokeachian values could successfully discriminate consumers from three culturally diverse groups, as well as distinguish between the stereotypes each culture held of the average American consumer. Values have also been found to be related to a person's choice between work and leisure activities (Jackson 1973), as well as the use of newspapers, magazines, and television (Becker and Connor 1981).

Given the fairly widespread use of the Rokeach Value Survey (RVS) to assess values in many of the studies mentioned here, a few researchers have investigated alternative techniques for assessing Rokeach's values, as well as the psychometric properties of the RVS. Among these, Munson and McIntyre (1979) demonstrated that Rokeach's values can be measured using a Likert-type rating approach rather than the more usual ranking approach; they found that the reliability coefficients using the rating method are not significantly different from those using ranking. However, Reynolds and Jolly (1980) found that rating was less reliable than either rank orderings or paired comparisons procedures, and concluded that a definitive statement cannot yet be made as to the most appropriate data collection method. Finally, Vinson, Munson, and Nakanishi (1976) showed that RVS data derived from ratings and subsequently factor analyzed, yielded factors consistent with Rokeach's conceptualizations of the terminal and instrumental value domains.

Values, Attitudes, and Behaviors

If research on values in marketing is to proceed in a systematic, organized fashion and findings are to be meaningfully compared across studies, it is important that unambiguous definitions be developed for values and such related constructs as attitude and behavior. What are values? How do they differ from attitudes and behaviors?

A review of the values literature discloses numerous approaches to definition and classification. For example, values have been defined by various scholars as being equivalent to, and/or synonymous with, the following: a need, a belief, a motive, any object of interest, a conception of the desirable and not something merely desired, a standard in terms of which evaluations are made, and a cognized belief of what ought to be required by society. Regarding classification schemas, values have been categorized as being asserted or operating; extrinsic, intrinsic, inherent, and instrumental; general and political; or as reflecting various content domains, including religious, social, theoretical, political, economic, and aesthetic. Along somewhat more philosophical lines perhaps, Kluckhohn and Strodtbeck (1961) contend that the individual's values can be indexed by five separate dimensions which reflect his or her value orientations: human nature is good or evil; past, present, or future time perspective; being, being-in-becoming, or doing; subjugation to, in harmony with, or mastery over nature; linearity, collaterality, or individualism.

While there has been no universally accepted definition of what a value is, in recent years a reasonably clear consensus seems to have emerged (Posner and Munson 1979). Posner and Munson observed that values consist of beliefs about what the individual considers right, fair, just, or desirable. As such, values are used, for example, in comparison processes when people establish standards, judge issues, debate options, plan activities, reach decisions, resolve differences, change patterns, or exert influence.

Milton Rokeach (1973, p. 25), perhaps the most seminal scholar on values, defines values as an enduring prescriptive or proscriptive belief that a specific mode of behavior or end-state of existence is preferred to an opposite mode of behavior or end-state. He further suggests that this belief transcends attitudes toward situations. As such, Rokeach contends it is a standard that guides and determines action, attitudes toward objects and situations, ideology, presentations of self to others, evaluations, judgments, justifications, comparisons of self with others, and attempts to influence others.

The distinction between preferable modes of behavior and preferable end-states of existence implies a differentiation between means and ends, or what Rokeach calls instrumental and terminal values. Instrumental values relate to modes of conduct and include such characteristics as ambition, independence, and responsibility. Terminal values describe the individual's desired end-state of existence and include such conditions as leading an exciting life, family security, and salvation.

An attitude differs from a value in that an attitude refers to an organization of several beliefs around a specific object or situation. On the other hand, a value refers to a single belief of a very specific kind (i.e., a proscriptive belief) (Rokeach 1973, p. 18). Whereas the individual may have many thousands of attitudes toward specific objects and situations, he may have only a few dozen values—only as many values as he has learned beliefs concerning desirable modes of conduct and end-states of existence.

Behavior can be viewed as the consequence or manifestation of the individual's underlying values and attitudes (Rokeach 1973). Behaviors, attitudes, and values can be cognitively interconnected in a hierarchical network such that they are psychologically consistent. Moreover, it seems plausible that attitudes and behaviors which spring from more centralized, salient values will be more resistant to change than those based on less central values.

Considerations in Conducting Values Research and Their Application to Specific Areas

Having briefly reviewed some of the major studies which typify prior values research in each of four disciplines and having examined prevalent conceptualizations of values as a construct, as well as the distinction between values, attitudes, and behaviors, we will now turn to various issues and considerations which appear relevant to conducting values research in general, as well as to their application to specific areas of research inquiry.

A review of the marketing literature to date, as well as most of the psychological and sociological literature, shows that virtually all studies have focused on using values only as independent or predictor variables and not as dependent or criterion variables. This one-sidedness in terms of a research orientation is unfortunate and perhaps dangerous, especially in the sense that it can cause researchers to overlook the true role played by values as both antecedents and consequences of human behavior. Researchers should not be cavalier in their hurried dismissal of research which focuses on values as dependent variables. Indeed, Rokeach (1973) has stated quite clearly that values must also be viewed as dependent phenomena. Although some studies have focused on the comparison of value structures along variables such as sex, education level, age, and religion (e.g., Williams 1979), the overriding intent of such studies is usually to demonstrate that values caused some specific attitude or behavior.

In view of the rather recent renaissance of values research among marketing academicians, and its overwhelming focus on values as antecedents rather than consequences of behavior, marketers should give increased attention to research which investigates those factors which might occur causally prior to the development and/or restructuring of the individual's personal value system. Possible antecedents to be considered in this context might be of two major types and categorized as either microindividual or macrosocial variables. The microindividual category would include, for example, variables such as age, education level, IQ, sex, self-image, job performance, and perceived success. The macrosocial category would include variables such as race, culture, subculture, reference group, and family influence.

Approaches to Values Segmentation

It would appear that researchers have a choice in determining how and when values research will be conducted. For example, in attempting to use values to identify target markets, researchers could follow the more traditional and frequently used approach, which might be termed the top-down values approach to market segmentation (TDVAMS). Here, personal values provide the initial basis for market segmentation. Value differences are viewed as the antecedent conditions which give rise to and are responsible for any differences in the various market-related behaviors (i.e., attitudes, beliefs, brand choices, product usage, etc.) observed in the people sampled. Specific demographic and personal variables of the microindividual type and/or the macrosocial type could next be applied to further segment, cluster, or otherwise group those people already found to have similar value structures into even more homogeneous clusters (i.e., similar value structures plus homogeneous age, sex, race, etc.).

On the other hand, researchers could pursue what might be termed a bottoms-up values approach to market segmentation (BUVAMS). Here, microindividual and macrosocial variables would be used initially to segment the market. These segmentation techniques could then be followed by values analysis to reveal, perhaps, even finer homogeneity within groupings.

In order to decide intelligently whether or not to use personal value analysis as a follow-up to conventional demographic segmentation techniques, the marketer would need to have knowledge of the extent to which values served as consequences of the various microindividual and/or macrosocial variables. For example, if previous research from marketing, psychology, sociology, etc., had shown that age, education, sex, or family influence was a significant correlate of personal values, then the marketer would appear more justified in initiating a follow-up value analysis.

In summary, although these notions regarding the existence or importance of either top-down or bottoms-up values segmentation are admittedly speculative and in need of considerable sharpening, hopefully they will serve to call attention to the complexity inherent in the values acquisition process. What is needed is more research investigating those factors which contribute to and/or govern how values are developed, as well as research designed to assess the possible contributions to consumer research of viewing values as a consequence rather than as antecedents of selected variables.

The majority of research studies investigating personal values in marketing, psychology, and organizational behavior are based on the Rokeach Value Survey (RVS). Therefore, several observations regarding two aspects of values measurement using this inventory are in order: those relating to the desirability of ranking versus rating, and those relating to the importance of the subjective ideal implied by the individual's ranking or rating of any value item.

Ranking Versus Rating

Regarding the first apsect, Munson and McIntyre (1979) demonstrated that both terminal and instrumental values in the RVS could be assessed using normal Likert-type scaling procedures and that their respective reliabilities are not significantly different from those based on the ranking procedure. The motivation for the scaling (rating) approach lies largely in the inherent weaknesses associated with Rokeach's (1973) ranking method. Major limitations have been noted by Clawson and Vinson (1977) and Munson and McIntyre (1979).

1. Rank order data provides less information than higher ordered interval or ratio-scaled data in that it forces values which may be viewed as equally important by the individual into separate ranked categories.
2. Ranking ignores differences in the intensity with which a particular value is held. Large differences in the importance attached to two consecutively ranked values cannot be distinguished from smaller differences. For example, the knowledge that the individual may place 40 percent greater importance on the value ranked ninth than tenth is lost with the ranking approach.
3. The ranking instructions (per Rokeach) do not permit the individual to distinguish between the situationally induced need for the value and the socially ascribed status attached to the value. For example, females considering entry into the work force may have a high need for equality and rank it first in importance, whereas their male counterparts feel this need to be much less and, therefore, rank it lower.
4. Rank ordered data preclude the use of more powerful parametric statistical procedures which many marketing and/or other problems in the social sciences require for their analysis.
5. Forced rank ordering which does not allow for ties (as used by Rokeach) can produce ipsativity in the data.

In light of these weaknesses, researchers may find the scaling approach more suitable in many problem applications. This may be true in spite of the fact that the scaling approach, as noted by Munson and McIntyre (1979), can suffer from end-piling (i.e., a respondent's tendency to rate a value toward the end of the scale labeled important). However, such end-piling generally has not been found to be detrimental to the testing of the values-related hypotheses.

The theoretical arguments of Rokeach (1973) for ranking values, although well articulated, may be outweighed in many instances by specific research objectives, problem statements, or pragmatic considerations which demand higher-order measurement procedures. It would seem that the researcher must weigh the trade-offs which implicate the desire for theoretical purity (i.e., ranking) against the need for what may be considered more pragmatic and strategically useful results (i.e., rating). Several studies using the RVS have successfully employed the rating approach (e.g., Munson and McIntyre 1978; Vinson, Scott, and Lamont 1977; Munson and Posner 1979, 1980; Posner and Munson 1981 a,b). Moreover, other studies have shown that the factor structures derived from scaled RVS data yield results which are consistent with Rokeach's terminal and instrumental value domains (e.g., Vinson, Munson, and Nakanishi 1976).

Measuring the Subjective Ideal

An additional aspect of value definition and measurement which appears to need more research attention is that which concerns the distinction between assessing the importance of a given value relative to other values and assessing the extent to which that same given value approximates the individual's subjective ideal.

For example, it is one thing to know that a person places more importance on the terminal value of wisdom than inner harmony. However, it is quite another matter to determine the extent to which that person perceives his actual (i.e., current) wisdom level to be adequate. Measurements of importance should not serve as surrogates for either actual levels or subjective ideals of the specific value. Without knowledge of the extent to which the individual perceives a discrepancy between his or her actual level of value realization and the subjective ideal, the motivational properties to be inferred from any value ranking or rating are considerably less clear. For example, although two individuals may rank (or rate) wisdom to be equally important, each may hold widely differing perceptions regarding their actual wisdom level, as well as their subjective ideal for wisdom.

Future research studies focusing on various aspects of values measurement are needed in several areas. Perhaps most important among these are studies addressing the trade-offs of ranking versus rating of RVS values (Rokeach 1973) with respect to their psychometric properties, as well as such practical considerations as inventory completion time, respondent cooperation and fatigue, the costs of data collection and analysis, and the overall usefulness of results. Replications of earlier work along these lines (e.g., Munson and McIntyre 1979; Reynolds and Jolly 1980) would provide additional insight.

In addition, other methods for both eliciting and analyzing values in the RVS should also be investigated for their appropriateness. Possible approaches include the following:

1. Transforming the respondent's ranked values (1–18 terminal or 1–18 instrumental) as per Rokeach's instructions into standard scores in order to obtain parametric data. Feather (1975) has utilized such transformed ranks and argues for their appropriateness based on the assumption that respondents have greater difficulty ranking values in the middle range than at either extreme of high or low importance.

2. Rating RVS values and then standardizing and/or normalizing the scores prior to subsequent analysis.

3. Having respondents initially rank order values per Rokeach and then follow with a value rating approach. The initial ranking could be expected to sensitize the respondent to all values in the RVS and therefore, perhaps, help to reduce the end-piling which might occur on the subsequent rating task.

4. Working with a reduced set of terminal or instrumental values by dropping out those ranked or rated in the middle range and dealing only with those at the high and low extremes. This may be necessitated in many research designs, especially where values are serving as predictor variables and (a) the sample size precludes consideration of the entire set of 36 value items, or (b) the theoretic basis for hypothesized relations between the total set of values and the criterion variable(s) is inadequate (i.e., only a few values are felt to be of theoretic importance to the criterion).

There is also considerable need for research which addresses how personal values may be linked to product (brand) attribute evaluations and product (brand) preferences and behaviors. Perhaps among the more promising techniques or methodologies for uncovering these linkages are those involving some type of laddering or variations in the repertory grid methodology (e.g., Reynolds and Gutman 1983) and causal modeling. Perhaps refinements in the laddering instructions and/or improvements in the procedures designed to construct the attribute-consequence-value hierarchies can be achieved.

Finally, some attention should be given to the use of anchor point values against which all other value items might be ranked or rated and to the possible use of measures involving the subjective ideal. It would seem that measures of the discrepancies between the individual's actual and subjective ideal level with respect to each value could serve as a relevant predictor of numerous criterion variables, including the following: generic product and store choice criteria, career selection, various indices of job performance, job satisfaction, and perceived congruity of organizational goals with personal goals.

Product and Brand Choice Behavior

Research to date which demonstrates relationships between values and marketing variables (attitudes, beliefs, behaviors) at the brand level as opposed to the generic level, are few. This is not surprising when one recognizes the possibility that in comparing any two people: (1) a different value or value system may lead to the same final behavior (Rokeach 1973, pp. 158–162) or (2) a similar value or value system may lead to a different final behavior and/or attitude. An example of the first possibility would be two people who decided against driving themselves home after drinking alcohol at a party—the first because he places high importance on the values of responsibility and being logical; the second because of dutiful obedience to legal statutes. (The second possibility) is illustrated by an individual who satisfies his need for both an exciting life and independence through a variety of diverse activities, including sports car racing, horseback riding, and listening to classical music.

These examples clearly point up the difficulty for the marketer who seeks to establish clear linkages between specific consumption behavior and the more psychologically removed, underlying values. They also suggest that values may prove more useful in discriminating choice behaviors among alternative generic product/service categories than among specific brands within a given generic category.

In other words, the potential for values to explain significant levels of variance in the consumer's choices between specific brands of such products as coffee, orange juice, or televisions seems much less likely than values' potential to explain variances in choices in such areas as nuclear versus conventional energy sources, attitudes and behaviors regarding birth control, euthanasia, capital punishment, violence in the media, pornography, obtaining a college education, career choice decisions, where and how to spend a vacation, or involvement in various political, social, and religious activities.

Values researchers interested in predicting brand choice behaviors should recognize that values might, at best, be only indirectly linked to most such behaviors. It seems more likely that any one value or value system will operate to influence brand choice through a system of intervening attitudes. Indeed, Howard (1977) suggests that within the Rokeach value paradigm terminal values will influence the consumer's choice criteria for, beliefs about, attitudes toward, and purchase of a particular product class. Vinson et al. (1977) suggest a linkage may exist between general or global values and more domain-specific values relating to product qualities, as well as descriptive and evaluative beliefs. Hence, if explaining various aspects of brand choice is the primary research consideration, the researcher should consider including various procedures to identify and assess relevant intervening attitudes.

Perhaps the most critical questions affecting the use of values in any strategic marketing sense are asked in order to determine the following: what needs the generic product/service fulfills; which specific value(s) may be associated with purchase and usage behaviors; and what are the relevant intervening attitudes which must be identified in order to link consumption choice to underlying values?

Clearly, answering these questions is no trivial task for the researcher. Attempting to show unambiguous linkages (for example, causal paths) between the consumer's values and brand preference requires several types of respondent input and fairly complex data analysis. These attempts are no doubt exacerbated by many factors, including the notion that for many consumption decisions the consumer's value system simply may not serve as the primary springboard for making the purchase decision. Given the hundreds of thousands of products and services from which the consumer must make his choices, it probably makes little sense to assume that more than a small fraction or subset will be of significant relevance to his personal value system.

However, at this juncture in consumer behavior-related values research, it is too early to know what products or services or what distinguishing characteristics may make them candidates for membership in this smaller subset. What is now needed are systematic research efforts which seek to identify those key dimensions that may distinguish objects (e.g., products, services, concepts, etc.) exhibiting strong linkages to personal values from those which do not. One might speculate that some of the following dimensions may prove to be useful in this regard: those related to the object's conspicuousness versus inconspicuousness, value-expressiveness versus utilitarianism (see, for example, Munson and Spivey 1981), susceptibility to reference group and family influence, susceptibility to opinion leadership, and involvement versus noninvolvement.

Cross-Cultural Values

Values lie at the heart of cross-cultural marketing research in that they serve as the springboard from which cultural norms are derived. Norms in turn operate to specify the boundaries within which the individual must behave. In their simplest form, cultural values can be viewed as beliefs which are widely held regarding what is desirable that may also impact the individual's activities (Nicosia and Mayer 1976, p. 67). Some recent empirical studies related to consumer behavior have used the Rokeach Value Survey to investigate cross-cultural value differences. For example, Munson and McIntyre (1978) found that the RVS could significantly discriminate among the values held by people from three diverse cultural backgrounds (Thailand, Mexico, and the United States), as well as discriminate between a culture's self-values and those used to stereotype an American consumer. They also note that the RVS may be particularly appropriate for investigating the potential role to be played by normatively based cultural differences in the formation of international market segmentation strategies (Munson and McIntyre 1979). Since the RVS is relatively inexpensive to administer and easily understood by most respondent groups (both in rating or ranking formats), it could be employed to develop value profiles for either the general population or individualized segments of a specific culture prior to the application of other more complex and costly segmentation techniques.

In spite of the extreme relevance of value analysis to cross-cultural research, marketers should not become deluded into thinking that merely knowing the value profiles (regardless of which values inventory may be used) of a foreign culture is sufficient to become an expert in the ways of that culture. Rather, they must view such value-related knowledge as simply a critical first step toward increasing their own understanding and appreciation of the functionings and inner workings of the foreign culture. This perspective should directly benefit the international marketer by increasing his sensitivity to the relevant norms which dictate how business should be conducted in the target culture, as well as increasing his self-awareness of how cultural values impact consumption within his home culture.

Cross-cultural values research should continue to grow in importance over the ensuing decades in tandem with the expansion of international trade. For international marketers, knowledge of traditional and emerging values may help to signal subsequent cultural and/or environmental change. Marketers must, however, remain sensitive to the notion that as the number and complexity of worldwide trading networks increase, so also does the potential for various forms of values conflict. These conflicts may manifest themselves in ways such as exposure to another culture's values, conflict between traditional and emerging cultural values, and value conflicts precipitated by technological change.

Future research efforts in the cross-cultural area such as that of Kluckholn and Strodtbeck (1961) should investigate the relevance of other value paradigms to consumption behavior. Also needed are studies investigating the extent to which the item content of the RVS is suitably reflective of the relevant value orientations within other cultures (particularly non-Western ones), and the extent to which translation of these value-items into foreign languages alters their individual meanings and the validity of the RVS.

Subcultures and Cross-Subcultures

In view of the close theoretical and empirical linkage between cultures and subcultures, marketers must be aware of the extent to which value systems impact the formation and maintenance of specific subcultures. Perhaps the most promising areas for values research in the United States over the next decade will be the disclosing of normative differences between both the dominant culture and various subcultures, as well as differences between specific subcultures.

A subculture might be viewed as any segment of the dominant culture which preserves important patternings of the dominant culture, but which also develops its own unique patternings of behavior. Subcultures within the United States which may be of most interest to marketers would include those defined by age, religion, marital status, nationality, and geographic location. Values and lifestyle constitute two major mechanisms through which subcultures may exert their uniqueness.

Although conflict and tension might surround the acceptance of the dominant culture's values, and facilitate the formation and maintenance of distinctive subcultural and lifestyle behaviors, marketers must realize that significant differences between the values of the dominant culture and the subculture are not likely to occur across all, or even the majority of value items. Differences are more likely to arise on only a small number of the total value set. This is because the prevalent subcultures (e.g., nationality, race, age, geographic, marital status, etc.) cannot escape (and/or do not wish to escape) from many of the patternings of the dominant culture. Sturdivant (1981) makes a related observation noting that one of the possible pitfalls in conducting subculture research is the propensity to focus on differences rather than on the more numerous shared values. In many instances, any differences may be as likely or more likely to arise due to variations in social class background than to a specific subcultural delimiter such as race, age, nationality, etc.

One must also take care not to overgeneralize about the homogeneity and/or stereotypic behaviors which characterize the members within a specific subculture. For example, upper-social-class Chinese from San Francisco and upper-class Hispanics from San Jose may exhibit greater homogeneity in their consumption and lifestyle patterns than would either group if compared to their respective lower-social-class counterparts.

The above observations regarding the expected number of value differences between a subculture and the dominant culture, coupled with those regarding the propensity of some researchers to overgeneralize about the homogeneity within a subculture, contain a key idea. Specifically, they suggest that it would be of considerable benefit for researchers concerned with subcultural and/or cross-subcultural differences to adopt what might be termed a *step-back* orientation from the all too prevalent tendency to seek and emphasize the homogeneity of behavior within a membership category and the heterogeneity across categories. Because it is normally irrelevant to the main research purpose of most subcultural or cross-subcultural studies, little effort ordinarily is given to discussion of variability within a membership category or of similarities across categories. To the extent that we ignore this step-back orientation and choose in its place one which focuses on a *model-man* approach emphasizing intergroup variations only, we run the risk of developing some largely unsubstantiated and remarkably tenacious and persistent sterotypes (Clausen and Williams 1963).

The practical implications of these observations are threefold. First, they caution marketers against assuming that all members within a specific subculture are homogeneous with respect to their consumption behaviors. Second, they indicate that any differences in consumption patterns observed between a specific subculture and the dominant culture probably can be attributed to a small set of value items. Third, in comparing one subculture with another, any cross-subcultural consumption-related differences might be as likely to arise from differences in such areas as social class or child-rearing practices as they are to arise from value-based differences. Other factors—beside values—for explaining subculture differences serve to considerably complicate values research for the marketer. They increase the probability of rejecting the null hypothesis of no difference in values across those subcultures being compared, when in fact it should be accepted. In summary, research studies to increase an understanding of the values acquisition process, as well as studies which view values as possible consequences of behavior, seem especially important to those doing subcultural research.

*Organizational Behavior and Job Placement, Career
Counseling, and Sales Force Management*

In addition to their more traditional role of explaining differences in cultural and subcultural behaviors and product/brand choice decisions, values offer equal or greater potential for explaining behavioral variations in several other areas relevant to marketers—especially organizational behavior and job placement, career and educational counseling, and sales force management.

The field of organizational behavior is characterized by an increasing number of studies focusing on personal values as important factors underlying such traditional managerial concerns as employee selection, motivation, conflict, and leadership. For example, values have been shown to influence manager-subordinate relationships (Brown 1976), the design of effective selection and reward systems (Mankoff 1974), and the degree of cooperation among work group members (Leifer and Loehr 1978). In a study comparing two values inventories, Munson and Posner (1980) found that both the Rokeach Value Survey (RVS) and England's (1967) Personal Values Questionnaire (PVQ) demonstrated acceptable concurrent validity in their capacity to significantly discriminate between managing and nonmanaging engineers, as well as between more successful and less successful employees. The direction of the differences in the value importance ratings found between managers and nonmanagers or between more successful versus less successful employees seem consistent with the literature and conventional wisdom. For example, managers placed significantly greater importance than nonmanagers on the PVQ values of profit maximization and subordinates, while nonmanagers attributed more importance to the PVQ values of employee welfare and my boss and the RVS values of being cheerful and independent. Employees who saw themselves as more successful than their peers attached greater importance to such PVQ work-related values as ability, competition, and me, and the RVS values of accomplishment, self-respect, and being capable and independent.

Munson and Posner (1980) observed that it is noteworthy that the levels of correct classification shown by the RVS were equal to or greater than those of the PVQ in discriminating managers from nonmanagers and employees with higher from those with lower perceived success. This finding suggests that differences in personal value structures exist across organizational job classifications not only for the more context-specific, managerially related PVQ-type values, but also for the more fundamental, global, and underlying Rokeach-type values.

Along somewhat different lines, in research of relevance to career and educational counseling and corporate recruiting strategy, several studies have reported sex-related differences in personal value structures (Rokeach 1968; Mahoney 1975; Posner and Munson 1981a), as well as value differences between university students, faculty, and corporate recruiters (Posner and Munson 1981b).

One key implication of these studies is the notion that faculty members, college career counselors, and corporate job recruiters should all be sensitive to the very real differences which may exist between their own values and those of the students they are advising or recruiting. More honest and open dialogue between the three groups regarding their mutual performance expectations could lead to more satisfying hiring results for all parties.

Collectively, the studies from the fields of organizational behavior and educational counseling suggest personal values research might be fruitfully extended to embrace marketing issues and problems which lie well beyond the more traditional research relating values to product and brand choice behavior or choice criteria. Given that the individual's values can influence his or her work-related behaviors in many ways, knowledge of personal values should prove highly useful to both the marketing and management arms of the organization. Knowing something about an individual's value system is a necessary prerequisite to designing (and probably maintaining) effective organizational motivation systems.

In view of the strong motivational character presumed to be inherent in the values construct and its presumed relevance to career choice, job performance, and work-place behavior, it is surprising that so few marketing studies have investigated personal values for their relation to any aspect of sales force management. Although various facets of sales force performance and satisfaction have been studied within the context of such approaches as expectancy theory (Walker, Churchill, and Ford 1977), exchange theory (Bagozzi 1978), and as a dyadic process (Weitz 1978), there has been no attempt to investigate the effect of personal values on such seemingly relevant areas as sales force selection, job performance, job satisfaction, job tenure, adequacy of reward and compensation plans, and the congruity of organizational goals with individual goals.

Yet it seems quite clear that much of a salesperson's conception of what constitutes desirable end-states or goals (i.e., terminal values) and his or her preferred modes of behaving (i.e., instrumental values) to achieve these goals, are inextricably linked and intertwined with his or her personal value system.

Personal values data may contribute to more effective sales force mangement in at least five major ways:

1. As supplements to other sales force selection techniques (i.e., objective testing, personal interview, background investigation).
2. As possible predictors of job performance, job success, job satisfaction, and job tenure when used in conjunction with such other predictors as personality, job context, and life history variables (Munson and Spivey 1980). Just as vocational interest tests are so often used to match employees and job/career openings, staffing and selection decisions might be supplemented by matching an individual employee's value profile to the value prototype of a new job position, occupation, or career.

3. As indicators of the types of reward and compensation plans which may be required for effective employee performance.

4. As indicators of the types of organizational atmosphere or corporate culture which an employee finds acceptable or repugnant.

5. As an index of the discrepancy between the salesperson's actual (i.e., current) and subjective ideal of the extent to which he or she possesses each value. Such an index of discrepancy (congruity) could be assumed to reflect motivational properties and influence the person's perception of numerous facets of his or her corporate experience, including job satisfaction, performance, tenure, perceived compatibility or organizational goals, and the perceived relevance of either hygenic and/or motivational factors (à la Herzberg) to job performance, satisfaction, reward, and tenure.

It would be of little or no surprise to learn several years hence that personal values have met with greater success in their ability to explain variations in the types of variables related to sales force management and organizational behavior (e.g., job performance, success, tenure, etc.) than they will meet in explaining variations in product and brand choice behavior.

Conclusion

This chapter has sought to provide an overview of values research across four disciplines: psychology, sociology, organizational behavior, and consumer behavior. The intent was not to provide an exhaustive detailing of all or even most of the values research within each discipline. Rather, the intention was more one of trying to give the reader an appreciation for the richness inherent within the values construct by noting its impressive history in explaining so many diverse forms of human behavior. Additionally, this study has raised some issues and concerns relating to values measurement and to using values as dependent variables, as well as raising some considerations for value researchers working in the areas of cross-culture, sub-culture, product and brand choice behavior, career counseling, and sales force management.

Hopefully, in ten to fifteen years when marketing researchers retrospectively assess the contribution of values to explaining consumer behavior, they will be pleased with the progress that will have been made. They might be gratified that what has evolved is a significant body of research which shows the numerous ways in which values relate to specific market behaviors. That which formerly could be described only as sentiment and notion about the significant role played by values in determining consumer behavior might henceforth be touted as fact. The status accorded by many researchers today to the construct of values as the very bedrock for explaining so much of consumer behavior will—at long last—have empirical foundation. For these reasons, we welcome the "values renaissance."

References

Allport, G.W., and P.E. Vernon. *The Study of Values.* Boston: Houghton Mifflin, 1931.

Bagozzi, R.P. Salesforce Performance and Satisfaction as a Function of Individual Difference, Interpersonal, and Situational Factors. *Journal of Marketing Research* 15 (1978):517–531.

Becker, B.W., and P.E. Connor. Personal Values of the Heavy User of Mass Media. *Journal of Advertising Research* 21 (1981):37–43.

Blau, P. *Exchange and Power in Social Life.* New York: Wiley, 1964.

Brown, M.A. Values—A Necessary but Neglected Ingredient of Motivation on the Job. *Academy of Management Review* 1 (1976):15–23.

Clare, D.A., and D.G. Sanford. Mapping Personal Value Space: A Study of Managers in Four Organizations. *Human Relations* 32 (1979): 659–666.

Clausen, J.A., and J.R. Williams. Sociological Correlates of Child Behavior. *Child Psychology,* Part 1. Chicago: National Society for the Study of Education, 1963. Pp. 62–107.

Clawson, C.J., and D.E. Vinson. Human Values: An Historical and Interdisciplinary Analysis. In *Contributions to Consumer Research,* V, edited by H.K. Hunt. Chicago: Association for Consumer Research, (Proceedings), 1978, 396–402.

Drake, J.W. The Backgrounds and Value Systems of Transportation Modeling Project Participants and Their Effect on Project Sources. *Transportation Research Forum Proceedings* 1 (1973):659–672.

Durkheim, E. *The Division of Labor in Society.* Glencoe, Ill.: Free Press, 1960.

England, G.W. Personal Value Systems of American Managers. *Academy of Management Journal* 10 (1967):53–68.

England, G.W., and R. Lee. The Relationship Between Managerial Values and Managerial Success in the United States, Japan, India, and Australia. *Journal of Applied Psychology* 59 (1974):411–419.

Feather, N.T. Value Differences in Relation to Ethnocentrism, Intolerance of Ambiguity, and Dogmatism. *Personality* 2 (1971):349–366.

Feather, N.T. *Values in Education and Society.* New York: Free Press, 1975.

Guth, W.D., and R. Tagiuri. Personal Values and Corporate Strategies. *Harvard Business Review* 43 (1965):123–132.

Henry, W.A. Cultural Values do Correlate with Consumer Discontent. *Journal of Marketing Research* 13 (1976):121–132.

Howard, J.A. *Consumer Behavior: Application of Theory.* New York: McGraw-Hill, 1977.

Jackson, R.G. A Preliminary Bicultural Study of Value Orientations and Leisure Attitudes. *Journal of Leisure Research* 5 (1973):10–22.

Kassarjian, H.H., and W.M. Kassarjian. Occupational Interests, Social Values, and Social Character. *Journal of Counseling Psychology* 12 (1966):48–54.

Kluckhohn, F.R., and R.L. Strodtbeck. *Variations in Value Orientations.* Evanston, Ill.: Row, Peterson and Co., 1961.

Leifer, R., and H.T. Loehr. Relationships of Personal Values with Group Process. In *Proceedings of the American Institute of Decision Science,* edited by R.J. Ebert, R.J. Monroe, and K.J. Roering, 2 (1978):130–132.

Levy, S.J. Social Class and Consumer Behavior. In *Perspectives in Consumer Behavior,* 3d ed. Glenview, Ill.: Scott Foresman and Co., 1981. Pp. 450–457.

Mahoney, J. An Analysis of the Axiological Structures of Traditional and Proliberation Men and Women. *Journal of Psychology* 90 (1975): 31–39.

Mankoff, A.W. Values—Not Attitudes—Are the Real Key to Motivation. *Management Review* 2 (1974):23–24.

Manzer, L., and S.J. Miller. An Examination of the Value-Attitude Structure in the Study of Donor Behavior. In *Proceedings of the American Institute of Decision Sciences,* 12, St. Louis, November 1978, 532–538.

McMurray, N.N. Conflict in Human Values. *Harvard Business Review* 40 (1963):130–145.

Munson, J.M. An Investigation of Value Inventories for Applications to Cross-Cultural Marketing Research. In *Proceedings of the American Institute of Decision Sciences,* 11 Chicago, 1977, 625–626.

Munson, J.M., and S.H. McIntyre. Personal Values: A Cross-Cultural Assessment of Self Values and Values Attributed to a Distant Cultural Stereotype. In *Contributions to Consumer Research,* V, edited by H.K. Hunt. Chicago: Association for Consumer Research, (Proceedings), 1978, 160–166.

Munson, J.M., and S.H. McIntyre. Developing Practical Procedures for the Measurement of Personal Values in Cross-Cultural Marketing. *Journal of Marketing Research* 16 (1979):55–60.

Munson, J.M. and B.Z. Posner. The Values of Engineers and Managing Engineers. *IEEE Transactions on Engineering Management,* E-26, 2 (1979):94–100.

Munson, J.M. and B.Z. Posner. Concurrent Validation of Two Value Inventories in Predicting Job Classification and Success for Organizational Personnel. *Journal of Applied Psychology* (1980):536–542.

Munson, J.M. and W.A. Spivey. Salesforce Selection that Meets Federal Regulation and Management Needs. *Journal of Industrial Marketing Management* 9 (1980):11-20.

Munson, J.M. and W.A. Spivey. Product and Brand User Stereotypes among Social Classes. *Journal of Advertising Research* 21 (1981):37-46.

Nicosia, F.M. and R.N. Mayer. Toward a Sociology of Consumption. *Journal of Consumer Research* 3 (1976):65-77.

Posner, B.Z. and J.M. Munson. The Importance of Personal Values in Understanding Organizational Behavior. *Journal of Human Resource Management* 18 (1979):9-14.

Posner, B.Z. and J.M. Munson. Gender Differences in Managerial Values. *Psychological Reports* 49 (1981):867-881. (a)

Posner, B.Z. and J.M. Munson. Comparing Value Systems of College Students, Faculty and Corporate Recruiters. *Psychological Reports* 48 (1981):107-113. (b)

Reynolds, T.J. and J. Gutman. Laddering: Extending the Repertory Grid Methodology to Construct Attribute-Consequence-Value Hierarchies. Paper presented at the Personal Values and Consumer Behavior Workshop, May 6-7, 1983, the University of Mississippi, Oxford, Mississippi.

Reynolds, T.J. and J.P. Jolly. Measuring Personal Values: An Evaluation of Alternative Methods. *Journal of Marketing Research* 17 (1980): 531-536.

Rim, Y. Values and Attitudes. *Personality* 1 (1970):243-250.

Rokeach, M. *Beliefs, Attitudes, and Values.* San Francisco: Jossey-Bass, 1968.

Rokeach, M. The Role of Values in Public Opinion Research. *Public Opinion Quarterly* 32 (1968-69):547-559.

Rokeach, M. *The Nature of Human Values.* New York: Free Press, 1973.

Rokeach, M. *Understanding Human Values: Individual and Societal.* New York: Free Press, 1979.

Rokeach, M. and E. Berman. *Values and Needs.* Unpublished paper, 1971.

Rosenberg, M.J. Cognitive Structure and Attitudinal Affect. *Journal of Abnormal and Social Psychology* 53 (1956):367-372.

Scott, J.E. and L.H. Lamont. Relating Consumer Values to Consumer Behavior: A Model and Method for Investigation. In *Increasing Marketing Productivity,* edited by T.V. Greer. Chicago: American Marketing Association, 1973, 283-288.

Sikula, A.F. A Study of the Values and Value Systems of College Roommates in Conflict and Nonconflict Situations, and an Investigation to Determine Whether Roommate Conflict can be Attributed to Differing Values and Value Systems. Unpublished doctoral dissertation, Michigan State University Library, 1970.

Sturdivant, F.D. Minority Markets and Subcultural Analysis. In *Perspectives in Consumer Behavior,* 3d ed., edited by H.H. Kassarjian and T.S. Robertson. Glenview, Ill.: Scott Foresman and Co., 1981, 429–443.

Tonnies, F. *Community and Society, Gemeinschaft and Gesellschaft.* East Lansing: Michigan State University Press, 1957.

Troldahl, V.C. and F.A. Powell. A Short-Form Dogmatism Scale for use in Field Studies. *Social Forces* 44 (1965):211–215.

Vinson, D.E. and J.M. Munson. Personal Values: An Approach to Market Segmentation. In *Marketing: 1776–1976 and Beyond,* 3 edited by K.L. Bernhardt. American Marketing Association, (Proceedings), Chicago, 1976, 313–318.

Vinson, D.E., J.M. Munson, and M. Nakanishi. An Investigation of the Rokeach Value Survey for Consumer Application. In *Advances in Consumer Research* IV, edited by W.D. Perreault. Association for Consumer Research, (Proceedings), Atlanta, 1976, 247–252.

Vinson, D.E. and J. Gutman. Personal Values and Consumer Discontent. In *Proceedings of the American Institute for Decision Sciences,* edited by R.J. Ebert, R.J. Monroe, and K.J. Roering. 2, November, 1978, 201–203.

Vinson, D.E., J.D. Scott, and L.M. Lamont. The Role of Personal Values in Marketing and Consumer Behavior. *Journal of Marketing* 41 (1977):44–50.

Walker, O.C., Jr., G.A. Churchill, Jr., and N.M. Ford. Motivation and Performance in Industrial Selling: Existing Knowledge and Needed Research. *Journal of Marketing Research* 14 1977:156–168.

Weitz, B.A. The Relationship Between Salesperson's Performance and Understanding of Consumer Decision Making. *Journal of Marketing Research* 15 1978:501–516.

Williams, R.M. Change and Stability in Values and Value Systems: A Sociological Perspective. In *Understanding Human Values: Individual and Societal,* edited by M. Rokeach. New York: Free Press, 1979. Pp. 15–44.

Yankelovich, D. New Criteria for Market Segmentation. *Harvard Business Review* (1964):83–90.

3

A Values and Lifestyles Perspective on Human Behavior

Rebecca H. Holman

VALS is an acronym for Values and Life Styles, a typology of the American consumer created by Arnold Mitchell of SRI, International (Mitchell 1978). The typology's theoretical roots lie largely in Maslow's need hierarchy (1954) and in the concept of social character (Riesman, Glazer, and Denney 1950). It was as a theoretical typology that VALS was first presented as part of a proprietary program offered by SRI in 1978. The typology remained primarily theoretical until 1980, when the first operationalization was attempted. Prior to then, the only evidence of the existence of the typology was inferential: NORC attitudinal data plus the accumulated years of evidence surrounding the work of Maslow and Riesman.

In the spring of 1980, SRI surveyed a national probability sample of 1,635 individuals. In addition to the 36 items comprising the typology classification system, respondents also answered more than 800 questions about attitudes, finances, media habits, product consumption, and activities. Respondents had first been qualified by telephone prior to their receipt of the questionnaire through the mail. A response rate of 79 percent of those agreeing to participate was obtained. It is from these data that the characteristics of each group reported here were derived.

Since then SRI has fielded another survey, this one in the fall of 1981, to a sample of 2,121. Its purpose was primarily to refine the system for classifying respondents by VALS types. To achieve that goal, more than a hundred attitudinal items were included as were standard demographics and limited product usage questions. SRI had decided, by that time, that one of the well-established annual surveys of media, product, and brand usage would provide a more comprehensive inventory of consumption patterns and would thus serve subscribers' needs better in the future. Therefore, an agreement was made with Simmons Market Research Bureau: VALS classification questions were to be administered to the respondents to Simmons' annual Survey of Media and Markets. For the 1981 survey, 8,600 respondents were classified in VALS terms; the 1982 survey yielded 12,438 respondents. SRI has only recently concluded similar joint ventures with four major commercial suppliers, classifying their respondents by VALS types: National Family Opinion (10,000 respondents now, 100,000 eventually); National Purchase Diary (13,000 members of their national panels); Mediamark (all respondents potentially); and National Demographics Limited (possibly 8 million respondents, available only for direct marketing efforts).

SRI's decision to delegate the product and media survey aspect of VALS types to other organizations undoubtedly derives from its organizational identity. SRI sees itself as a social science organization primarily concerned with human evolution and growth, personal maturity and the future of man within extant socio-political structures. As such, the more pragmatic concerns of many of the VALS subscribers, namely how to market goods and services more effectively, are of less interest to SRI.

The VALS typology, because it has a firm foundation in theories about human behavior and values, is quite different from other commercially available typologies. Most of the others have a structure that is data-driven, the result of massive data-reduction exercises. As such, these typologies are limited by their input, apply only to one point in time for a single population, and contain a relatively fragile basis for hypothesis generation. Because VALS is derived from propositions about human behavior in general (and adult Americans in particular) one is able to speculate about changes over time, other spheres of behavior, and other cultures. The VALS typology forms a basis for generating data to test specific hypotheses, not vice versa.

Young and Rubicam (Y&R), the largest American advertising agency, was one of the charter subscribers to the VALS program. Its researchers have worked closely with those at SRI, sharing not only perspectives on applications, but results of analyses and input to upcoming projects.

The VALS typology is particularly useful for an advertising agency in that it offers a view of people as whole individuals, not as just demographics and/or consumption statistics. It is particularly important that those who create advertisements be able to understand the people in the target audience as complete persons, not just sets of numbers. It was from this perspective that Y&R combined qualitative research with the quantitative database (generated initially by the 1980 SRI survey and coupled with subsequent surveys) to arrive at an understanding of the VALS types not obtainable elsewhere.

The qualitative work consisted of in-depth interviews with people representative of each of the VALS types. Respondents were asked to discuss their personal histories, their current life situations, their relationships with family and friends, their hopes for the future, the things they liked to buy, which entertainment media they liked and disliked, and what was meaningful for them in their lives. Interviews were conducted in participants' homes and places of business. Pictures were taken of selected respondents, their families, possessions, pantries, homes, bedrooms, closets and baths, pets, and anything else that would tell their stories visually. The interviews were transcribed and extracts coupled with the slides, forming what were referred to as profiles. These profiles, when combined with the statistical information about the types, forms a powerful communication tool, plus a multifaceted way of knowing what the types really are. The usual practice is to augment the typical "researchese" of tables and graphs with several profiles typical of the target audience.

An Overview of the Typology

The VALS typology has three main segments, each divided into subgroups depicted in figure 3–1. The first segment is referred to as the Need Driven and

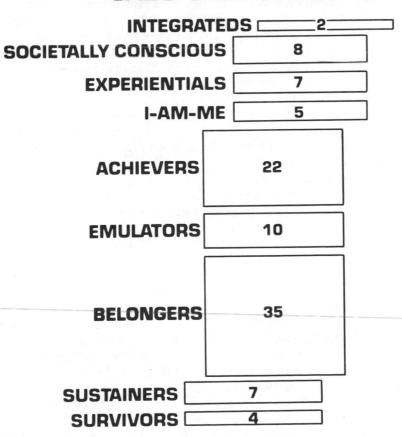

Figure 3–1.   Overview of the Vals Typology

represents the American poor. Here the word *need* refers to physiological needs which, as pointed out by Maslow (1954), take precedence over the higher-order psychological needs until a certain level of satiation is obtained. The Need Driven represent about 11 percent of the American population. The segment is comprised of two types: Survivors and Sustainers.

The major segment of the typology is called the Outer Directed, containing about two-thirds of the American population. The term *Outer Directed* is derived from the concept of social character (Reisman, Glazer, and Denney 1950).[1] For the people contained in this group, psychological needs are best fulfilled by looking to the expectations of others and by adhering to the norms of the society at large. Outer Direction manifests itself in the United States in three lifestyle types: Belongers, Emulators, and Achievers.

Contrasting somewhat with the Outer Directed are the Inner Directed, for whom personal needs and priorities often take precedence over the expectations of others. This group currently contains about one-fifth of the adult population of the United States, but it is a group that has grown most rapidly in the past decade and, under certain assumptions about the future, is likely to be the one to grow most rapidly in the decade to come. It is comprised of I-Am-Mes, Experientials, and Societally Conscious, each representing a different stage of maturity.

A very small fourth segment is referred to by SRI as the Integrateds. Analogous in some ways to Maslow's self-actualizing people (Maslow 1968), they are individuals who have combined the best of outer- and inner-direction into unique and diverse lifestyles. Currently they number about 2 percent of the adult population of the United States.

As the types are presented in figure 3-1, it appears that the typology might also be a hierarchy—not only a statement of what people are, but also a model of how they grow and mature. The strong theoretical foundation in Maslow's need hierarchy (with Need Driven at the bottom and Integrateds at the top) reinforces such a notion (Maslow 1954). While there are hierarchical components, it is not a strict hierarchy. For example, it is rare that Achievers mature into I-Am-Mes; SRI's solution is the Double Hierarchy depicted in figure 3-2. In this model, the traditional developmental path in the U.S. culture is located on the left—the Outer Directed route to Integration. An alternative route, the Inner Directed one on the right, has emerged as a vital force in the United States since the end of World War II. Most of the Inner Directeds were born after World War II and were nurtured in the relative affluence of the 1950s and 1960s. Now they have turned away from the intense materialism that seems to be a correlate of Outer Direction in this culture, to seek gratification in other facets of life.

The developmental aspects of the typology are a fascinating and fruitful area of inquiry, stimulating questions such as:

VALUE AND LIFE-STYLE SEGMENTS (VALS)

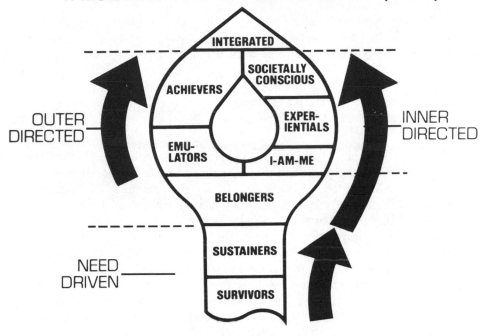

Source: Arnold Mitchell, *Social Change: Implications of Trends in Values and Lifestyles,* Menlo Park, Calif.: SRI International, 1979, p. 9.

Figure 3–2. The VALS Double Hierarchy

What are the generational flows in the typology and how will the children of the Inner Directeds differ from their parents?

What changes in the typology will result from the increasing maturity of the post World War II baby boom?

What within-household accommodations result when one decision-maker is from the right half of the typology and another from the left half?

The investigation of these and other such issues are part of ongoing Y&R research efforts, and serve as key inputs to planning for the future. However, the bulk of the research focuses on characteristics of the discrete segments and how consumer insights provided by the typology offer input into the creation of advertising which touches people. It is with this in mind that the balance of this article focuses on characterizing each type and illustrating how such a characterization coupled with product usage information, leads to a deeper understanding of consumer motivations.

Need Driven

The Need Driven, the poorest people in the U.S. culture, are constrained psychologically by economic circumstances. As they must spend much of their time struggling to obtain the bare minimum needed for survival they have little time for paying attention to psychological needs like love and esteem. The so-called "culture of poverty" is well-documented (Harrington 1962; Irelan 1966; Miller 1966; Caplovitz 1967). SRI has subdivided the Need Driven into two types: Survivors and Sustainers.

Survivors. Survivors are the poorest in the U.S. culture and are, in fact, the elderly poor. They comprise about 4 percent of the adult population and reported median household incomes of $3,200 per year in 1979 (as reported in SRI's 1980 survey). Indeed, none of those classified as Survivors had household incomes of more than $7,500 per year, which was derived largely from Social Security and pensions; of those that worked, half did so on a part-time basis. With a median age of 66, they are the oldest of the VALS types; as with survival statistics for Americans, most are women (77 percent in 1980). Fully 60 percent reported broken marriages, either through divorce or death of a spouse. Twenty-eight percent were nonwhite, living in urban areas. Their education levels are low: 60 percent of those in the 1980 survey had not graduated from high school.

Attitudinally, Survivors show the depressed mentality one might expect to be associated with their demographic profile. They are unhappy because their expectations for a comfortable old age, economically secure with the benefits of their earlier labor, have simply not been fulfilled. Social Security is not enough to support them and they have to make do with less. Many of them live alone; those that have families cling desperately to them, while those that don't yearn sadly for the past. They spend much of their time at home not only because of infirmity, but also because the home is their last refuge against a hostile world. They feel insecure in their ability to cope with the demands that life makes on them. They have conventional views generally, as well as in such areas as whether women can work and still be good mothers, the use of drugs, and the propriety of unmarried persons having sexual relations.

Rose. Rose is a Survivor who was in her early sixties when interviewed. She was a recent widow whose husband had died from a service-related injury, although she said that the Veterans Administration (VA) had refused to acknowledge his condition as being service-related. When he died, the only insurance he left was a $7,500 Veteran's benefit. Rose, having no skills, was unable to find a job and was only able to live for a while on the $7,500. Her first move was to live with an elder sister. When that didn't work out, she moved in with her daughter and son-in-law.

During this time, Rose felt a great deal of anger toward her husband for dying and leaving her with absolutely nothing. In response, Rose turned to alcohol and became an alcoholic. It was through her church that Rose joined an Alcoholics Anonymous (AA) group and finally got control over her life. A person she met in AA was able to intercede in her behalf with the VA, which resulted in a reversal of their position in her husband's case. She started receiving Veteran's benefits of a little more than $200 per month and immediately looked for a new place to live. The one-room apartment she found cost more to rent than she received from the VA, but luckily she qualified for a CETA program which enabled her to live on her own. When the CETA program was cancelled, Rose was fortunate to find a part-time job with the Red Cross, where she was working at the time of the interview.

Her apartment was at the back up two flights of stairs. It was scrupulously clean and neat and she had tried to make the best of it with what little she had left over from paying rent and buying groceries. She couldn't afford many luxuries, but a recent purchase of hand cream was a small indulgence even though it meant scrimping on food that week. She was proud of the fact that she could find bargains in clothing at a nearby Salvation Army thrift shop.

Rose spent a lot of her spare time reading. She checked books out from the public library—it was free—and she kept a Bible by her bedside. She made up the small single bed like a sofa so that during the day the room looked less like a bedroom; she would undoubtedly believe it improper for a lady to receive visitors in her bedroom. The walls were decorated with pictures of her grandchildren, whom she talked about with great warmth. She occasionally baby-sat with them to give her daughter a break. Rose said that this was the only way she could help her daughter; she'd like to do more, but that's all she could. The only furniture she had in the apartment that dated from before her husband's death was his armchair. She kept it to remind her of a better time that she hadn't a hope of returning to.

Sustainers. Sustainers are quite different from Survivors in that for them, hope is not yet extinguished. Indeed, they are angry people, struggling against the odds to break out of their poverty and into the middle class. A slightly larger group than Survivors (around 7 percent of the adult population), their household incomes are also higher, with a 1979 median of $8,600. Their income, however, fluctuates from year to year; they are on and off the welfare rolls as the local economy prospers and suffers. At a median age of 28, about half of the Sustainers are post World War II baby boomers. In the 1980 survey, 54 percent of the Sustainers reported that they were currently married, but a significant number of those (21%) were second and third marriages. Sustainers contain the highest proportion of non-whites (36%), equally divided among blacks and Hispanics. Sustainers, like Survivors, live primarily in urban areas. Sustainers also have low education levels: only 3 percent from the 1980 survey were college graduates.

Sustainers are also unhappy as a group, but their unhappiness has different roots from those generating the Survivors' discontent. Sustainers believe that the system is somehow profoundly biased against them. They are suspicious of others and claim that they are rebelling against their upbringing, as well as things in general. While this is the group that has the largest number of children living at home, they value their family the least of any of the VALS types. Where they seek personal gratification is among their peers who give them the status that the larger society denies them. They value money very highly and spend it when they have it; for Sustainers, there is little benefit in trying to save for a rainy day, perhaps because the rainy day is always today.

Josephine. Josephine was in her mid-30s when interviewed and was living with her five children and one grandchild. When Josephine's oldest daughter had the baby, she was the same age as Josephine was when she was born. Neither woman had ever been married. Josephine took on the added burden of her grandchild because she hoped that this would enable her daughter to graduate from high school only a year behind her class. The family lived in a sparsely furnished apartment in a project.

Josephine expressed a great deal of concern for her children's future, primarily because they didn't do well in school. They had all been classified as slow learners, and she was upset because mainstreaming meant that they didn't get special tutoring like they used to. She didn't really know how to arrange for extra help for them, although she knew it was needed.

While Josephine saw little hope for an improvement in her own life condition, she had encouraged her sons to develop their athletic skills as a way out of their poverty. She was undoubtedly unaware of the very low probability of this actually happening. Arthur Ashe's statement that athletics is the new opiate of the lower-class masses characterizes Josephine's inability to comprehend the reality of a world that she observes from afar.

Outer Directeds

Outer Directeds, because they look to others for a definition of what is appropriate, tend to be very normative—not only establishing, but also maintaining the societal standards of conduct. For many years, Outer Directeds have been a primary motivating force in the U.S. culture. It is from their ranks that both the Middle (or Silent) Majority and the Country's leaders emerge. The Outer Directed's three lifestyle groups are named for basic social needs that characterize primary motivations for their members. Such a characterization is not exclusionary, however. While Achievers, for example, live lives characterized by achievement motivation, they are not the only individuals in the culture with high levels of need for achievement.

Belongers. As their name implies, Belongers are more interested in fitting in than standing out. For them, it is important to know their place and what is expected of them. They also need to know how others fit into the overall scheme of things. Belongers will exert a lot of effort seeing to it that everyone performs up to expectations.

This is the largest group in the VALS typology, representing more than one third of the U.S. adult population. Their income levels are modest (a median of $15,800 in 1979) as are their education levels; most have graduated from high school. They hold blue-collar, crafts worker, and service jobs; many of the women define themselves as housewives and many of the men are retired. Unlike Survivors, however, Belongers retire with pensions sufficient for their ordinary living expenses. At a median age of 52, Belongers are the second-oldest group, although there are large numbers of young Belongers as well. There are more female Belongers than male. This doesn't mean that men shun this group, but instead that women are more attracted to it. There are, for example, as many male Achievers (the group that is predominantly male) as male Belongers. Belongers are mostly married and white, living in rural areas or small towns. Even those who inhabit large central cities probably treat their neighborhoods like small towns, limiting much of their activities to the neighborhood.

Attitudinally, Belongers are among the happiest of the VALS types, very contented with the lives they lead. They are trusting of others and enjoy establishing strong linkages with others in their community. While being a part of a group is important to them, the most important group is their family, of whom they speak with great depth of emotion. They are homebodies, preferring to stay at home rather than go out in the evening for a party. Belongers are also averse to taking risks, not only in fiscal matters but also along personal dimensions. They prefer guaranteed investments and will trade off security against growth at every turn. They are very cautious about trying new and different things. If it was good enough for past generations, it's good enough for them.

Henry. Henry exemplifies a man who has chosen a Belonger lifestyle, probably because of his personal history. Henry's father was born in the United

States, but returned to Germany with his father (Henry's grandfather) shortly after birth, because of his mother's death. As a young man, Henry's father was drafted into the German army during World War I. He announced that he would fight English or Russians but not Americans, since those were his people. Such a statement was tantamount to treason but fortunately, Henry's father had an uncle in the German high command who managed to save him: Henry's father spent World War I at the Russian front. After the war, he emigrated to the United States, settled in New England, and lived there for the rest of his life.

When World War II began, Henry enlisted in the U.S. Army Air Corps. After mustering out of the Army, Henry joined the Army Reserves, eventually rising to the rank of colonel. When age forced him into retirement, he promptly joined the Retired Army Officers Association. Henry went to college on the GI bill and obtained a master's degree from Columbia University. He was offered a chance to teach at West Point, but declined it because it would entail so much traveling, commuting back and forth from his home. At no time did he seriously consider moving his nuclear family to West Point. They lived next door to his parents; his parents needed them; they needed his parents; so why move?

Henry and his wife had six children. Five had moved away from home at the time of the interview and all joined some branch of the military, clearly with their father's approval. He kept in touch with his children by long distance—even the daughter stationed abroad. The telephone bills might be high but Henry considered it money well-spent.

Henry's primary occupation was teaching history at the local public high school. In commenting on discipline problems in the schools, he admitted that while some teachers had problems, he had an easy solution: he identified the offenders and simply threw them out of the room.

Both his truck and his car had CB radios, and he had a home station in the basement of his home. Henry started one of the first CB clubs in the area and was instrumental in community service using CB radios. He also belonged to the local Republican party and proudly displayed a bumper sticker reading "Happiness is a Republican Governor" on his car. Henry, like other Belongers, expressed a great deal of respect for elected officials. He told the interviewer how sad he was during the Watergate debacle and how outraged at the impeachment proceedings against Nixon. He felt that the American public wronged Nixon by not giving him the respect that should accrue to the office of the Presidency.

Henry enjoyed the contacts he had with others in his community. They often exchanged favors of essential services; such bartering undoubtedly had economic benefits, but for Henry, it was the social benefits that prevailed.

Emulators. Emulators are psychologically more mature than Belongers, in that they demand more of themselves as they strive to climb the social class ladder. Belongers are much more content with where events and circumstances take them. The Emulators model much of their behavior after Achievers, the most materially successful group in the culture.

This group is one of the smaller ones, comprising around 10 percent of the adult population. While half of the Emulators had 1979 incomes of more than $17,900 per year, none of them characterized themselves as upper-middle or upper class. Additionally, only about 6 percent have college degrees and almost a third of those from the 1980 survey were college dropouts. Perhaps these statistics reflect the fact that Emulators do not have a great deal of self-confidence. Emulators are young (median age of 28) and live mostly in urban areas. They have diverse marital statuses (only 59 percent reported current marriages) and more than one-fifth are nonwhite.

Emulators are not particularly happy, perhaps because they realize they will not be able to reach the goals they have set for themselves. They tend to blame the system for keeping them back but, at heart, they probably recognize that it is their own inadequacies that detain them. As compensation, they often affect the external trappings of those who have "made it," spending their scarce resources on items that they think display high social status. They love to spend money and often spend beyond their means; they have the highest credit-card balances of any group in the VALS typology. Emulators often display a plethora of contradictions. When asked to characterize themselves, they picked "conservative," even though their attitudes toward issues such as use of drugs, premarital sex, and working women were quite liberal.

Chet. The interview with Chet began in the office of a small electronics manufacturer where Chet worked as a sales representative. After graduation from high school, Chet worked as a furnace repairman until he met his future boss. While repairing a furnace one day, Chet struck up a conversation with a man who recognized Chet as a personable fellow and offered him a job with his new company. Chet accepted the offer, had been with the firm six years, and expected a promotion (his first) to manager in the very near future.

Chet explained that he was very concerned about the impression he made on the job. For the interview, he wore a three-piece suit and a flower on his lapel. He said that he tried always to wear three-piece suits and usually a flower. Accordingly, the guys in the plant named him "best-dressed man," a title they created for him. Chet also had his hair styled and wore a beard, so that he would appear to be older than he was.

On the wall of Chet's bedroom was a poster for Corvette. (Actually, it was a poster-size advertisement.) One might think that this poster served to remind Chet of the material benefits he was striving for but had not yet attained. But in fact, Chet owned a Corvette, so the significance of the poster was initially puzzling. When one reassessed the poster in the context of Chet's life situation the symbolism became clear: Chet had obtained the actual object (the car) but not the other accoutrements of the symbol, namely the glamorous women pictured with the car in the poster.

Chet said that he read very little and rarely watched television, preferring to go out at night to popular nightclubs or to his athletic club. When he did read, he preferred to focus on material which would help him with his career. Chet was clearly trying to prepare for success. He didn't have any immediate plans to seek a formal college education, however, and one wonders if his drive and ambition would be enough in the competitive business environment of his future.

Achievers. Achievers are the successful and success-oriented builders of the American dream. Leaders of business and government, these individuals are very happy with the fruits of their considerable labors and often indulge themselves and their families with the luxuries of life.

Achievers as a group number approximately 20 percent of the adult population and, of this number, approximately 60 percent are males. Their incomes are the highest of all the VALS groups (median income was $32,000 in 1979 terms). Although well-educated (about a third have college degrees), they are not the best-educated of the VALS groups. With a median age of 42, some Achievers are undoubtedly World War II veterans who have bootstrapped themselves to the top of their professions without benefit of a formal college education. Mostly white and married, Achievers inhabit the elegant urban and suburban sections of the country.

A primary characteristic distinguishing Achievers from Emulators is their almost overwhelming self-confidence. Achievers take on the world as a challenge and conceive of themselves as superior players, able to master any situation. They are, accordingly, highly career-oriented, devoting both psychic and mental energy to advancing themselves toward the goals they have set for themselves.

While Achievers accept risk as an opportunity for considerable gain, a primary motive for them is to retain control over their lives and environments. Innovations which demonstrate a marked advantage over what they replace are welcomed; radical change is not. Politically, they are very conservative and conventional.

Stuart. Unlike many Achievers, Stuart had been with one firm throughout his career. Many Achievers, finding their career paths blocked at one company, will move around, always moving upward. Stuart had had an opportunity to change firms (including a promotion and a salary increase) but when the president of his company called to offer Stuart the same package, Stuart decided to stay. He reasoned that when the president called him personally, it was a signal that his personal success would be tied to that of the president's. At the time of the interview, Stuart was the comptroller of his company. Shortly afterwards, he became a special assistant to the president; then executive vice-president; and finally, at age 38, president and chief executive officer.

Stuart lived with his wife and three children in a large suburban house. Stuart explained that they needed more room, especially for entertaining. He said that he felt that by bringing business associates to his home instead of taking them to a restaurant, he would have an advantage over his competition.

For relaxation, Stuart constructed fine-quality furniture in his basement workshop. While it is not typical that Achievers engage in handicrafts, it is true that they become masters at whatever they undertake and Stuart was no exception. His workshop was neatly organized with all the tools necessary to produce professional-quality products.

Achievers will generally buy top-of-the-line products, feeling that they've worked hard and deserve to enjoy the fruits of their labors. Stuart, however, pointed out an important feature of Achievers when discussing a recent purchase of a dishwasher. It was not top of line, but next down. The top model would have cost $80 more and would only have had a few extra buttons that his wife wouldn't use. Achievers are quite willing to spend money when there is a significant price/quality trade-off. Otherwise, they are shrewd purchasers who feel competent to evaluate the utility of their purchases.

Stuart, like many Achievers, brought work home from the office, reasoning that one could not really get ahead in one's career without spending 10 to 12 hours a day at it. He also went into the office on Saturday, where he would be observed working overtime by his colleagues. His attention to his career kept him away from his family more than he would prefer, but he felt that working hard, providing the best for them, was better in the long run.

Inner Directeds

Inner Directeds form a relatively new group in the U.S. culture, emerging primarily from the relative affluence of the 1950s and 1960s and seeking something other than the intense materialism that Outer Direction engenders. While they acknowledge the expectations that others have of them, they reserve for themselves the right not to behave up to expectations. For Inner Directeds, personal priorities often take precedence over the wishes of others.

While the Inner Directeds are currently small in number (approximately 22 percent of the adult population) this group is the one that has grown most rapidly in the past decade and, under certain assumptions about the future, is the one to proliferate in the decade to come (Mitchell 1981). The influence of Inner Directeds also exceeds their numbers. They are the most open to change of all the VALS groups and, consequently, are the source of much innovation. Additionally, they are vocal in asserting their rights and the rights of others, and frequently become the spokespersons for other groups in the VALS typology.

I-Am-Me's. The I-Am-Me group represents a transition stage from Outer to Inner Direction. Typically children of Achievers, I-Am-Me's are in the rebellious stage that many go through when emerging from puberty. Relative to their peers, I-Am-Me's express their rebellion more flamboyantly, exhibitionistically, and egocentrically, thus gaining a lot of attention for themselves.

At any one point in time, I-Am-Me's represent only around 5 percent of the adult population. But, as this is a short-lived phase for most who pass through it, it is characterized by enormous turnover in membership. As many I-Am-Me's either live at home with their Achiever parents or attend college while being supported by their parents, their income levels are low (less than $10,000 per year). This is the youngest group in the VALS typology, with 91 percent under 25. There are also more males than females in this group (64% male). Most are single (98%) and white (95%).

I-Am-Me's are not the happiest of the VALS groups, but their discontent stems more from immaturity than from an ingrained cynicism. They are at the phase of their lives where their elders do not give them the respect they feel they deserve. Accordingly, they seek out their peers, who will grant them the status and esteem that the larger culture withholds. As can be predicted, they are vehemently nonfamilial, greatly preferring to go out in the evening rather than to stay at home.

I-Am-Me's embrace change more than any of the other VALS groups and delight in experimenting with the unconventional. They are spenders rather than savers but, being single, all that they spend goes for themselves.

Veronica. Like many I-Am-Me's, Veronica lived at home with her Achiever parents. She moved back home after completing her college education (she was an art major), but she didn't get a job that related directly to her education. She worked part-time at the cosmetics counter of a large department store. When probed during the interview, she agreed that showing people how to use makeup was "sort of like painting on faces," but that was not her primary motive in seeking the job. Rather, she didn't want to be tied down to something permanent. Being able to leave a job on short notice was a primary criterion for her.

Veronica's car, a Volkswagen Rabbit, was a symbol to her of the personal freedom she sought at this time in her life. With it, she could take off at a moment's notice to get away from home for a day, weekend, or several weeks (all of which she had done). Veronica was clearly resisting growing up, and made an active effort to retain a youthful irresponsibility.

One of her creative outlets was making huge papier mache masks of cartoon characters and Muppets. She told the story of a dirty trick she and three others played on a friend who recently got married. During the formal reception after the ceremony the four of them briefly disappeared to reappear in full costume at a signal from the band leader. She, as Miss Piggy, started dancing with the father of the bride. Veronica said that they didn't have any idea about what the reactions would be, but their friend deserved it. The notion of flouting conventionality would appeal to an I-Am-Me mentality and was undoubtedly a primary motivator.

Veronica was uncertain about her future. She thought that she would move to somewhere distant from her parents and live a life different from theirs, but she was vague about it. At the moment, her artistic interests and her own personal pleasure dominated her thoughts and consumed most of her energy.

Experientials. As I-Am-Me's mature, they often become Experientials. As their name implies, Experientials are interested in direct experience with life, trying out the various possibilities. Unlike the I-Am-Me's, the Experientials have turned their focus from themselves to concentrate on interactions and on specific others.

This is also a small group, comprising only about 7 percent of the adult population. If they are grown-up I-Am-Me's (median age is 28), many have completed their college degrees (more than a third) and have gotten well-paying jobs (median income was $22,300 in 1979). They are equally split among males and females. Experientials have a high (of all of the VALS groups) of 9 percent *mingles* (the Census Bureau's word for unrelated cohabitation). Mostly white, they live in both urban and suburban areas.

Experientials are happy people who have emerged from the disgruntled state typical of I-Am-Me's. Experientials have formed satisfying life conditions for themselves. They obtain most of their gratification from nonwork activities and do not look on their jobs as careers. In Achiever terms, they are unambitious.

Experientials characterize themselves as liberated, experimental, and impulsive. They will try almost anything once, and like to be free to react to whatever life presents them. Accordingly, they dislike being committed and do not seek long-term relationships of any sort, whether work or personal.

Jared. Jared exemplifies a person who had emerged into the Experiential group out of an intense, and prolonged I-Am-Me phase. For the interview, he wore black leather pants and boots, a sleeveless undershirt, and studded bracelets and belt. His hair fell below his shoulders, his beard to midchest. Jared lived with his Belonger parents and obviously derived much gratification from shocking his father (the owner of a fleet of taxicabs) on a daily basis. Nevertheless, Jared showed a growing maturity and acceptance of his father's perspective (even acknowledging the similarities between them). One would predict that Jared would soon drop these external trappings of rebellion, feeling that they had lost their utility.

Experientials tend to have active fantasy lives and to surround themselves with the objects of their fantasies. Jared is no exception: an entire wall of his bedroom was covered with photographs of Marilyn Monroe, a woman he had adored since childhood.

Jared's spirituality took many forms. He believed in the power of astrology, commenting on this several times during the interview. He had also experimented with Eastern religions, but was fundamentally a devout Catholic. He kept a *New Testament* by his bedside and attended Mass regularly.

Jared had a bachelor's degree and graduate credits in speech pathology, but did not work in speech therapy. Rather, Jared chose an occupation that provided him high income for little time commitment, maximum flexibility over hours and location for doing business, and minimum commitment. Jared worked as a hairdresser, moving from shop to shop, and making house (or office) calls.

Like many Experientials, Jared purchased many products for their hedonistic or aesthetic qualities. He had an impressive collection of colognes and body perfumes, used facial moisturizers, and even indulged his love of comfort by purchasing a white Cadillac with white seat covers. His behavior in caring for the Cadillac demonstrated his strong Belonger background.

Jared was a happy, loving person. When asked which of the objects in his room best described what he was, he chose an acrylic "Love" sign. He said that he would one day like to raise a child, but was not necessarily interested in a permanent relationship with another adult. His focus on the breadth of possibilities for relationships, rather than limiting himself to a single significant other, is very typical of Experientials.

Societally Conscious. An even more psychologically mature group, analogous to Achievers in this regard, is the Societally Conscious. Their focus has turned from relationships with others to concern for the world at large. Impassioned individuals who have a concern with trying to improve things in general, the Societally Conscious are often leaders of single-issue movements and spokespersons for those who have been harmed by the larger culture (as they see it).

Currently, Societally Conscious represent around 9 percent of the adult population and their numbers include the highest concentration of nonwhites among the Inner Directeds (13%). Mostly married (73%), this is the oldest of the Inner Directed group, with a median age of 37. They also have the highest education level of all the VALS groups, with 39 percent reporting graduate school attendance.

Their education level, coupled with the fact that this group contains the highest proportion of dual-earner incomes and the highest concentration of managerial/professional occupations, means that this group has the highest potential household income. At a median income level of $25,500, they are second to Achievers. This may be because a significant number of Societally Conscious live in rural areas, perhaps practicing what SRI has called *voluntary simplicity* (Elgin 1981). Voluntary simplicity is characterized by a movement away from the large central cities to live "at one" with nature in an undeveloped area, perhaps bartering with neighbors for essential goods and services. Societally Conscious tend to share the Experientials' lack of ambition (in Achiever terms) and thus may have decided not to strive for promotions and salary increases.

Societally Conscious individuals exhibit the most traditional liberal political and social ideas, supporting most of the recent liberal movements. They get involved in their communities, often showing a great deal of interest in civic events.

Like Achievers, they have a great deal of personal self-confidence, but this expresses itself in the compromises they decide to accept and those they will not tolerate. Many of them, for example, eschew the external signs of status, believing that it is more important to acknowledge the inner man than the shell that is projected to the world.

Margaret. Margaret, her husband, and two children lived in a modest house with a natural wood exterior. The stream running through the property appealed to them all, but they converted the conventional fireplace into a more fuel-efficient wood burner in order to preserve scarce natural resources.

Both Margaret and her husband had master's degrees in library science. Their house was filled with books, but some of the most important ones for Margaret were her cookbooks. Margaret tried to eat nothing but natural foods and had done so, under her mother's tutelage, since childhood. Margaret's concern for nutritional well-being extended beyond her family. She organized a group of women to try to impose a boycott on ice cream in the public schools and she was a delegate to a national conference on world hunger. In speculating on the future, Margaret mentioned that because of inflation, she might have to discontinue her volunteer work and take a job. The interviewer pointed out that Margaret's husband, working as a public school teacher, could get a better-paying job. Margaret acknowledged that, but explained how happy he was teaching and working with children. He had tried other jobs but was happiest where he was. She concluded that she would rather that the family compromise their material requirements than her husband compromise his happiness. Margaret's attitude on this clearly matches the views of other Societally Conscious about the proper place of work in one's life.

Integrateds

Integrateds are difficult to conceptualize and to identify. Their complex lifestyles, the result of unique efforts to meld inner and outer directed tendencies into something personally agreeable, are probably found in diverse segments of the culture. Few in number (approximately 2 percent), SRI does not have a direct method for identifying these people from survey data. For the 1980 survey, SRI classified no Integrateds, although they later pinpointed 42 of them in their 1981 survey (Mitchell 1982). For marketing purposes, this is currently not as critical a segment as the others. If their numbers expand or if they become what SRI envisages, the new leaders of the country, then their impact will be much greater than it is at present.

Measuring VALS Types

SRI currently uses a 30-item questionnaire to classify individuals by VALS types. The questionnaire is comprised of 22 attitudinal items (measured by 6-point agree-disagree scales) and 8 demographic items. The questionnaire is easily answered by survey respondents.

The classification algorithm, based on discriminant function analysis, is proprietary with SRI. Commercial firms may become members of the VALS program for as little as $4,500, after which they may obtain the rights to use of the classification questionnaire for an incremental $5,000. SRI will then process respondents' data for a small additional fee.

Respondents are actually assigned probabilities of membership in each of the VALS segments. Thus, one may exhibit tendencies toward several groups, while belonging primarily in one of them. It has proved useful in certain instances to examine not only primary VALS classification, but secondary ones as well (Mitchell 1983). This is particularly helpful when exploring differences among members of the larger VALS segments.

Conclusions

If one were to explore secondary or tertiary classifications and were to incorporate magnitudes of difference in probability of assignment to groups in one's appraisal, it would be possible to generate as many different lifestyle subtypes as there are people. In truth, this is an accurate assessment of the diversity of individuals, but it is hardly actionable from a marketing perspective. At the individual level, the VALS typology, as it is operationalized and theorized, is too broad a generalization, almost stereotypical. Yet, when the marketer deals at arm's length with millions of people, VALS is a better way to humanize those people than many other conceptualizations currently available. Furthermore, the ability to speculate about behavior not previously studied or about future trends are strong points in favor of VALS. It is its strong conceptual base that makes this possible, and also uniquely characterizes VALS among commercially available segmentation systems.

Notes

1. While Riesman, Glazer, and Denney coined the term "other directed," SRI has chosen to use "outer directed" instead. Although the appropriateness of these terms can be debated, this is not the forum for doing so. For better or worse, those using the VALS typology are obliged to use "outer directed" if for no other reason than to keep consistent with SRI's published documents. Kind acknowledgements go to Hal Kassarjian (U.C.L.A.) for pointing out this discrepancy.

References

Banfield, Edward. *The Unheavenly City, Revisited.* Boston: Little, Brown and Company, 1974.

Caplovitz, David. *The Poor Pay More.* New York: The Free Press, 1967.

Elgin, Duane. *Voluntary Simplicity.* New York: Wm. Morrow & Co., 1981.

Harrington, Michael. *The Other America.* New York: The Macmillan Company, 1962.

Irelan, Lola M. *Low Income Life Styles.* Washington, D.C.: U.S. Department of Health, Education, and Welfare, 1966.

Maslow, Abraham H. *Motivation and Personality.* New York: Harper & Row, 1954.

Maslow, Abraham H. *Toward a Psychology of Being.* New York: Van Nostrand Reinhold, 1968.

Miller, Herman P. *Poverty: American Style.* Belmont, Calif.: Wadsworth Publishing Co., 1966.

Mitchell, Arnold *Consumer Values: A Typology.* Menlo Park, Calif.: SRI International, 1978.

Mitchell, Arnold. *Values Scenarios for the 1980's.* Menlo Park, Calif.: SRI International, 1981.

Mitchell, Arnold. *The Integrateds.* Menlo Park, Calif.: SRI International, 1982.

Mitchell, Arnold. *Types of Achievers.* Menlo Park, Calif.: SRI International, 1983.

Riesman, David, Nathan Glazer, and Reuel Denney. *The Lonely Crowd.* New Haven, Conn.: Yale University Press, 1950.

4

Personal Values and Market Segmentation: Applying the Value Construct

Robert E. Pitts and
Arch G. Woodside

Values are generally defined as closely held, abstract beliefs centrally located within one's belief system (Lessig 1976). Further, values are thought to exist as members of hierarchical groups of beliefs about preferable end-states of existence or preferable modes of behavior (Rokeach 1968). Rokeach contended that a value is either consciously or unconsciously a standard or criterion for guiding action and for developing and maintaining attitudes toward relevant objects and situations (Rokeach 1968, p. 160). Thus, the values which individuals hold are considered a major influence on human behavior (Parsons and Shils 1951).

The postulate that values do influence individuals has long been accepted in psychological research. Values were presented as an integral part of attitude and, consequently, a causal influence on behavior by Tolman (1951). In the original attitude model presented by Rosenburg, attitude toward an object was modeled as a function of value importance and the evaluation of the object as a means of obtaining the value (Rosenburg 1956).

Rokeach (1968, p. 15) contended that values, as the central beliefs of the individual, are causally related to attitudes. He stated that all attitudes are value expressive. According to Rokeach, if one focuses on attitudes, specific attitudes must be examined. An examination of values, however, provides both an overall picture of the most central cognitive structure of the individual, as well as a means of linking central beliefs to attitudes (Rokeach 1968). Thus, Rokeach contended that values may be more useful than attitudes in understanding human behavior.

Market researchers have built on this foundation, using values as a means to better understand consumer motivations. Lessig examined a four-level value-based model of consumer behavior. Boote (1975) studied both instrumental and terminal value influence on product and brand decisions. Henry (1976) looked at value influence on automobile purchase behavior. Boote (1981) related personal values to specific product attributes in a study of preferences for restaurant services.

Values also appear to hold promise as useful market segmentation variables. They may indicate underlying consumer motivations and, at the same time, define market segments desiring similar product benefits (Vinson and Munson 1976). Values have been suggested both as a means of enriching segment descriptions and as a substitute for personality traits, lifestyle(s), and other socioeconomic segmentation variables (Dhalla and Mahatto 1976; Howard 1977). Howard linked values and choice criteria directly, contending that consumers with similar values will exhibit similar choice criteria and final behavior.

From Rokeach's (1968) theoretical delineation of values as terminal (end-states of existence) and instrumental (modes of behavior), Howard (1977) proposed a complex relationship between values and consumer behavior variables. Howard (1977, pp. 96–102) postulated a two-level model of value influence for extensive problem solving (EPS), for which a consumer needs to form choice criteria to use in evaluating both the product class and brand. His model described two levels of choice, with terminal values guiding choice among product classes and instrumental values guiding choice among brands.

This study examines the application of values to market segmentation using both benefit (choice criteria) segmentation and product class and brand-within-class preference segmentation. The first research hypothesis is that personal values are effective in the differentiation of benefit segments. This hypothesis is drawn from the theoretical linkages between values and benefits desired. The second and third study hypotheses are drawn from Howard's (1977) contentions concerning the linkage between personal values and preferences and separate terminal/instrumental value linkages in the class and brand decision structure. The second research hypothesis is that values may be used to discriminate between groups of consumers with different product class and brand-within-class preferences. A third hypothesis to be examined is that terminal values are related to class decisions, while instrumental values are linked to brand decisions.

Method

Value Measurement

Respondents' values were measured with the Rokeach Value Scale (Rokeach 1973). The scale consisted of two lists of eighteen items or values to be ranked in order of importance. One list contained values classified by Rokeach as terminal (ideal end-states of existence) and the other was made up of instrumental values (ideal modes of behavior). The individual value ranks were rescaled with a normal (z) transformation for analysis with parametric techniques (Feather 1975; Hayes, 1967; Hollen 1967).

Product-Choice Criteria Stimuli

The present study examines the applicability of value segmentation as a means for understanding consumer needs for two widely varying products. Automobiles were selected as an infrequently purchased, major durable good. Previous research has linked values to specific automobile choice criteria (Munson 1977; Vinson, Scott, and Lamont 1977) and to product class ownership (Henry 1976). In addition, the magnitude and complexity of the automobile decision process is believed to lead to a significant need for information and an extended decision time, which are the characteristics of EPS.

The automobile models selected represent several manufacturers and provide a wide range of product characteristics. The models included: Cadillac Seville, Chevrolet Corvette, Chevrolet Impala, Chevrolet Monza, Ford Granada, Ford Mustang II, Lincoln Continental, Mercedes 450 SE, and Oldsmobile Cutlass.

Underarm deodorant was the other product stimulus used in the study. The decision processes associated with this frequently purchased, very personal product were selected as a vivid contrast to the automobile decision. For example, the very nature of this product type is such that it is impossible to confidently establish the purchase and decision structure. As with the automobile study, however, a set of deodorant brand stimuli of varying types (i.e., well-known major brands, specialty, antiperspirant, and powder brands) was presented as a means of positioning study respondents into a more complex decision stage. Nine brands of underarm products were included: Arm in Arm, Arm and Hammer, Arrid, Ban, Body All, Right Guard, Secret, Sure, and Tussy.

For each product type, a list of 10 product choice criteria was developed for evaluation on a 5-point scale ranging from very important to very unimportant. The choice criteria for automobile decisions were developed from previous studies (Alpert 1971; Green, Maheshwari, and Roa 1969). An exploratory study was used to determine criteria for deodorant decisions.

Multidimensional scaling techniques were used to operationalize the product class for automobiles and deodorants; subjects were asked to evaluate the similarities of all possible pairings of the product brands. Data were also collected on the perception of each choice criteria attribute for each brand.

Finally, respondents ranked all stimulus brands according to personal preference and current brand usage. Product classes were not listed for evaluations of brand dissimilarities, but were derived from the brand perceptions.

Data Source

The University of South Carolina consumer panel was the data source for the study. The panel was randomly recruited and generally reflected the characteristics of households in the urban areas of South Carolina with gross annual incomes over $6,000. An extensive demographic profile of each member family was maintained.

Two groups of 280 panel members each were randomly chosen from the panel for the study. Each group examined the decision processes related to one of the product type stimuli. In order to control for any contamination between responses to the value instrument and the choice criteria measured, data were collected from separate panel mailings approximately two weeks apart. Care was taken to ensure that the same member of the panel family responded to both study waves. A total of 176 usable automobile responses and 125 usable underarm deodorant responses were matched from the two waves (response rates of 63 percent and 45 percent, respectively).

Results

A preliminary step in testing the first hypothesis was the determination of segments with similar choice criteria relative to each of the two products. Hierarchical cluster analysis was used to develop the segments based on stated importance of choice criteria in personal product decisions.

Correlations between respondent evaluations of the importance of choice criteria for product class decisions (described in the questionnaire as the class or type of product) and brand evaluations were extremely high. No significant differences were found between segment membership based on brand versus class criteria at the $p < .05$ level. Thus, subsequent benefit analysis was based on mean importance ratings for both class and brand evaluations for deodorants and automobiles.

From the cluster analysis, a four-group structure based on choice criteria was selected for automobiles, with one large segment containing 50 percent of the respondents and the three other segments dividing the remaining 50 percent. A three-segment structure was developed for analysis of deodorant decisions. (See table 4–1.)

The benefit segments (clusters) and individual personal values were submitted to discriminant analysis using the 36 transformed value system ranks as the independent variables. A 10-step value function provided for the correct classification of 51 percent of the observations for the four automobile choice criteria segments (table 4–2).

A 10-value discriminant analysis model was also produced for deodorants, correctly classifying 69 percent of respondents as to choice criteria

Table 4–1
Benefit (Choice Criteria) Segments—Most Important Criteria

Automobiles			
Group 1	Group 2	Group 3	Group 4
style	not exciting	friends own	price
luxury	price	style	economy
space	style unimportant	space	dependability
	performance		

Underarm Deodorant		
Group 1	Group 2	Group 3
price	prevents odor	(weak rankings
familiar brand	prevents wetness	on all criteria)
fragrance		

segment membership for the three benefit groups. An indication of the effectiveness of the value model was its ability to classify correctly a large proportion of the members of groups 2 and 3 (64 and 83 percent of the group members, respectively), even though these groups were relatively small in size (table 4–3). A dummy variable for sex was included in the data set for

Table 4–2
Stepwise Discriminant Analysis Results—Automobile Benefit Segments

	Classification Function Coefficients			
	Group 1	Group 2	Group 3	Group 4
Term 4	−0.03	−0.16	0.33	0.44
Term 6	0.18	0.41	−0.46	−0.32
Term 11	0.19	0.38	−0.67	−0.10
Term 12	−0.09	−0.00	−0.80	0.02
Inst 2	−0.21	0.40	−0.06	−0.14
Inst 5	0.11	−0.48	−0.12	0.19
Inst 6	−0.10	0.34	−0.05	0.23
Inst 8	−0.41	−0.07	0.50	0.09
Inst 14	−0.03	0.29	−0.19	−0.64
Inst 16	−0.15	0.18	0.06	0.83
Constant	−0.12	−0.34	−0.44	−0.43

		Prediction Results			
	No. of	Predicted Group Membership			
Actual Group	Cases	Group 1	Group 2	Group 3	Group 4
Group 1	92	50	14	13	15
		54.3%	15.2%	14.1%	16.3%
Group 2	36	12	16	5	3
		33.3%	44.4%	13.9%	8.3%
Group 3	25	7	0	11	7
		28.0%	0.0%	44.0%	28.0%
Group 4	32	6	5	4	17
		18.8%	15.6%	12.5%	53.1%

Percent of Grouped Cases Correctly Classified: 50.81

Table 4–3
Stepwise Discriminate Analysis Results—Membership in Deodorant Benefit Segments

| | Classification Function Coefficients | | |
	Group 1	Group 2	Group 3
Term 1	0.15	−0.16	−1.90
Term 7	0.12	−0.32	−1.09
Term 11	0.03	0.56	1.46
Term 14	−0.06	0.52	0.38
Term 17	−0.18	−0.38	−1.40
Inst 8	0.18	0.54	−0.38
Inst 12	−0.01	−0.57	−1.82
Inst 17	0.11	0.29	−0.76
Inst 18	−0.05	0.12	−0.63
Sex	0.94	1.16	2.48
Constant	−0.29	−0.71	−4.48

| | | Prediction Results | | |
| Actual Group | No. of Cases | Predicted Group Membership | | |
		Group 1	Group 2	Group 3
Group 1	93	65	23	5
		69.9%	24.7%	5.4%
Group 2	25	5	16	4
		20.0%	64.0%	16.0%
Group 3	6	0	1	5
		0.0%	16.7%	83.3%
Ungrouped Cases	3	2	1	0
		66.7%	33.3%	0.0%

Percent of Grouped Cases Correctly Classified: 69.35

the deodorant discriminant models. The sex variable was thought to be a useful covariant for this product, because certain brands are marketed to the members of a single sex.

Analysis of the second hypothesis required the identification of product class structure. The INDSCALE multidimensional scaling technique was used to determine perceptual configurations for each product type. These perceptual spaces were then submitted to cluster analysis for the specification of perceptually based product classes for automobile and deodorant decisions.

For automobiles, a six-class grouping appeared most appropriate. The perceptual classes were: class 2, Mercedes; class 2, Monza; class 3, Continental and Cutlass; class 4, Seville and Mustang; class 5, Corvette; class 6, Impala and Granada. Five product classifications were chosen for deodorants: class 1, Arm-in-Arm, Arm and Hammer, and Body All; class 2, Secret and Sure; class 3, Arrid and Right Guard; class 4, Tussy; and class 5, Ban. Thus, the three powder brands formed one class. Two female-oriented products, Secret and Sure, composed the second class. Right Guard and Arrid were grouped into a third class, while Ban and Tussy each formed a unitary brand class.

Derived preference measures were used for each of the product classes and each brand within each class. Preference for a product class was operationalized by evaluating each class relative to the rank of the most preferred offering in that class. Brand preference within a product class was defined as the relative preference for the brand stimuli. For details of product class determination, see Pitts (1977) and Pitts and Woodside (1983).

Most preferred product class and most preferred brand-within-class models were developed with class or brand preferences as the dependent variables in a discriminant analysis for each product. Summaries of the eight discriminant models developed are shown in table 4-4.

For automobile class preference, a ten-variable value model was selected which correctly classified 50 percent of the respondents (table 4-5). The correct classification of the respondents preferring Corvette was especially enlightening. These individuals seemed to be clearly distinguishable from the members of the other groups. Examination of the classification function indicated that inner harmony and cheerful were two of the primary values of those respondents identifying a preference for Corvette over the other automobile classes. These two values had relatively large positive nonzero classification coefficients, which indicated that these values were important for those individuals relative to members of the other groups.

As shown in table 4-5, the discriminant models indicated that values were also useful in classifying respondents on the basis of preferences for deodorant classes and brands-within-classes. For example, a five-value model correctly classified 72 percent of those respondents expressing an Arrid versus Right Guard brand preference (table 4-6). This particular model provided results indicating important values for only one product in the two-product comparison. For example, the model indicates that mature love was much more important to members of the segment preferring Right Guard; however, no information concerning the importance of values for those preferring Arrid can be drawn from the model. Further consideration of additional value variables provided for little improvement in the classification results for any of the three brand preference models.

Discussion

First, it must be remembered that the study components—choice criteria and value importance measures—were generated from two separate waves with a time elapse of several weeks between each wave. Thus, the likelihood of contamination of data between choice criteria and values was minimized.

Table 4-4
Discriminant Analysis Results for Product Class and Brand-Within-Class

Segmentation Criterion	Number of Variables in Model	Percent Correctly Classified	Terminal Values in Model	Instrumental Values in Model
Automobiles				
most preferred class	10	50	5	5
within class preference:				
Cutlass/Continental	5	69	3	2
Impala/Granada	10	62	5	5
Mustang/Seville	10	76	5	5
Deodorant				
Most preferred class	10	52	9	1
within class preference:				
Secret/Sure	5	66	4	1
Arrid/Right Guard	5	72	3	1
Arm in Arm/Body All/ Arm and Hammer	5	52	4	1

Table 4-5

Value Models for Most Preferred Automobile Class: Discriminant Analysis Results

(Perceptual Classifications: MERCEDES (1); MONZA (2);[a] CUTLASS & CONTINENTAL (3); SEVILLE & MUSTANG (4); IMPALA & GRANADA (5); CORVETTE (6))

	Classification Function Coefficients				
	Group 1	Group 3	Group 4	Group 5	Group 6
Term 2	0.21	-0.36	0.30	0.17	1.27
Term 7	0.00	0.27	-0.27	-0.13	-2.63
Term 10	0.10	-0.07	0.11	-0.27	2.17
Term 13	-0.01	0.24	-0.43	0.24	0.68
Term 14	-0.49	-0.02	-0.13	0.92	-1.83
Inst 3	-0.14	0.26	-0.43	-0.07	-1.26
Inst 4	-0.25	-0.15	0.32	-0.19	1.63
Inst 7	0.18	0.23	-0.41	-0.56	-0.76
Inst 8	-0.38	-0.12	0.05	0.52	-0.32
Inst 16	0.19	-0.01	-0.15	0.31	1.36
Constant	-0.22	-0.16	-0.29	-0.51	-11.89

Prediction Results

		Predicted Group Membership				
Actual Group	No. of Cases	Group 1	Group 3	Group 4	Group 5	Group 6
Group 1	45	19 42.2%	13 28.9%	9 20.0%	4 8.9%	0 0.0%
Group 3	58	11 19.0%	29 50.0%	6 10.3%	11 19.0%	1 1.7%
Group 4	35	7 20.0%	3 8.6%	19 54.3%	6 17.1%	0 0.0%
Group 5	19	2 10.5%	4 21.1%	3 15.8%	10 52.6%	0 0.0%
Group 6	2	0 0.0%	0 0.0%	0 0.0%	0 0.0%	2 100.0%
Ungrouped Cases	26	1 3.8%	24 92.3%	0 0.0%	1 3.8%	0 0.0%

Percent of Grouped Cases Correctly Classified: 49.69

[a]Group 2 results are not shown.

Table 4–6
Stepwise Discriminant Analysis Results—Preference for Arrid (1) Versus Right Guard (2)

	Classification Function Coefficients	
	Group 1	Group 2
Term 4	−0.33	0.33
Term 11	−0.19	0.45
Term 16	−0.22	0.19
Inst 2	−0.19	0.23
Sex	0.43	1.39
Constant	−0.15	−0.55

	Prediction Results		
	No. of	Predicted Group Membership	
Actual Group	Cases	Group 1	Group 2
Group 1	59	45	14
		76.3%	23.7%
Group 2	68	22	46
		32.4%	67.6%

Percent of Grouped Cases Correctly Classified: 72.65

Results may be examined as long-term cognitive relationships with little probability that a respondent may have attempted to match stated values with choice criteria.

The study's findings support current conceptualizations of value influence on the individual. Values were shown to be related to differences in choice criteria; therefore, there is evidence that values do influence the cognitive decision structure of the individual.

The first two research hypotheses were generally supported for both products. Significant multivariate value models were determined for each market segment examined. For the first hypotheses, ten-variable value models were shown to be efficient discriminators of choice criteria segments.

Examination of the choice criteria classification functions revealed the emergence of several salient values (i.e., nonzero positive coefficients) for each segment (group). These values provide the basis for differentiating members of one segment from members of the other segments.

Personal values, however, were much more effective descriptors of deodorant than of automobile choice criteria segment membership. This probably reflects the family orientation of the automobile decision and, perhaps to some extent, the second hypothesis was tested through the determination of a number of discriminant models for class and brand preference. Market segments were based on preferences for both product class and brand. Respondents were grouped into market segments on the basis of the most preferred product class. To examine the applicability of values to brand preference segmentation, market segments based on brand preferences were determined for each of the brand classes with more than one brand. Respondents were assigned to brand market segments based on their relative brand preference rankings within each product class. The models developed indicated that only a few values were needed to differentiate market segment membership based on preference, with accuracies varying from about 50 percent for class preference up to 76 percent for brand preference comparisons.

A strict relationship of terminal values to class preference and of instrumental values to brand-within-a-class preference was not supported. Further research is needed to examine the two-level hypothesis in a more controlled EPS environment. The lack of dichotomy may be a function of the decision structure or the number and type of relationships examined. It may even be conjectured that in this case the importance of the automobile and deodorant decisions are related to the predominance of terminal value correlations.

From a theoretical viewpoint, the study provides further evidence of the impact of individual values. Thus, the findings relative to value segmentation are supportive of value theory.

The primary purpose of market segmentation is the development of marketing strategy. Insight into the values of members of market segments provides a means for developing this strategy. Recognizing that values are often based on needs and motives, it follows that knowledge of the values provides the marketer with a very powerful and practical tool for achieving need/motive satisfaction. While it is unlikely that the marketer would attempt to modify need structure, he could design new products or structure product/brand advertising such that a product/brand is perceived as a means of satisfying the particular needs of the individual values segment.

References

Alpert, Mark I. "A Canonical Analysis of Personality and the Determinants of Automobile Choice." Proceedings of the American Marketing Association, 1971.

Boote, Alfred S. "An Exploratory Investigation of the Roles of Needs and Personal Values in the Theory of Buyer Behavior." Unpublished doctoral dissertation, Columbia University, 1975.

Boote, Alfred S. "Market Segmentation by Personal Values and Salient Product Attributes." *Journal of Advertising Research* 21 (February 1981):29–35.

Dhalla, Nariman K. and Winston H. Mahatto. "Expanding the Scope of Segmentation Research." *Journal of Marketing* 40 (April 1976):34–41.

Green, P.E., Arun Maheshwari, and Vitala Rao. "Dimensional Interpretation and Configuration Invariance in Multidimensional Scaling: An Empirical Study." *Multivariate Behavioral Research* 4 (April 1969): 159–180.

Feather, Norman T. *Values in Education and Society*. New York: The Free Press, 1975.

Hayes, William L. *Quantification in Psychology*. Belmont: Cole Publishing Company, 1967.

Henry, Walter A. "Cultural Values do Correlate with Consumer Behavior." *Journal of Marketing Research* 8 (May 1976):121–127.

Hollen, Charles C. "The Stability of Values and Value System." Unpublished master's thesis, Michigan State University, 1967.

Howard, John A. *Consumer Behavior: Application of Theory*. New York: McGraw-Hill Book Company, 1977.

Lessig, V. Parker. "Measurement of Dependencies Between Values and Other Levels of the Consumer's Belief Space." *Journal of Business Research* 83 (1976):227–239.

Munson, J.M. "An Investigation of Value Inventories for Appliations to Cross Cultural Marketing Research. In *American Institute of Decision Sciences Proceedings*, edited by J. Stolen and T. Conway. Chicago, 1977, pp. 624–626.

Parsons, Talcott and Edward A. Shils. *Toward a General Theory of Action*. Cambridge: Harvard University Press, 1951.

Pitts, Robert E. "The Influence of Personal Value Systems on Product Classes and Brand Preferences: A Segmentation Approach." Unpublished doctoral dissertation, University of South Carolina, 1977.

Pitts, Robert E. and Arch G. Woodside. "Personal Value Influences on Consumer Product Class and Brand Preferences." *The Journal of Social Psychology* 119 (1983):37–53.

Rokeach, Milton. *Beliefs, Attitudes and Values*. San Francisco: Jossey-Bass, Inc., 1968.

Rokeach, Milton. *The Nature of Human Values*. New York: Free Press, 1973.

Rosenberg, Milton J. "Cognitive Structure and Attitudinal Effect." *Journal of Abnormal and Social Psychology* 53 (November 1956):367–372.

Tolman, Edward C. "A Psychological Model." In *Toward a General Theory of Action*, edited by T. Parsons and E.A. Shils. Cambridge: Harvard University Press, 1951.

Vinson, Donald E. and J. Michael Munson. "Personal Values: An Approach to Market Segmentation." In *Marketing: 1776–1976* and

Beyond, edited by K.L. Bernhardt. *American Marketing Association Proceedings*, Chicago, Illinois, 1976, pp. 313–318.

Vinson, Donald E., Jerome E. Scott, and Lawrence M. Lamont. "The Role of Personal Values in Marketing and Consumer Behavior." *Journal of Marketing* 41 (April 1977):44–50.

Part II
Monitoring Values and Value Change in Society

In part II, value monitors are examined as a means of establishing and tracing values in a culture or subculture. A survey-derived profile of American values and two content methodologies provide examples of measurement methodologies and clarification of values and value changes over time.

Robin introduces value monitors in chapter 5. He examines the case for value monitors and presents an example of their use in studying social responsibility.

Chapter 6 by Lynn Kahle reviews the results of a study of the values from a probability sample of 2,264 Americans. This national survey examined the relationship of personal background, role adaptation, and psychological functioning to nine personal values. Kahle then suggests possible consumer behavior implications from the value monitors.

Harold Kassarjian, in chapter 7, uses a content analysis methodology to explore the changes in values over two decades as depicted in the Sunday comics. He contends that the comics are a major yet virtually unexplored medium which presents a capsule view of the culture to which they are directed. The study examines values, goals, and other stimulus variables.

Chapter 8 presents another content analysis of value orientation from a communication medium. Richard Pollay operationalizes 42 value categories in a study of 2,000 magazine ads from 1900 to 1980. Particular attention is given to the methodology used and its application as a reliable research tool. Overall, practicality and family values are discussed as the dominant central theme in the ads.

5 The Logic of Establishing Value Monitors

Donald P. Robin

This article has two basic objectives. The first of these objectives is to establish the reasons for using value monitors, while the second objective is to provide an example of their importance. Thus, the first section is an attempt to establish the benefits of value monitors for use by business and industry, while the second section analyzes the example of social responsibility.

Benefits Derived from Knowledge of Values

There are many benefits to business and industry which would accrue with the establishment of value monitors by organizations or industry associations. One benefit lies simply in the establishment of the meaning of ethical behavior. A major problem of many marketing managers who want to do the right thing is simply knowing what is right and wrong. An extension of this idea would be for the marketing manager to know and understand the impact of any of his actions on the perceptions of that organization's publics. Knowing how people feel initially and what their reactions might be to potential organizational behaviors should be a great aid to marketing managers who wish to behave ethically.

A second benefit to be achieved from the use of value monitors represents the further extension of the first idea. Understanding the values of the many publics faced by an organization should help them avoid regulatory intrusions by governmental agencies. Further, value monitors should aid organizations that face action by regulatory agencies. For example, the recent rapid growth in the use of consumer research by the Federal Trade Commission of the United States government (Guerard 1980; Snyder 1979) has forced many organizations facing litigation to use short-term research geared to the particular problem under attack. The availability of a long-term value monitor would provide research with a higher validity and reliability than that used by the regulatory agency. This recent increase in the use of consumer research by the U.S. Federal Trade Commission may well be the precursor of an expanded use of research by regulatory agencies all over the world. If that situation were true, consumer policy decisions by these agencies might better reflect the true costs and benefits of those decisions.

The third benefit of establishing value monitors occurs when potential pressure groups are identified. In the broadest context of society and in business as part of that broader society, certain individuals and groups of individuals often have much more influence on social policies than their numbers would seem to dictate. The increase in class action suits of all types is an example of their influence on organizations. Value monitors, which identify segments of the population according to their potential for action, would help organizations spot potential pressure groups before they acted. The organization involved could then determine whether the concerns of these pressure groups were legitimate and in the best interest of society and either react to their concerns if they are legitimate or attempt to defuse those concerns if they are not.

A fourth rather obvious benefit of understanding societal values comes from improving lobbying efforts in the political arena. If legislators of policy at all levels of government can be shown that a particular action is in the best interest of society, lobbying for that position should be enhanced. Obviously, a potential for misuse in this same arena also exists. However, if the societal benefits compared to costs are to be maximized, both parties must have access to information about what society deems right and wrong. Thus, one group of organizations which should maintain value monitors are the same governmental and regulatory groups already discussed.

A further significant benefit from maintaining value monitors in those areas of concern to a particular organization is an increased sensitivity to changes over time. The ability of an organization to identify culturally based trends that are determined by values places an organization in the best possible position to take advantage of these trends. The benefits to micro-marketers could be substantial, and that potentiality could be enough reason to justify the establishment of value monitors.

Perhaps the most important benefit to an organization is simply in understanding the impact of its marketing activities on human values. Unquestionably, different segments of a given population are influenced in different ways by marketing activities. These changes in cultural and subcultural mores and behaviors can be both positive or negative in nature but, in either case, both the marketer and the society within which he operates is better off knowing exactly what these influences are. Opinion polls, advertising, and other promotional activities, organizational/political-legal-regulatory interfaces may do more to establish or change values in an unintended or covert way than any overt attempts made by the same organization. If this covert impact is as real as it seems to be, organizations are less likely to understand the full impact of their actions than if their original intent was overtly to affect values in a prescribed way. Of course, unintended changes may produce important effects in the same way that intended changes would, and it is important for the marketing practitioner to understand the nature of these influences.

Why Values Should be Monitored

In trying to establish the importance of understanding values in the preceding section, no effort was made to explain why a conditional monitoring system was desirable. Values are often viewed as relatively stable, and constant monitoring of even those values of obvious importance to the organization may seem excessive. However, values, or at least the constructs used to measure them, do change over relatively short time periods, and this section will use an example to illustrate how rapidly such changes can occur.

The concept of social responsibility has been examined extensively (Berkowitz and Daniels 1964; Berkowitz and Lutterman 1968). An 8-item scale was used to measure the construct (Robinson and Shaver 1973). The items used in the scale to measure this construct are tied into traditional values and are therefore likely to have essentially a conservative individualist theme (Robinson and Shaver 1973, p. 467).

This scale has been used by marketers as a surrogate for socially conscious consumers (Anderson and Cunningham 1972), as a comparison to a Socially Conscious Consumer Index and actual recycling behavior by Webster (1975 and 1976), to identify Sierra Club and/or Audubon Club members in the general population (Tucker, Dolich, and Wilson 1981), to determine ecological opinion leaders (Henion, Anderson, and Batsell 1976), and to predict environmental behavior and knowledge (Arbuthnot 1977). Further, the social responsibility scale was an important consideration in the development of other research by marketers (e.g., Kinnear, Taylor, and Ahmed 1974; Antil and Bennett 1979; Crosby, Gill, and Taylor 1981; Belch 1982). Thus, it is apparent that the scale and the construct has become important to marketing as a field and to its theoretical development. However, Webster (1975, p. 194) sounded a note of caution about the scale, indicating that it might not be measuring modern social values.

In order to pursue Webster's concern, the scale was administered to 155 undergraduate students and the results were analyzed for internal consistency. Simple interitem correlations of the eight scales ranged from (absolute values) 0.002 to 0.464. Of the 28 possible combinations, 3 were less than 0.10, 13 were between 0.10 and 0.20, 9 were between 0.20 and 0.03, while only 3 were between 0.03 and 0.47. The resulting Coefficient Alpha was a very poor 0.14. The best combination of scale items to maximize Coefficient Alpha occurred when five of the eight items were eliminated. Factor loading for each of the scale items appear in table 5-1. With three of the best fitting items in the scale, Alpha increased to 0.74, but they seem to be measuring only a small part of the generalized construct originally intended by Berkowitz and Lutterman (1968).

The time frame for this change in the measuring of social responsibility is not long—1968 to 1983. Recognition of that change in specific terms

Table 5-1
Summary Statistics for Social Responsibility Scale

Questions	Factor Loadings
1. It is no use worrying about current events or public affairs; I can't do anything about them anyway.	−.124[a]
2. Every person should give some of his/her time for the good of his town or country.	.277[b]
3. Our country would be a lot better off if we didn't have so many elections and people didn't have to vote so often.	−.140
4. Letting your friends down is not so bad because you can't do good all the time for everybody.	−.135
5. It is the duty of each person to do his/her job the very best he/she can.	.654[b]
6. People would be a lot better off if they could live far away from other people and never have to do anything for them.	−.752[b]
7. At school I usually volunteered for special projects.	.140
8. I feel very bad when I have failed to finish a job I promised I would do.	.182

Adapted from L. Berkowitz and K. Lutterman, "The Traditionally Socially Responsible Personality," *Public Opinion Quarterly*, 32 (1968):169-185.

[a]Question 1 loaded heavily on another scale being used at the time entitled "Powerlessness."
[b]Coefficient Alpha (3 selected items) = 0.74.
Coefficient Alpha (all 8 items) = 0.14.

could be extremely important to marketers in both profit and nonprofit settings. Thus, monitoring key values seems to be a desirable practice for academics and practitioners alike.

References

Anderson, Thomas W., Jr. and William H. Cunningham. The Socially Conscious Consumer. *Journal of Marketing* 36 (July 1972):23-31.

Antil, John H. and Peter D. Bennett. Construction and Validation of a Scale to Measure Socially Responsible Consumption Behavior. In *The Conserver Society*, edited by Karl E. Henison, II and Thomas C. Kinnear. Chicago: American Marketing Association, 1979. Pp. 51-68.

Arbuthnot, Jack. The Roles of Attitudinal and Personality Variables in the Prediction of Environmental Behavior and Knowledge. *Environment and Behavior* 9 (June 1977):217-232.

Belch, Michael A. A Segmentation Strategy for the 1980's: Profiling the Socially-Concerned Market through Life-Style Analysis. *Journal of the Academy of Marketing Science* 10 (Fall 1982):345–358.

Berkowitz, Leonard and Louise R. Daniels. Affecting the Salience of the Social Responsibility Norm. *Journal of Abnormal and Social Psychology* 68 (March 1964):275–281.

Berkowitz, Leonard and Kenneth G. Lutterman. The Traditional Socially Responsible Personality. *Public Opinion Quarterly* 32 (Summer 1968): 169–185.

Crosby, Lawrence A., James D. Gill, and James R. Taylor. Consumer/ Voter Behavior in the Passage of the Michigan Container Law. *Journal of Marketing* 45 (Spring 1981):19–32.

Guerad, Collot. Remarks of Deputy Assistant Director for the Division of Advertising Practices. Federal Trade Commission before the 11th Annual Midwest Research Conference of the American Marketing Association, Chicago, Illinois, 1980.

Henion, Karl E., II, W. Thomas Anderson, Jr., and R.R. Batsell. Psychographic Characteristics of Ecologically Concerned Chief Executives of 76 Major Corporations. In *Ecological Marketing*, edited by Karl E. Henion and Thomas C. Kinnear. Chicago: American Marketing Association, 1976. Pp. 79–95.

Kinnear, Thomas C., James R. Taylor, and Sadrudin A. Ahmed. Ecologically Concerned Consumers: Who Are They? *Journal of Marketing* 38 (April 1974):20–24.

Robinson, John P. and Phillip R. Shaver. *Measures of Social Psychological Attitudes*. Ann Arbor, Mich.: Institute for Social Research, 1973.

Snyder, Wallace S. Remarks of Assistant Director for the Division of Advertising Practices, Federal Trade Commission, before the Advertising Research Conference of the American Marketing Association, New York, N.Y., 1979.

Tucker, Lewis R., Karl J. Dolich, and David Wilson. Profiling Environmentally Responsible Consumer-Citizens. *Journal of the Academy of Marketing Science* 9 (Fall 1981):454–478.

Webster, Frederick E., Jr. 1981. Determining the Characteristics of the Socially Conscious Consumer. *Journal of Consumer Research* 2 (December 1975):188–196.

Webster, Frederick E. Who is the Socially-Ecologically Concerned Consumer? In *Ecologically Marketing*, edited by Karl E. Henion, II and Thomas C. Kinnear. Chicago: American Marketing Association, 1976. Pp. 121–130.

6 The Values of Americans: Implications for Consumer Adaptation

Lynn R. Kahle

Many textbooks of consumer behavior recognize the importance of attitudes in consumer behavior and give the obligatory reference to the theory of Daniel Katz (1960) on the functions of attitudes, including the important function of value expression. Yet far fewer of these texts proceed to the next logical step and critically evaluate what values are being expressed through attitudes. This shortcoming undoubtedly, in part, reflects the shortage of recent, adequate national studies of consumer values. I hope here to take a step toward rectifying this problem by describing the major findings of a recent national study of social values (Kahle, 1984b) and considering some of the implications for consumer behavior.

A good place to start is with a brief theoretical consideration of the nature of values. Values and attitudes both are abstractions about adaptation. A basic goal of humans is adaptation. Piaget (1952) has articulately defined this concept as the environment transforming the organism, resulting in an increase in the interchanges between the environment and the organism that favor preservation. Because the memory capacity of humans is not adequate to remember every instance of previous experience relevant to adaptation, abstractions such as attitudes and values are formed to summarize previous experience. Most humans cannot, for example, recall every interaction they have had with ice cream, but it is adaptively sufficient simply to remember the attitudinal abstraction "I like ice cream." Likewise, one cannot remember the exact results of every interaction one has heard about between humans and rattlesnakes, but it is adaptively sufficient for most of us to remember only the attitudinal abstraction "I dislike rattlesnakes." Values, which differ from attitudes primarily in that they do not have objects, are one step more abstract than attitudes. A more elaborate expression of these ideas, which are part of social adaptation theory, is presented elsewhere (Kahle, Kulka, and Klingel 1980; Kahle 1984a, 1984b).

Method

The data reported here summarize some of the major findings from *Social Values and Adaptation to Life in America* (Kahle, in press-b). Those data, in turn, are part of a larger study, the principal report of which is contained in *The Inner American* (Veroff, Douvan, and Kulka 1981). That study was carried out to replicate and extend the now-classic survey of mental health, *Americans View Their Mental Health* (Gurin, Veroff, and Feld 1960). The new study included a question that asked respondents to identify their first and second most important values from a list of nine Rokeach-like (Rokeach 1973) terminal values, which were selected because of their applicability to all of life's major roles: sense of belonging, excitement, fun and enjoyment in life, warm relationships with others, self-fulfillment, being well-respected, a sense of accomplishment, security, and self-respect. Rokeach's list was viewed as somewhat difficult for some respondents to conquer and as including values that would probably be fulfilled only within one role.

Since only five respondents selected excitement, that category was collapsed together with fun and enjoyment in life. The availability of these data on values within a study that measured standard background characteristics, functioning in life's major roles, and subjective mental health provided a unique opportunity to study values and adaptation.

Rokeach's (1973) list was not used because with 18 items it was viewed as somewhat difficult for respondents to conquer, because it is only marginally relevant to Maslow's (1954) theory, and because Rokeach's list included some values that may not be applicable to fulfillment in some important life roles. Furthermore, Rokeach asked respondents to rank order all 18 terminal values from his list, whereas respondents in the present research only ranked their 2 most important values. Theoretically the complete list of value rankings may provide additional information, but in our experience it often is only the top values or two that have the greatest significance in people's lives. Furthermore, the statistical complexities from detailed rankings add problems to inferences. The present data-collection method also differs from the VALS system in that it is simpler to administer. Both the Rokeach and the present system differ from the VALS system in that the methodology is public information. At this time, methodological experimentation, diversity, and tolerance should probably dominate research on values, although science works best when information is public.

The respondents were 2,264 adults selected from the sampling units of the University of Michigan's Survey Research Center, the organization which conducted the study. The sampling procedure was designed to yield a representative probability sample of noninstitutionalized adults living in the coterminous United States. At each stage of the study the rigorous standards of the Survey Research Center were followed. The response rate for this face-to-face interview was approximately 70 percent.

Results

Because the detailed account of the statistical inferences has been presented for the scientist elsewhere (Kahle, in press-b), here only verbal summaries of the major findings will be presented, with special emphasis given to the topics of potential interest in consumer behavior. The reader should bear in mind, however, that inferences are of the probabilistic kind rather than the absolute kind. For example, the comment "warm relationships with others was primarily selected by women" represents a summary of a trend. It does not imply that no men selected warm relationships as their primary value. The form of presentation will be based on giving a description of the basic characteristics of the people who selected each value as their primary value. Because one of the most important uses of data such as the present data may be for market segmentation, it was felt that a description of each value segment would be most useful. We will consider the values in order of frequency of selection, from most to least.

Self-Respect

About 21.1 percent of the sample selected self-respect as the primary value, making it the most frequently endorsed primary value in the entire study. Ironically, the people who selected self-respect were among the least distinctive in other regards. On only one item in the entire study did this group show extreme differentiation from other groups, and that item asked people to describe how they differed from others. The proponents of self-respect were far less able to differentiate themselves from others than were the other value groups. These people, then, tended to be middle-of-the-road types in most respects—middle Americans.

The respondents who endorsed self-respect do have some attributes on which they differed from respondents in general. They tended to have good jobs that involved a lot of data, a lot of work with people, considerable complexity, and high prestige. They tended to be Jewish or Presbyterian and middle-aged. Their incomes were not likely to fall below $4,000 or to exceed $20,000.

As the modal value endorsed by Americans, self-respect may be the single value to which one would want to link a product if the product could be linked to just one value and if the product could have wide appeal or disallowed segmentation. Americans want to be at peace with themselves. They hope to look inside themselves and like what they see, not find a guilt-laden, neurotic, or evil self.

People who value self-respect probably prefer normal products—items that do not deviate drastically from the norm. They may be less innovative in use of new products and perhaps rely on name-brand products more than other groups. Their purchases of durable goods are probably especially important to them.

Security

The second most frequently selected primary value was security. The 20.6 percent of the sample that selected security was far more distinctive than the self-respect group. People who endorsed security tended to be retired or to have jobs that gave them little complexity, involvement with data, prestige, or pay. In the last case, valuers of security constituted a large part of the people in our sample who earned less than $4,000. Widows and blacks were likely to value security. People who valued security also lacked psychological security in that they had shortness of breath, trouble sleeping, dizziness, and anxiety.

People who value security live with constant awareness of the economic and existential uncertainty of these times, worrying about what the future may bring. They have some concern about life's potential for catastrophy. That this value is selected frequently implies that not all Americans are enamored with the cultural ideals of riskiness and freedom. At least a fifth of the people prefer security over all of the other values.

Marketers may have already considered the value of security, perhaps to the point of saturation. It is already possible to purchase securities and home security devices, as well as "social security" through vaginal deodorants and mouthwashes. People who value security probably constitute a significant market for used cars and TV sets, for medical remedies and appliances, for sources of affection and social support.

Warm Relationships with Others

The third most frequently selected primary value (16.2%) and the most frequently selected secondary value was warm relationships with others. Combining the first and second value, we found that more people selected warm relationships than any other value for one of their two values. Women were especially likely to endorse warm relationships with others, particularly housewives and married or single women. On the other hand, divorced men frequently selected warm relationships with others as a primary value, quite unlike divorced women. Divorced men wanted a woman desperately, but divorced women believed that a relationship with a man was not important.

Lutherans, fundamentalists, and frequent church-goers also endorse warm relationships. First-borns were unlikely to select this value. Clerical workers often liked this value. Weight loss and nightmares sometimes bother people who selected warm relationships, but generally they were psychologically well-adjusted. Marriage and parenting were important for these people, and they had good social support networks, although they would have liked to have had even more friends.

People who advocate warm relationships with others as their fundamental value tend to live on a social level. Their entanglements and involvements guide their lives, especially the positive aspects of the entanglements.

These people may be more likely to give gifts than members of other value groups, and their purchases probably show more about their social situation than the purchases of other valuers. They probably spend more on entertaining, on community activities, and on their families.

Sense of Accomplishment

In contrast to the value of security, which is advocated by people who feel insecure, most people from the 11.4 percent of the sample who selected sense of accomplishment as their primary value have accomplished a lot. They were well-educated and well-payed managers and professionals with jobs that have prestige, complexity, involvement with data and people, and a high degree of self-direction. These people were often young and male. Religiously, they may have been Jews or Methodists, or they may simply not have attended church. They were healthy, well-adjusted, rarely depressed or nervous. They felt self-confident and capable. Sometimes, however, relationships distracted from accomplishment.

The work ethic is glorified by this group. These people are the achievers who want to be and are successful. They are able to consume, with a high degree of discretionary income. What they want for the future is probably more manifestation of success and of task completion.

These people may consume more conspicuously than other groups. Quality homes, cars, furniture, and clothing tend to characterize these people. They probably enjoy symbols of achievement, such as fine wines, swimming pools, and boats. Products that foster accomplishment, such as books and home computers, may interest this group. Finally, they may enjoy innovative products.

Self-Fulfillment

Maslow (1954) ranked self-actualization as the top value in his hierarchy of values, and 9.6 percent of the respondents in this study apparently did too.

Self-fulfillment tended to be quite similar to sense of accomplishment in terms of the proponents it attracted. For example, self-fillers were young, educated, well-to-do, successful, and healthy. They displayed more optimism than any other group. Both sexes selected self-fulfillment equally. Self-fulfillers were very internal in that they had a high degree of self-confidence and rarely felt depressed or out of control.

Most unhappiness for people who value self-fulfillment resulted from family roles. Self-fulfillers were dissatisfied with their marriages and with parenting. They felt that they could have been better parents, and they strongly disliked housework, finding less satisfaction from housework than any other group. Interestingly, however, people who value self-fulfillment did find that their relationship with their spouse was the nicest thing about their marriage more than any other value group. It therefore seems that the trouble with marriage is the demands it makes on time rather than the social commitment, from the perspective of a proponent of self-fulfillment.

Self-fulfillment combines several traditional American virtues into a hybrid value. Individuality, accomplishment, and freedom are all aspects of self-fulfillment.

Marketers already seem well aware of the importance of this value in contemporary America. Products that increase the convenience of life, such as fast foods, disposable diapers, and domestic services, probably appeal to self-fulfillers. Likewise, self-enhancing products, such as exercise equipment and hot tubs, may have a special attraction for these people. Finally, products that require mastery, such as home computers and musical instruments, may interest self-fulfillers. Many purchasing characteristics of accomplishment valuers may be interchangeable with fulfillment valuers.

Being Well-Respected

People who value being well-respected (8.8 percent of the sample) believed that they did not get the respect that they deserved. These people were often over 50 and tended to be craftsmen, operators, farmers, or retired. They were likely to earn $8,000 per year or less, putting them near the bottom of society economically. These people have worked hard, followed the social and behavioral demands of society, gone often to their Baptist, Methodist, or fundamentalist churches, yet other people have not fully admired them because people who valued the respect of others had jobs that lacked prestige and allowed little self-direction. They also lacked education, often only having completed grade school. Even though the pay and value fulfillment from their jobs was low, people who valued the respect of others loved their jobs and had no intention of leaving those jobs. Ironically, these people did not view themselves as especially good at their jobs. The same type of irony can be seen in family roles. These people believed that they were very good spouses but that their marriages were not based on good relationships. Housework gave them satisfaction and fulfillment, even though they often were divorced.

Psychologically, these people had their share of problems. They tended to be depressed, defensive, and external. In fact, being well-respected may require an external orientation more than any other value. Perhaps this fact relates to the lack of happiness, health, and optimism in these people's lives. The internal versus external difference between the respect values, as well as the difference between warm relations and belonging, underscore the problem with Maslow's (1954) theory—the failure to consider the internal-external dimension in values.

These people may be more likely than others to purchase items to enhance respect, but unlike the people who value self-respect, these people cannot afford status symbols that foster prestige through cost. Yet with a more external set of standards than the people who value self-respect, these people must of necessity accept the standards of respect that others provide them. In order to be well-respected you must march to the beat of someone else's drum.

This value segment probably prefers conventional clothing, furniture, and cars. These people constitute an excellent segment for over-the-counter drugs and vitamins, since these products may be attractive to people with an external orientation. This group may also attend with care to information about inexpensive nondurables, since cleanliness and housework interest them.

Sense of Belonging

Just as being well-respected is the external partner of self respect, likewise sense of belonging is the external partner of warm relationships with others. Only 7.9 percent of the respondents selected this value as primary. Women, housewives, clerical workers, and people with a high school education tended to espouse this value. The sense of belonging group tended to experience many psychosomatic symptoms and to take drugs to find relief. They tended to be nervous, anxious, dizzy, and have frequent headaches.

These valuers attended church once a week and were likely to be Presbyterian, Lutheran, or Catholic. These people earned a middle income and were middle-aged. Most importantly, however, they were married. They experienced a great deal of marital satisfaction and derived much value fulfillment from marriage, although they felt that they could be better spouses. Likewise, they derived much satisfaction and fulfillment from parenting. In a sense, one could say that many of the people who endorsed sense of belonging were women who see themselves as belonging to their husbands. These women devote their lives to their families, and when they decide to shop, they have their families in mind.

If this value group did not exist, Procter and Gamble probably would have created it. Its members prize clean laundry, clean teeth, inoffensive underarms, and tasty coffee. Toys fascinate them. These people share externality and probably some product preferences with people who value the respect of others, such as interest in over-the-counter drugs.

Fun-Enjoyment-Excitement

Only 4.5 percent of the respondents selected either fun and enjoyment in life or an exciting life as a primary value. The people who selected fun-enjoyment-excitement tended to be young males. These respondents often were unemployed or had poor, unfulfilling jobs. Sales and labor people often selected this value. These respondents rarely attended church and often did not prefer one religion over another. They found fulfillment from leisure. This group of respondents tended to be childless, and they viewed parenting and housework as unfulfilling. They lacked social support and drank alcohol too much, but otherwise these valuers were remarkably well-adjusted. They did not have trouble with nerves, headaches, dizziness, sleep, or anxiety.

Obviously leisure activities are ones which especially interest the fun-enjoyment-excitement crowd. These people do not avoid pleasure nor hide from amusement. The fun-enjoyment-excitement people seem to be ones who want to "stop and smell the roses," appreciating whatever life is giving them at the moment. In spite of an often bleak present, these people enjoy what they have and feel optimistic and confident about the future.

This group probably spends money on exercise equipment, sporty cars, and vacations. Recreational equipment and products that enhance attractiveness to the opposite sex may also be important.

Discussion

The list of values seems useful simply as a descriptive device to define what now exists. Too often in the marketing literature more attention is given to trends in values than to values per se. For example, one encounters frequent consideration of the trend toward increased leisure and the correlated increase in value placed on fun and enjoyment in life. Given that the value of fun-enjoyment-excitement is especially characteristic of the young, the existence of this trend is probably corroborated by the data presented here; however, marketers should not overlook the fact that more than 4.5 times as many Americans selected self-respect as their primary value as selected fun-enjoyment-excitement. When one considers both respect values and both the primary and secondary value, it is clear that nearly half of Americans value respect a lot. Fun-enjoyment-excitement pales by comparison. Clearly traditional values, even if they are fading, still exert influence on Americans (compare Berkman and Gilson 1978).

Vinson, Scott, and Lamont (1982) suggest four ways in which values may be useful in marketing: market analysis and segmentation, product planning, promotional strategy, and public policy. Positioning and repositioning might be added to that list. Clearly marketers could benefit from information about values at each phase of marketing. Understanding the fundamental values of consumers and linking products to the implicated desires would certainly seem to create new opportunities. Although the list of values presented here has not yet been directly tested within a marketing context, the potential benefit would seem to justify such an attempt, particularly when applied in the context of a specific product. Perhaps the major finding from this research to date is the pervasive importance of values.

Nevertheless, we should exercise prudence in applying values to any area of research, since values certainly have no magical or miraculous properties. Values will probably prove most useful when applied thoughtfully and carefully to a specific product area in conjunction with other useful measures and with an understanding of the adaptive significance of the values in respondents' lives.

The adaptation role of values may be most evident in their interplay with attitudes, as suggested by the functional theory of Katz (1960). Katz proposed that one of four functions attitudes serve is value expression. These attitudes may be aroused through salience of cues associated with values, through appeals for self-image assertion, and through ambiguities that threaten self-esteem. These attitudes may be changed by undermining values or self-concept. Probably most ethical marketing efforts would involve values with attitudes by seeking to establish a link between values and attitudes and by showing that certain attitudes can foster value fulfillment.

When a consumer accepts a link between a value and an attitude, purchasing behavior still has not been established, for we know that considerable complexity intervenes between attitude and behavior (Kahle and Berman 1979; Kahle, Klingel, and Kulka 1981). For example, attitudes best predict behavior when both are measured carefully and have commensurate abstractness. Since values are highly abstract, this generalization implies that predicting very specific behaviors will not be simple.

Much about values and consumer behavior remains to be learned. Only as more sophisticated theoretical (e.g., Hawkins, Best, and Coney 1983) and empirical (e.g., Pitts and Woodside 1983) evidence accumulates can we expect additional progress. This chapter and others in this book suggest, however, that the effort is promising.

References

Berkman, W.W. and C.C. Gilson. *Consumer Behavior: Concepts and Strategies*. Encino, Calif.: Dickenson Publishing, 1978.

Gurin, G., J. Veroff, and S. Feld. *Americans View their Mental Health*. New York: Basic Books, 1960.

Hawkins, D., R. Best, and K. Coney. *Consumer Behavior: Implications for Marketing Strategy*, 2d ed. Dallas: Business Publications, 1983.

Kahle, L.R. *Attitudes and Social Adaptation: A Person-Situation Interaction Approach*. London: Pergamon, 1983, 1984(a).

Kahle, L.R. (ed.) *Social Values and Adaption to Life in America*. New York: Praeger, 1984(b).

Kahle, L.R. and J.J. Berman. Attitudes Cause Behaviors: A Cross-Lagged Panel Analysis. *Journal of Personality and Social Psychology* 37 (1979):315–321.

Kahle, L.R., D.M. Klingel, and R.A. Kulka. A Longitudinal Study of Adolescents' Attitude-Behavior Consistency. *Public Opinion Quarterly* 45 (1981):402–414.

Kahle, L.R., R.A. Kulka, and D.M. Klingel. Low Adolescent Self-Esteem Leads to Multiple Interpersonal Problems: A Test of Social Adaptation Theory. *Journal of Personality and Social Psychology* 39 (1980):496–502.

Katz, D. The Functional Approach to the Study of Attitudes. *Public Opinion Quarterly* 24 (1960):163–204.

Maslow, A.H. *Motivation and Personality*. New York: Harper & Row, 1954.

Piaget, J. *The Origins of Intelligence in Children*. New York: International University Press, 1952.

Pitts, R.E. and A.G. Woodside. Personal Value Influences on Consumer Product Class and Brand Preferences. *Journal of Social Psychology* 119 (1983):37–53.

Rokeach, M. *The Nature of Human Values*. New York: Free Press, 1973.

Veroff, J., E. Douvan, and R.A. Kulka. *The Inner American: A Self-Portrait from 1957 to 1976*. New York: Basic Books, 1981.

Vinson, D.E., J.E. Scott, and L.M. Lamont. The Role of Personal Values in Marketing and Consumer Behavior. In *Consumer Behavior: Classical and Contemporary Dimensions*, edited by J.U. McNeal and S.W. McDaniel. Boston: Little Brown & Co., 1982.

7 Males and Females in the Funnies: A Content Analysis

Harold H. Kassarjian

The influence of mass communication has long been debated with classic studies on the content of advertising, television and magazine fiction, values presented in newpapers, the motion picture, the daytime serial, and dozens of others. This study examines still another medium aimed at both children and adults, but one that simply has not been taken seriously in the scholarly research in consumer behavior—the Sunday comics.

The comics are a serious business. Born during a circulation war between William Randolph Hearst's *New York Journal* and Joseph Pulitzer's *New York World,* the Yellow Kid appeared on July 7, 1895. It was yellow because the foreman in Pulitzer's color press room needed the chance to print a solid block of yellow, a difficult color to print at the time. Under other conditions, the Yellow Kid might have been a different color and yellow journalism, named after the Yellow Kid, probably would be tied to a different hue (Berger 1973). More a political cartoon than a comic strip, it led the way for the strips as we know them today: Katzenjammer Kids, 1898; Buster Brown, 1902; Mutt and Jeff, 1907; Bringing Up Father, 1913; Doonesbury, Andy Capp, Cathy, and Sally Forth in the 1970s.

Peanuts, with its gentle humor and almost universal appeal, is a $150-million-a-year empire. Peanuts appears in more than 1,400 papers around the world, and it has generated hundreds of books in a dozen languages, as well as a Broadway play, a line of greeting cards, annual TV specials, and an entire products industry including sweatshirts, baseball caps, dolls, bedsheets, tie clips, stuffed animals, and calendars. In 1976, the *New York Daily News* paid about $2,000 per week for rights to print the strip, while other newspapers now pay from $300 a week to as little as $5 or $10 per week, depending on what the traffic will bear. Cities with competing newspapers pay considerably more than newspapers without competition. A few years ago, the *Philadelphia Bulletin* paid $200,000 a year to buy an entire package of King Syndicate features and comics from a competitor. "When you lose Blondie and Beetle Bailey, it is no laughing matter" (Shaw 1977).

According to David Shaw, *Los Angeles Times* staff writer, comic readers are intensely—sometimes fanatically—loyal, and when a newspaper drops one of their favorites, the howls of outrage are at times enough to intimidate even the most intrepid editor. For example, Roberts, executive editor of the *Philadelphia Inquirer*, discontinued two comics about dogs—Fred Basset and Rivets. According to Roberts, "the readers went absolutely crazy. I learned a valuable lesson: the only immutable law in this business is never, never, never, run a dog strip unless you plan to stick with it forever. You stop using it and the readers will burn your damn building down." When the *Los Angeles Times* dropped a comic strip featuring a cat, Heathcliff, an editor commented, "We received 1,500 calls and letters. I didn't think we'd escape with our lives" (Shaw 1977).

With such brand loyalty, unheard of in consumer goods, it is strange indeed that the comics have not been studied seriously. Other aspects of the mass media have been dissected and analyzed. But the comics have been relegated to a bit of socially oriented criticism (Wolfe and Fiske 1949) or to informal, casual analyses (Berger 1973; Brabant 1976) in which the researcher examines a sample of strips in an unsystemic way and derives conclusions. In 1955, Saenger studied male and female relations in comic strips from 1950. Some years later, a more thorough study was conducted by Barcus (1963) on comics appearing in the years 1943 to 1958. This study had been heavily influenced by a still earlier study on strips run in 1950 in the *Los Angeles Sunday Times* and *Los Angeles Sunday Examiner* by Spiegelman, Terwilliger, and Fearing (1952, 1953a, 1953b).

In many ways, the present study has been patterned after the Spiegelman paper, allowing for some comparisons between these three studies. However, note the dates of these works: 1943, 1950, 1958, etc. Little in the way of systematic research over the past two-and-a-half decades was uncovered. This may have been due in part to the fact that content analysis lost favor as a research technique and that research in the social sciences turned more to surveys and to the experimental approach to data collection in the laboratory. In consumer research, no work was conducted on the comics, outside of some commercial readership surveys.

Hence the purpose of this study was to examine the Sunday comics over a period of two decades. What kind of people live in the world of comic strips? What is the world in which the characters live, work, die, marry, love, eat, and vote. What are the values expressed and transmitted from the mass media to the populace? How are subgroups handled? What is their role in the fantasy world of the Sunday comics? Has the role of the woman changed from the sweet domesticated role of housewife to that of a modern Brenda Star or Wonder Woman? Is the male presented as a Superman or a bumbling Dagwood Bumstead, and has his role changed over time?

This study, then, is a systematic, formal content analysis of a sample of Sunday comics. It is a measurement of the stimulus material itself, not of the intent of the artist or the newspaper editor, nor is it a measure of how readers perceived the strip. The question is What is in the strips and how has it changed over time?

Method

Years Selected

The first year selected for the study was 1979. Two decades earlier (1959) was the earliest comparison point selected. The third year selected was 1976 to provide a feel for recent trends in the comics.

Selection of Comic Strips

Some 300 strips are available to papers by distributing syndicates. Since microfilm or microfiche files simply would not do and other archival material for a 20-year period was not easily available, the decision was made to use strips as actually published in a major newspaper, rather than a sampling of comics that may have been in existence but little used.

The unit of analysis was three strips per year (three consecutive Sundays). Using random numbers, the three-week unit for each year was selected from the *Los Angeles Times.* The final sample consisted of all comic strips published in the *Los Angeles Times* on October 4, 11, 18, 1959; March 14, 21, 28, 1976; and August 5, 12, 19, 1979. Since some issues of the *Los Angeles Examiner* (later the *Los Angeles Herald—Examiner*) were available, those comics appearing on March 21, 28, April 4, 1976; and August 5, 12, 19, 1979 were also included.[1] The strips used in the study for each year are listed in table 7-1. These strips contained 691 characters—about 9 percent were animals and 91 percent humans (a figure consistent with earlier studies).

Categories of Analysis

The content analysis required judges to examine the comic sections of the Sunday papers during the three consecutive weeks and answer a series of questions. The first set of questions concerned the strip as a whole—whether it was a caricature, whether the strip was a serial or a discrete episode each Sunday, as well as the time and location of action.

Judges were then asked to list the name (or description) of each character appearing in any of the panels for each of the three weeks for each strip and then asked to judge each separately. Categories included demographic characteristics such as sex, age, occupation, and ethnic group, judgments about the values or goals in life, the means for achieving these goals, and, if the character was an animal, whether or not it was anthropomorphized. A list of the categories and an abbreviated definition of each is presented in appendix 7A.

Table 7-1
Newspaper Comic Strips Studied[a]

Los Angeles Times			Los Angeles Examiner	
1979	1976	1959	1979	1976
Rex Morgan	Rex Morgan	Rex Morgan	Snuffy Smith	Snuffy Smith
Mary Worth	Mary Worth	Mary Worth	Bringing Up Father	Bringing Up Father
Peanuts	Peanuts	Peanuts	Prince Valient	Prince Valient
Rick O'Shay	Rick O'Shay	Rick O'Shay	Popeye	Popeye
Dennis the Menace	Dennis the Menace	Dennis the Menace	Blondie	Blondie
Andy Capp	Andy Capp	Dotti	Steve Canyon	Steve Canyon
BC	BC	Dick Tracy	Hagar	Hagar
Heathcliff	Heathcliff	Lil Abner	Juliet Jones	Juliet Jones
Apartment 3G	Apartment 3G	Gasoline Alley	Hi and Lois	Hi and Lois
Crock	Crock	Ferdnand	They'll Do It Everytime	They'll Do It Everytime
Better Half	Better Half	Joe Palooka	Beetle Bailey	Beetle Bailey
Doonesbury	Doonesbury	Nancy	Redeye	Redeye
Momma	Momma	Tarza	Lockhorns	Lockhorns
Broom Hilda	Broom Hilda	Terry and The Pirates	Shoe	Little Iodine
Wizard of Id	Wizard of Id	Mickey Finn	Latigo	Donald Duck
Star Wars	Kelley and Duke	Moon Mullins	Tank McNamara	Mickey Mouse
Drabble	Yankee Doodles	Brenda Star	Agatha Crum	Tiger
Tumbleweeds	Ziggy[b]	Buck Rogers	Spiderman	Scamp
		On Stage	Marmaduke	Hubert
		Dondi	Ziggy[b]	
		Little Orphan Annie		
		Mr. Mum		
		Judge Parker		
		Willy Woo		
		Short Ribs		
		Grin and Bear It		
		Nebbishes		
		Gordo		
		Emmy Lou		

[a] Advertisements and "Believe it or Not by Ripley" were not considered comic strips and were omitted. Also not included were those strips that did not appear in all three consecutive issues for each year: Better Half (1959 *Times*), Dunagins People, Berry's World, Tucker (appearing once in 1979 *Times*).
[b] Ziggy appeared in the 1976 *Times* and 1979 *Examiner*.

The various categories and coding instructions were pretested on pilot studies using comic strips from the 1958 and 1977 *Los Angeles Times* and *Los Angeles Herald Examiner.* All disagreements among pretest judges were discussed and new definitions or clarifications developed until the data clearly indicated that the judges agreed on the precise meanings of the categories and the shades of difference between responses. Consensus was necessary since the purpose of this study was not to measure individual perceptual differences between judges, but rather to establish and define categories describing the stimulus material (comics) across time.

Final Judging

The final set of judges consisted of graduate and undergraduate students recruited from Pennsylvania State University and UCLA who had volunteered several hours of their time. In groups of one to three, they were presented with 1958 and 1977 comic strips and the instructions or coding categories (as summarized in appendix 7A). Their task was to follow those instructions and definitions precisely. Under ideal conditions, the only disagreements should have been clerical errors. Once judges were familiar with the rules, they were presented with a final sample of the Sunday comics and asked to read and judge the strips for about two hours. Each judge worked alone. Typically, individuals processed 5 or 6 different comic strip units each, for a total of 15 to 18 separate installments per judge.

Typically, each strip was processed by two or three judges (table 7-2). As can be seen in table 7-2, about 10,000 separate judgments were made with about 800 disagreements for a reliability figure of .92, quite respectable in content analysis. The errors and disagreements tended to cluster around age (Is Snoopy a teenager or adult? Is Andy Capp classified as adult

Table 7-2
Reliability

	Number of Strips
Strips originally processed by	
Single judge	5
Two judges	99
Three judges	27
Four judges	2
Total number of judgments made	9964
Number of disagreements	789
Total errors in judgment	7.9%
Interjudge reliability	92.1%

or older?) and around the goals and values of characters (Is the goal of Broom Hilda on a lazy Sunday afternoon one of comfort or recreation?). However, all reliability figures were within reasonable limits.[2]

Next, an independent judge was presented with the responses of the original judges and the actual strips. His task was to consider only the disagreements, reread the strip, and adjudicate any differences between judges. In most cases errors were in fact clerical. When substantative differences did occur, this judge was to make the final determination using only the definitions spelled out in the instructions. These judgments were the final data used in this study.

Results

Because a portion of this study has been previously published (Kassarjian 1983), those data will be summarized rather than repeated and then the previously unpublished data will be presented. Since there were no significant overall differences between the two newspapers or between 1976 and 1979, the data were aggregated.

The world of comics is a world of males. Males outnumber females more than two to one. In 1976–1979, 67 percent of the characters were male and 28 percent were female. In 1959, the ratio was 71 percent male to 28 percent female. These results have been consistent for 50 years. Spiegelman et al. (1952) found the population to be 70 percent male. Barcus (1963) in his study of comics from 1943 to 1958 found 72 percent to be male. The consistency is remarkable, for not only do the studies get virtually identical results, but these data agree with the studies in other mass media such as fiction and radio. Women are simply not all that numerous in the mass media, whether it be in the world of books or the world of comics.

Similarly, two-thirds of the characters were classified as middle or working class. There are very few poor and any skewing is toward the upper class. Again, these data are in agreement with earlier studies (Spiegelman et al. 1952; Barcus 1963). As might be expected, those comic characters who work are found mostly in the professional and white collar occupations (e.g., Judge Parker, Dagwood Bumstead) and much less in the unskilled and craftsman categories. This may reflect the interests of the suburban, better-educated readership of newspapers. However, the stability over time is interesting, for there has been little change in occupational distribution over the 20-year period of this study or in earlier studies going back to 1943. Somehow the funnies have ignored the societal changes that have occurred over the past three or four decades.

The world of the comics is consistently an adult world and has been for decades. Fully four-fifths of the characters are adult or older. The comic strip world is one of tranquility and racial harmony. There is no class conflict nor are there racial problems, for there are no minorities. In 1959, 87 percent of the characters were American and of Anglo-Saxon heritage. Interestingly, some changes did occur in the following two decades, with the number of Anglo-Americans dropping to 71 percent. The number of Europeans (e.g., Andy Capp, Wizard of Id) increased from zero to 12 percent during the same time period. American minorities remained an insignificant percentage throughout the 20 years: one Jew (Agatha Crum, 1979), two Mexican-Americans (Gordo, 1969), two Blacks (Doonesbury, 1976; Beetle Bailey, 1979), two Asian-Americans (Doonesbury, 1976), and a few Indians here and there.

The most surprising lack of change, other than the continued paucity of women, was in the categories of minorities. With the changes that have occurred in American society since 1959, one surely could have expected that greater numbers of blacks and other minorities would appear in the comics, but that did not happen.

Finally, how funny are the funnies? The data indicated a slight preponderance of humor strips over adventure strips in 1959, but hardly enough to justify the title *funnies* or *comics* at that time. By the late 1970s, however, about four-fifths of the strips were classified as humorous. It is in this sphere that significant changes have occurred over time. Whether one considers the intent of the strip, the use of caricatures, or the style of the artist, the funnies have become funnier and informal perusal indicated a far subtler brand of humor than the buffoonery of days past. Specific details can be found in Kassarjian (1983).

Males and Females in the Funnies

Saenger (1955), using 1960 strips in an informal analysis, claimed that in the comics, women are presented as less intelligent, less suggestible, and as primarily interested in social life rather than business affairs. Brabant (1976), in her casual analysis of four 1974 strips (Blondie, The Born Loser, Dennis the Menace, and Priscilla's Pop), claimed that women tend to be presented as homebodies engaging in fewer leisure activities than the male and often dressed in an apron. However, Brabent specifically selected four domestic strips in which much of the activity takes place in the home and kitchen.

Table 7–3 presents the results from this study.[3] First, female characters are noticeably younger than males; they are more often depicted as children or teenagers and less often as older folks. Over the 20-year time span, the age of men has not changed, but women did get somewhat older. Further, women are significantly more middle class. Seldom are women presented as upper class, and very rarely is a female presented as lower class. This dif-

Table 7–3
Male-Female Demographics[a]

		Male		Female	
		1959	*1976–1979*	*1959*	*1976–1979*
			(in percent)		
	N^a =	*149*	*283*	*62*	*128*
Age					
Child, teen		15	15	24	20
Adult		75	75	70	71
Older		10	10	6	9
		100	100	100	100
Social class					
Upper		18	17	19	10
Middle		38	42	55	59
Working		32	25	23	23
Lower		10	15	2	3
Don't know		2	1	1	5
		100	100	100	100
Ethnicity					
Anglo-American		87	74	90	81
Hyphenated American		2	2	2	2
Minority		1	1	—	—
American Indian		4	3	—	6[a]
European		—	15	—	6
Other, don't know[b]		6	5	8	5
		100	100	100	100

[a]Human characters only

[b]Arabs in Crock (1976, 1979) and Broom Hilda (1979)
  Black Africans in Tarzan (1959)
  Asians in Steve Canyon (1976)
  Outerspace in Star Wars (1979)

ference between men and women is particularly striking. In the 1970s, 15 percent of men and a mere 3 percent of women were judged as lower class (Maw on Snuffy Smith, an Indian squaw in Redeye, an Indian maiden in Steve Canyon, and Andy Capp's wife). Note that only one of these could be classified as Anglo-American (Maw, a hillbilly).

Turning to ethnic classifications, detailed categories of nationality and ethnic groups were originally devised, but it soon became evident that they would have to be collapsed. Hence the Berelson and Salter (1946) concept of the one hundred percent American was used as the first category of ethnicity. This group includes such characters as Mary Worth, Blondie, Dennis the Menace, and Steve Canyon—white, probably Protestant, and of Anglo-Saxon or Nordic Heritage. It does not include Irish, Italian Catholics, Greeks, or Hungarians. These characters were called *Hyphenate Americans,* American by nationality but not Anglo-Saxon-Nordic by heritage. The category of American minorities included blacks, Jews, Asians, and Chicanos, but did not include American Indians, who had their own category. The rest of the world was divided into European and other.

In fact, in examining the ethnic character of males and females in the comics, one finds that women are even more one hundred percent American than are men. In the 1970s, about 74 percent of men were considered Anglo-Saxon-Nordic, while 80 percent of the women were so classified. There were no female blacks, Mexicans, Orientals, or Jews. Also note that there were significantly fewer female Europeans than male Europeans. Women were primarily depicted as younger, middle-class, one hundred percent Americans.

As for occupations of men and women (table 7-4), the results are consistent with these findings. Very few women held upper-level jobs relative to men. Whereas the number of men in professional careers seems to have increased slightly over the 20 years, it dropped for women from 13 percent to 9 percent. When women do work, it is primarily in white collar positions (secretary, sales clerk, telephone operator), and even so, the percentage has dropped from 21 percent to 13 percent in the past two decades, while unskilled labor (waitress, maid) increased a little. Hence when women do work, it tends to be in the stereotypic female role. Also note that while 10 percent of men could be classified as bums, hobos, or on the dole, among women it was a mere 3 percent. Even then women are never hobos or undesirables.

What is it that female characters do? They are housewives, a role that has increased from 1959 to 1979, or children, or presented in some unde-

Table 7-4
Male-Female Occupation and Role

		Male		Female	
		1959	*1976–1979*	*1959*	*1976–1979*
			(in percent)		
	N^a =	149	283	62	128
Occupation					
Professional		26	28	13	9
White-collar, sales		17	18	21	13
Skilled labor		11	9	1	—
Unskilled, waitress		10	16	3	6
Housewife		—	—[a]	34	38
Student, child		15	14	24	18
No job		12	10	—	3
Retired, don't know		9	5	4	13
		100	100	100	100

[a]One house-husband in Apartment 3-G (1979).

finable category where occupation could not be judged. Simply stated, the comics do not reflect the dramatic changes that have occurred in American society since 1959.

Sexism in the Comics

The issue of sex-role stereotyping and blatant sexism has been studied in television, children's picture books, textbooks, and a variety of other media. In consumer research, the role of women in advertising has been heavily researched in about a dozen papers. In one of these (Venkatesan and Losco 1975), the authors studied thousands of magazine ads in the years 1959 to 1973 in a well-designed content analysis. They had operationalized some of the complaints made by feminist groups about the treatment of women in the media. For example, the National Organization for Women had complained that women were presented as dependent on men, needing male instruction, encouragement, and protection, and as overachieving housewives obsessed with menial tasks.

To examine the treatment of women in the comics, the Venkatesan and Losco categories were used in this study with minor modifications to fit the funnies rather than magazine advertising. The definitions of the categories are in appendix 7A. A portion of the Venkatesan-Losco results are presented in table 7–5. Women were primarily presented in magazine advertising as sex objects, physically concerned about cosmetics and accessories to enhance beauty and appeal, and dependent on men. Only 13 percent of the thousands of ads examined over a dozen years were not free from these classifications of sexism.

Table 7–5
Human Female Role and Sexism

		Venkatesan and Losco[a]		*This Study*	
		1959–1963	*1969–1971*	*1959*	*1976–1979*
			(in percent)		
	N =	4100	5314	62	128
Dependent on man		24	26	14	13
Overachieving housewife		13	8	7	8
High living		9	8	3	6
Physically beautiful		25	39	10	5
Sexual object		54	53	3	6
None of the above		14	13	63	62
		139	147	100	100

[a]Venkatesan and Losco (1975) used multiple answers in their study. In this study judges selected the single best category rather than multiple responses, hence the results are not directly comparable.

In the comics, the picture is quite different (table 7–5). Two-thirds of the comic strips simply did not display the blatant sexism found in magazine ads. About 13 percent of the women were presented as dependent on men, 8 percent as overachieving housewives, and minimal percentages in the other categories. A mere 3 percent to 6 percent of women in the comics were presented as sexy or sex objects, as compared to 53 percent in magazine advertising. Perhaps it is difficult for a Blondie, Brenda Star, or Momma to compete with a Cheryl Tiegs or Farrah Fawcett. Things simply do not change much or very fast in the comic pages. The percentages have remained relatively stable over the past two decades.

The Task of Men and Women

If women in the comics are not sex objects or overachieving housewives, what is it that they do? Table 7–6 presents these data. Women are primarily interested in recreation and leisure, and the percentages have increased dramatically since 1959. Men also show a greater interest in recreation over the past two decades (31 percent to 42 percent) but for women the change has been from 32 percent to 53 percent. When women do work, it is much less at an outside job or in a decorative role than it used to be and more often in the home. Men, on the other hand, are almost never seen working in the home, garden, or workshop. Marketing activities, not important for either sex, are less important for men than for women in the comics in recent years.

Table 7–6
Setting or Task of Males and Females

		Male		Female	
		1959	1976–1979	1959	1976–1979
			(in percent)		
	N =	149	283	62	128
Task					
Recreation, leisure		32	42	32	53
Working at job		54	50	27	15
Working at home, garden, workshop		1	3	17	21
Marketing (selling, buying)		3	1	3	4
Student, decorative other		10	4	21	7
		100	100	100	100
Hero or Villain?					
Hero, good, kind		75	78	82	89
Villain, mean, bad		20	19	11	4
Don't know		5	3	7	5
		100	100	100	100

In the comics, women are neither ignored nor presented as sex symbols; the differences between men and women are more subtle. The woman seems to be treated very gently. She is the sweet, young, white, middle-class housewife concerned about her home and presented, not as an overachieving pot-scrubber, but as a soul interested in recreation and leisure activities.

From this, one would assume that women are seldom presented in villainous roles, which are, indeed, usually reserved for males (primarily minorities and foreigners). The lower section of table 7-6 presents these data. In recent years, 89 percent of women in the funnies have been presented as good and kind heroines as compared to 78 percent of men cast in heroic roles. Such positive depiction has increased for women over the past two decades, more than it has for men. Typically, male villains tend to be evil knights, spies, bandits, and burglars. Female villains are characters like Fat Girl (Crock), an Indian Squaw (Redeye), and Lucy in Peanuts, who really are not all that bad.

In general, the characters in the strips are good people, and for women the pattern is even more exaggerated. Women are a bit more American and a bit nicer than men, and although they obviously don't work as hard, they also don't do mean things other than occasionally enticing a male or pulling a football away from an unsuspecting Charlie Brown. The sexually attractive Wonder Woman and the beautiful but evil Dragon Lady (Terry and the Pirates) belong to another era.

Goals and Values

Consistent with the setting or task of the characters, when one turns to the goals or values (table 7-7), one again finds that leisure and relaxed living are important. For both men and women, recreation and comfort were major goals (40 percent for men and 33 percent for women in 1979, up from about 25 percent each in 1959). A comfortable state, physical integrity, and psychological well-being best describe the modal value system of the funnies. Interestingly, there is little difference between men and women. Although women were more often presented in a recreational setting (table 7-6), the expressed or implied goals of both sexes are similar. Women do tend to be somewhat more interested in group success, family enhancement, and group welfare than men, while men tend to be more interested in freedom, personal independence, and escape from authority.

Although wealth and the accumulation of property and luxury items are not all that important in the comics, men are more concerned about money and what it buys than are women, and more so in the past than in the present.

Justice, maintenance, and administration of law, the apprehension of law-breakers, and the rectification of wrongs to society are also in the male

Table 7-7
Male-Female Values and Goals

		Male		Female	
		1959	1976-1979	1959	1976-1979
			(in percent)		
	N =	149	283	62	128
Recreation, sports, visiting		15	19	11	16
Comfort, relaxed living		11	13	14	19
Physical and psychological well-being		14	15	13	15
Group, family enhancement		12	10	15	15
Romantic love		3	1	14	13
Wealth		14	10	8	7
Freedom, personal independence		5	8	1	2
Adventure		5	7	1	4
Power, dominance		13	14	15	14
Vengeance		9	6	3	3
Brutality, violence		5	6	1	—
Altruism, service		11	12	15	12
Justice		15	4	3	2
Science, wisdom, theoretic		5	4	1	3
Others, don't know		4	5	7	2
Total[a]		141	134	122	127

[a]Multiple answers add to more than 100 percent.

domain, although these values have dropped precipitously as goals in the past 20 years. This may be due to a decrease of adventure strips and to a corresponding increase in humorous strips over the years. Revenge, brutality, and physical violence are also in the male domain, but again, these are not major values promulgated in the comics.

The picture of men that emerges is the stereotypic one of virility, strength, and macho interest. Women, on the other hand, are stereotyped as soft, tender housewives interested in family and group enhancement. Romance and need for passionate affection from the opposite sex are reserved for women; love and tenderness are simply not for men. These differences are fairly consistent over the 20-year period. Compared across studies, the results are once again amazingly similar. My 1979 data seldom show more than minor differences from the 1950 data of Spiegelman or the 1943-1958 data of Barcus.

The only counterindication to the conclusion that males are presented as tough and aggressive while women are passive, tender, and romantically inclined is in the category of power and dominance in interpersonal relations. One would expect that this goal would better fit the male macho stereotype than the soft and unassuming role reserved for the female. Power is simply not a tender, romantic behavior pattern. However, there is no difference between men and women on power and domination needs and goals.

These data could not be easily explained except for a fortuitous stroke of luck. The Barcus study was uncovered after this study had been designed, the data collected, and processed. Barcus had asked a question not thought of or considered in this study—namely, is the comic character single or married? That single moderator variable made a significant difference on a few of the goals and values expressed by comic characters. Single men were portrayed as stronger and more active than married ones. Married men were shorter, fatter, uglier, balder, and generally less attractive than their single compatriots.

According to Barcus (1963, pp. 204, 213), "When single, the male exceeds the female in power goals, but when married, there is a reversal." In short, marriage seems to change people—at least in the fantasy world of the funnies. The aggressive power-seeking single male is rapidly socialized into a milder, perhaps more henpecked "Milktoast," whereas the married female also is transformed such that "The married female exceeds all other groups in power goals." In short, married men and single women are less dominating and power-oriented than are single males or married females.

What changes may have occurred on this variable over the past twenty years are not known and, if this study is ever replicated, it clearly should include the marital status of the characters. Nevertheless, the conclusions do not change. The goals of the women in the comic strips are more those of the stereotyped female—soft, tender, romantically inclined seeking a relaxed life of comfort and recreation. Males are the strong, masculine, aggressive "better half," seeking power and domination (at least while single, and perhaps relinquishing it after marriage).

Means to the Goal

The means employed to reach these goals are presented in table 7–8. Men and women again differ and in the expected direction. Both use industry and hard work, and both men and women have changed such that fate, luck, and external forces are relied on far more now than two decades ago. However force and violence are used by men much more than women. Also, sponging and imposing on others is a male characteristic rather than female (in fact, the only female categorized as a sponge was a prehistoric woman in B.C.).

The means women use consists of personal charm and affability. However, charm shows a significant drop as a means to the end for both men and women in the past 20 years, to be replaced by diligence for men and by luck for both sexes. These data corroborate earlier findings and stereotypes.

Table 7–8
Male-Female Means to the Goal

	N =	Male		Female	
		1959	1976–1979	1959	1976–1979
			(in percent)		
	N =	149	283	62	128
Industry, diligence		36	34	23	34
Personal charm		23	15	53	37
Trickery, cunning		16	9	14	9
Violence, force		11	9	2	4
Sponging, imposition		3	4	—	1
Fate, luck		15	27	11	23
Established authority		17	15	18	10
Others, don't know		7	5	5	3
Total[a]		128	118	126	121

[a]Multiple answers add to more than 100 percent.

Summary and Conclusion

As many as 100 million people in the United States, and perhaps two or three times that number worldwide are exposed to the comics.[4] The purpose of this study was to determine the major values, goals, means to the goal, and messages that this amazing medium of communication has been promulgating to these readers. The technique used as a formal, systematic content analysis of the Sunday comics during the years 1959, 1976, and 1979.

The values held by the characters revolved around recreation, a relaxed lifestyle, and their own psychological and physical integrity; there was little room for romantic love, aggression, brutality, or vengeance. To reach these goals, the comic characters use industry, hard work, charm, established power, and fate—the Protestant ethic of middle America. There is little emphasis on deceit, threats, force, or sponging. Interestingly, very few changes occurred over the two decades measured in this study. In fact, combined with other studies to account for an even longer period of time, the comics simply do not change all that much. In many ways the comics reflect reality; in many others, they are a fantasy world that is not much affected by the day-to-day changes of society.

Women are not depicted all that differently from men. There is some stereotyping, but not as much as one finds in advertising or perhaps even television. Women are a bit younger, a bit more white Anglo-Saxon-Nordic and a bit more middle-class than males. Prime occupations for females are housewife, waitress, sales clerk, or student; seldom does one see a professional, and almost never a manager or business executive. They spend much more time working in the home, whereas men seldom work there, even in the garden or basement. The goals of women are more delicate—romance, recreation, and family enhancement—and they strive toward these goals through hard work, charm, and fate. Men are also interested in recreation and the good life, but unlike women, love is inconsequential. Wealth, justice, vengeance, and brutality—macho virile characteristics—are more important to them than to women. Men, too, primarily use industry, diligence, charm, and fate to reach their goals, but also use violence and force a bit more often.

Notes

1. In reality this study was conceived some 25 years ago when the author was a graduate student. Since that time, the Sunday comics from the *Los Angeles Times* and the *Los Angeles Examiner* were saved and stored in the garage on an irregular basis. Hence, the sample consisted of a random selection of selected strips that were available. If deteriorating newspapers in a suburban garage can be defined as a statistical universe, the sample was a representative one.

2. Another measure of the reliability of the judging occurred serendipitously. Due to author stupidity, several judges at Penn State were informed of the purpose of the study and the hypotheses. These judges knew what the researcher was looking for before they saw the study. When this error was pointed out by several marketing department colleagues, those data were put aside and new judges recruited for the actual study. Next, these strips were processed a third time using judges recruited from the UCLA student body. On a small subsample of strips, we thus had judgments made by knowledgeable Penn State students, naive Penn State students, and naive UCLA students. The reliability between these sets of judges was almost identical to the overall reliability presented in table 7-2. It simply did not matter whether the judges know the hypotheses or were from the East coast or the West coast. That is as it should have been, for this study was not measuring interpreter or audience characteristics, but stimulus characteristics which did not change.

3. In comparing males and females (table 7-3 through 7-8), animals were not included, although they were in the earlier calculations. Since the animal population was so small, it would have made no difference, and the conclusions would be identical; however, the sex role of male and female ducks or domestic relations among a family of mice did not seem appropriate.

4. In the United States, newspaper sales are about 60 million. Obviously, not all papers carry comics and not all buyers read them. However, most newspapers are read by more than one person, hence an estimate of 100 million.

References

Barcus, Francis E. The World of Sunday Comics. In *The Funnies: An American Idiom,* edited by D.M. White and Robert H. Abel. New York: The Free Press, 1963. Pp. 190–218.

Berelson, Bernard, and Patricia J. Salter. Majority and Minority Americans: An Analysis of Magazine Fiction. *Public Opinion Quarterly* 10 (1946):168–190.

Berger, Arthur A. *The Comic-Stripped American.* Baltimore: Penguin Books, 1973.

Brabant, Sarah. Sex Role Stereotyping in the Sunday Comics. *Sex Roles* 2 (1976):331–337.

Fearing, Franklin. Toward a Psychological Theory of Human Communication. *Journal of Personality* 22 (1953):71–88.

Kassarjian, Harold H. Content Analysis in Consumer Research. *Journal of Consumer Research* 4 (June 1977):8–18.

Kassarjian, Harold H. Social Values and the Sunday Comics: A Content Analysis. In *Advances in Consumer Research,* Vol. 10, edited by R.P. Bagozzi and A.M. Tybout. Ann Arbor, Mich.: Association for Consumer Research, 1983. Pp. 434–438.

Saenger, Gerhart. Male and Female Relations in the American Comic Strip. *Public Opinion Quarterly* 19 (Summer 1955):195–205.

Shaw, David. The Comics—A Serious Business. *Los Angeles Times,* Part 1, April 28, 1977, p. 1ff.

Spiegelman, Marvin, Carl Terwilliger, and Franklin Fearing. The Content of Comic Strips: A Study of a Mass Medium of Communication. *Journal of Social Psychology* 36 (1952):37–57.

Spielgelman, Marvin, Carl Terwilliger, and Franklin Fearing. The Content of Comics: Goals and Means to Goals of Comic Strip Characters. *Journal of Social Psychology* 37 (1953):189–203. (a)

Spielgelman, Marvin, Carl Terwilliger, and Franklin Fearing. The Reliability of Agreement in Content Analysis. *Journal of Social Psychology* 37 (1953):175–187. (b)

Venkatesan, M., and Jean Losco. Women in Magazine Ads: 1959–71. *Journal of Advertising Research* 15 (October 1975):49–54.

Wolfe, K., and M. Fiske. The Children Talk about Comics. In *Communications Research 1948–49,* edited by Paul Lazarsfeld and F.N. Stanton. New York: Prentice-Hall, 1949.

Appendix 7A
Categories of Analysis

I. Strip as a Whole

Drawing
1. Caricature: distortion of physical characteristics (e.g., Andy Capp)
2. Noncaricature: likeness to recognizable human beings (e.g., Mary Worth)

Continuity
1. Serial: continuity of plot in two or more strips (e.g., Mary Worth)
2. Discrete: complete and discrete episode (e.g., Peanuts)
3. Panel: unique and separate cartoons in each strip (e.g., The Better Half)

Humor versus Adventure
1. Laughter: intent of strip is to arouse laughter or a smile. A humorous strip.
2. Adventure: excitement or nonhumorous interest aroused
3. Can't tell

Location
1. On earth
2. Other plant/outer space
3. Can't tell

If the action takes place on earth, complete the three blocks which follow.
1. Historical: reasonably accurate depiction of events, although particular individuals need not be historical characters
2. Contemporary: occurs at present time
3. Future
4. Can't tell

1. In United States
2. Not in United States
3. Can't tell

1. Urban: set in a city or town
2. Suburban
3. Rural: farm or ranch, rural areas
4. Can't tell

II. Characters in the Strip

Part A

Description: Describe or name the character you are evaluating. For each character go to Part B.

Part B

Importance
1. Character plays a vital role; plot impossible without character
2. Supporting character: character is important in plot development but not vital
3. Extra character: serves as background to the main action

Sex
1. Male
2. Female
3. Don't know

Age (If animal, estimate approximate age category)
1. Child
2. Teen-age (13–19)
3. Adult (20–49)
4. Older (50 plus)
5. Don't know

Socioeconomic Class
1. Upper Class: indications of wealth (perhaps inherited), prosperity, high social prestige
2. Middle Class: indications of moderate income and somewhat higher than average social prestige, comfortable living
3. Working Class: fair economic status, a lower than average prestige and social status
4. Lower Class: impoverished to poor, no prestige or social status
5. Simply cannot say

Apparent Occupation
1. Professional: doctor, lawyer, high-level business executive, nurse
2. Entertainer: professional sports (highly paid, not piano player in a bar)
3. Nonprofessional white collar: sales, clerical, low-level manager, bank teller
4. Skilled craftsman: foreman, mechanic, police, fireman, blue collar job

  5. Semiskilled blue collar: truck driver, waiter, waitress, janitor
  6. No job: no skills, untrained, perhaps on welfare, hobo
  7. Student
  8. Housewife
  9. Child (also pet or animal without a job)
 10. Retired
 11. Don't know

Ethnic Group
  1. White American, no ancestry indicated, 100 percent WASP
  2. American black
  3. American Indian
  4. American, Jewish ancestry
  5. American, Oriental ancestry
  6. American, Mexican ancestry
  7. American, other ethnic ancestry (e.g., Irish, British, German)
  8. Non American: African
  9. Non American: European
 10. Non American: Asian
 11. Non American: other area
 12. From outer space
 13. Don't know

Setting or Role of the Character
  1. Working on a job (other than marketing activity)
  2. Shopping, buying, selling, or other marketing activity dealing with products
  3. Working in the home, gardening, cleaning, kitchen, or workshop
  4. Recreational or leisure role
  5. Student activities such as studying, reading, or in class
  6. Decorative role (no apparent role other than to decorate the scene; e.g., beautiful girl walking by)
  7. Other (write in on answer sheet)
  8. Don't know

Interaction of female with other characters (for female characters only: if male character, skip to next section)
More than one may apply:
  1. Woman as dependent on man

     Needs male instruction, encouragement, reinforcement; requires male for affection, instruction, happiness, leisure, protection

  2. Woman as overachieving housewife

Overly concerned with menial tasks; concerned with ultimate cleanliness; being a good housewife or mother

3. Woman as high living

   Concerned with luxurious leisure, material possessions, expensive adornments, decorative products

4. Woman as physically beautiful

   Concerned with cosmetics, accessories to enhance physical beauty; concerned with looking more youthful, slimmer, more appealing

5. Woman as a sexual object

   Presented in a decorative role to attract man; sexy poses; partially clad or nude

6. None of the above categories fit

Sympathy
1. Character is likeable; a "good guy"
2. Character has negative expectation; villain; thwarts efforts of hero or friends; a "bad guy"
3. Don't know

Goals: Select the primary goals that seem to be guiding the character's actions. (If there is an important secondary goal, place in next column.)
1. Brutality: physical violence for satisfaction, pleasure, as an end in itself
2. Vengeance: retribution of revenge for some wrong or mistreatment imagined or actually inflicted on individual character (not society)
3. Power-Status: dominance in interpersonal relations; self-advancement in social status
4. Wealth: accumulation of money, land, property, luxury items
5. Freedom: escape from authority, personal independence
6. Physical and psychological integrity: maintenance of well-being of self under threat of injury, illness, tension, etc.
7. Adventure: new experience as an end in itself; may be hazardous enterprise for pleasure
8. Remantic love: tender and passionate affection for and from person of opposite sex
9. Recreation: play, diversion, visiting, sports
10. Comfort: relaxed living, settled family state
11. Justice: maintenance and administration of law; apprehension of lawbreakers; rectification of wrongs to groups, society
12. Group success: protection or enhancement of family or group welfare, prestige; may be ethnic or sports group, for example, or family success and status

13. Service-Benefactor: altruism; regard for and devotion to interests of others
14. Theoretical goals: science, wisdom, knowedge for its own sake
15. Aesthetic goals: beauty, art, music for its own sake
16. Religion: mysticism, belief in God or evil
17. Other: write in on answer sheet
18. Don't know

Means: Select the primary means used by the character in striving for their goals. (If there is an important secondary means use next column.)
1. Industry: diligence, planning, doggedness, determination
2. Personal charm: cordiality or affability; natural or consciously assumed
3. Fate: acceptance of, or resignation to, control by other persons or environmental forces
4. Authority: legal or rightful power; a right to command or act as a result of a public prestige position or cultural role
5. Trickery: artifice or stratagem; crafty procedure or practice; nonviolent
6. Violence: physical force
7. Sponging: imposition on others; living parasitically without cost; does not refer to children or housewives
8. Other: (write on answer sheet)
9. Don't know

If character is animal, continue. If character is a human, go on to next character or next set of strips.

Anthropomorphization
1. Animal character demonstrates human characteristics, expressions of physiognomic character; emotion, intelligence, insight, not usually associated with animals (e.g., Snoopy in Peanuts)
2. Animal character demonstrates no human characteristics of any kind

Situation
1. Appropriate: animal is usually associated with the scene in which it appears (e.g., city has dogs, farm has cows)
2. Inappropriate: animal is not usually associated with the scene (e.g., ducks do not have television sets or drive automobiles)

Type of Animal: Write in the type of animal being considered.

8

The Identification and Distribution of Values Manifest in Print Advertising 1900–1980

Richard W. Pollay

Values are probably the single most important dimension of advertising, despite the paucity of research on the subject. Values are important from both the sender's and receiver's point of view, because it is the goodness of products that lies at the heart of the whole communication. Despite the economist's concern for information transmittal, it is clear that advertising's primary function is to transmit value to a product and brand, and information is of tactical usefulness only to the extent that consumers are responsive to it, effecting a communication of values.

As William Phillips, the chairman and CEO of Ogilvy and Mather International, recently noted to the Conference Board, because of "the added value in psychological terms, advertising has become the last stage in the manufacturing process . . . In very real ways, advertising turns the product into the 'brand'" (Kaselow 1982). It is by the effective transmission of values that alternatives that might be otherwise indistinguishable, veritable commodities become transformed into goods. The package contains the product, but the advertising delivers the goods.

Since the transmission of values always involves the implicit message that these are the appropriate values, there has long been concern from social critics about the value profile of advertising. These voices raise doubts about advertising's social and cultural consequences and come from diverse academic and professional disciplines within commercial cultures like our own. Similar concerns are now being expressed in forceful ways about the effects of transnational advertising on developing countries. UNESCO's recent MacBride Commission report, chaired by a Nobel Peace Prize winner, notes that "advertising is seen by many as a threat to cultural identity and self-realization; it brings to many people alien ethical values; it affects and can often deform ways of life and life-style." Because of this and other effects, "there is a real need for an independent, comprehensive and systematic comparative inquiry . . . into both the direct and indirect, the intended and the unintended effects" (MacBride 1980, pp. 111, 154).

This research takes the first step toward that end by developing a measurement methodology suitable to analysis of values manifest in advertising.

Why Advertising?

> (As) the maintenance, enhancement, and transmission of values within a culture typically become institutionalized, then an identification of the major institutions of a society should provide us with a reasonable point of departure for a comprehensive compilation and classification of human values (Rokeach 1973, p. 25).

Many institutions perform a value transmission function. There is good reason, however, to pay particularly close attention to advertising as a carrier of cultural values. Unlike the other institutions of the family, church, courts, universities, etc., advertising plays a major role in the mass media, thereby giving it far more universal influence. It also employs a full spectrum of artists in various media to create communications of potency. Thus, study of advertising's cultural character is essential to understanding the cultural evolution of commercialized societies.

Historians, led largely by Potter's influential *People of Plenty* (1954), feel that despite the relatively pedestrian motivation of each advertiser to simply sell more, advertising's greater significance lies in its aggregate impact, providing an omnipresent rhetorical environment which surrounds people of all ages, classes, and interests.

> Advertising has joined the charmed circle of institutions which fix the values and standards of society and it has done this without being linked to any of the socially defined objectives which usually guide such institutions in the use of their power . . . then it becomes necessary to consider with special care the extent and nature of its influence, how far it extends and in what way it makes itself felt (Potter 1954, p. 177).

Toward Definitions

Values are those properties of objects, individuals, or communities which make them good, worthy, or respectable. It is difficult to write a definition without the tautological circularity of such terms as *ought* or *should*, but we can borrow from the work of Rokeach, who defines values as

> A value is an enduring belief that a specific mode of conduct or end-state of existence is personally or socially preferable to an opposite or converse mode of conduct or end-state of existence. A value system is an enduring organization of beliefs concerning preferable modes of conduct or end-states of existence along a continuum of relative importance (Rokeach 1973, p. 5).

Both personalities and cultures can be characterized by the behavior and consequences valued, their hierarchy of these values, the rules of dominance in their application, and the general balancing of apparently contradictory value states (e.g., pride versus modesty, natural versus technological).

> A value is a selective orientation toward experience, implying deep commitment or repudiation, which influences the ordering of "choices" between possible alternatives in action. These orientations may be cognitive and expressed verbally or merely inferable from recurrent trends in behavior (Kluckhohn 1961, p. 18).

Virtually all kinds of behavior and attitudes, from simple purchasing acts to political and religious ideology, are derived from values. Values restrain or canalize an individual's impulse toward culturally approved acts and attitudes. They guide the presentation of self and the evaluation and judging of both self and others. They are standards that govern what beliefs and behaviors are worth preserving, trying to change, and even going to war and dying for.

> Values, then, are images formulating positive or negative action commitments, a set of hierarchically ordered prescriptions and proscriptions. Without a hierarchy of values, human behavior could be described by a list of instincts and a probabilistic calculus. Human life would become a sequence of reactions to unconfigured stimuli (Kluckhohn 1961, p. 20).

How Do Advertisements Utilize Values?

From the practitioner's viewpoint, advertisements utilize values in every way possible. It is exactly the business of the creative process to create values such that products become goods. Contemporary advertising takes a slightly different tack toward the same end by portraying the manner in which the consumers of products become good, either to themselves or to others. The creative process uses everything at its disposal, all the tools of rhetoric and the artistry of illustration, to portray the product or its consumers as idealized and deserving of adoration or envy.

Hayakawa (1964) likens advertising to poetry and notes that the "copywriter, like the poet, must invest [the product] with significance so that it becomes symbolic of something beyond itself . . . the task of the copywriter is the poeticizing of consumer goods." Price (1978) describes commercials as contemporary myths encouraging us to "perform a substitute act, a symbolic gesture, in which we put coins on a counter and pick up a magic potion or a symbolic object." Levi-Strauss (1966) uses the concept of *bricoleur* to describe the process by which the creators of advertisements assemble the oddments of cultural symbols to invest products with new meanings.

Let us examine how this is done. The copywriting often manifests values by simple assertion, stating quite plainly that a particular product is good because it has certain properties. If we share a value with the author, we ask no further questions when he says that the product is worthy because it is cheap, modern, or popular. We understand that to be cheap, new, or popular is to be good. Thus, a simple claim that a soap will get you clean presumes the valuation of cleanliness.

It is not always the case that such a valuation is presumed. Often argument is extended to demonstrate how such a property is instrumental to the attaining of some other valued end-state. For example, cleanliness might be shown as instrumental toward social acceptance among peers, sexuality and romance, or economic achievement, not to mention health. In these cases, it is the ultimate rationale or the ulterior motive that manifests the value presumed by the copywriter. It is this rhetorical frontier, where the goodness of the product goes without further elaboration, that identifies the principal values that the advertisement depends on, implicity ratifies, and hence reinforces.

Values are also manifest in the visual imagery of the advertisement, and often quite directly. The quality being communicated can be displayed in a manner that parallels the direct rhetorical assertion. The classic styling of dinnerware may be displayed or the capacity of a product to enhance the consumer's sexual attractiveness may be evidenced. Often the process relies on simple association, where a mood, feeling, or affect communicated by the art surrounds the product, like so much sugar-coating on a bitter pill.

Imagery can also communicate values in a somewhat more artful but oblique fashion. The artistic presentation of a person, object, setting, or event which contains the properties to be transferred to the product accomplishes this transformation by simply bringing the source and the recipient of these properties into a contiguous relationship. This contiguity asks us to see an essential similarity between the product and the presented reference, and to treat this similarity as a metaphoric one. Visual metaphors, like their verbal counterparts, are often quite evocative, transmitting multiple meanings or dimensions of both similarity and difference. To prevent ambiguity in the communication, the property to be transferred to the product is often reiterated or clarified in the text. Cues from the captioning and body copy, as well as a general redundancy, typically clarify which properties of the referent are to be transferred to the product or manufacturer.

For example, Kodak, desiring to communicate the trustworthiness of their film products, recently ran a magazine advertisement with a charming picture of a grandfatherly farmer surrounded by small children all gently stroking a baby pig. The entire text read "Trust Kodak," but the power of the communication is contained in the trust displayed in the pictoral imagery at multiple levels. The small children are entrusted to the care of the farmer and the baby pig is similarly entrusted to the care of all of those present. Thus, the value of trustworthiness is communicated in a metaphoric way. The same group of children might be portrayed in a manner that lends their youth, innocence, or excitement to the product, but the text, as sparse as it is, explicates any ambiguity in the photography and makes clear the advertiser's intent. (For additional discussion, see McCracken and Pollay 1981.)

The Inventory of Values in Advertising

Many sources might be drawn on to develop a universe of value concepts appropriate to the analysis of the content of ads. Starch (1923) identified 48 different motives utilized in advertising, ranging in apparent effectiveness from hunger, appetite, and love of offspring to shyness and teasing. Andren et al. (1980) generated an ad hoc list of 24 rhetorical approaches. Berger (1980) raised many provocative questions, although he provided no specific methods. A widely known list of motives is represented by Henry Murray's needs (1938). Fowles (1976) used an abbreviated form of Murray's 26 needs and coded advertisements according to 18 needs. Murray's needs were more extensively adapted for the content analysis of values by White (1951) in his study of propaganda.

Although not yet used in content analysis, the most widely cited and recognized contemporary work on value analysis is Rokeach's (1973) identification of 18 instrumental and 18 terminal values for a self-descriptive task. The terminal values were distilled from a large list drawn from a literature review and an interview process (not unlike focus groups) through which citizens' own values were elicited. After identifying several hundred concepts, these were reduced through recognition of synonymous meanings and the elimination of items that were too specific or that did not represent end-states of existence.

The instrumental values were a result of a pruning from 555 personality traits. Again, the pruning was done on the basis of judgment of synonymity; the values apparently most important in American society; those likely to be maximally discriminating across social status, race, age, and other demographic variables; and those minimally intercorrelated. The final set of values used by Rokeach were organized into the two lists presented to respondents for their self-descriptive ranking, clearly a different task from the coding of content. Munson and McIntyre (1979) suggested these personal values can also be measured with Likert scales, although Reynolds and Jolly (1980) rejected this methodology as less reliable than either rank ordering or paired comparison methods.

Necessary Conditions for a Value Inventory

Analytical Flexibility. Minimal intercorrelation between categories is desirable, making each category unique and the coding task minimally ambiguous. Categories hopefully will provide for maximal discrimination between the cultural content of advertising and the values promoted by other social institutions. The more detailed the coding system, the greater the opportunity for a refactoring and the recognition of the patterns of joint utilization of values in the promotional process. The categories should also facilitate the ready identification of the changing relative utilizations of those values which occur in natural dualisms. This means that items like safety and adventure must be measured independently and cannot be used jointly to anchor a single scale, as in methodologies like the semantic differential.

Consistency with the Literature. The final set of categories ought to be consistent not only with the literature that discusses the measurement of values in other contexts, but also with the literature commenting on the social role of advertising. The best known of these works is Greyser's (1972) "Advertising: Attacks and Counters." A more recent and thorough discussion focusing on the cultural consequences of advertising as evidenced in the conventional wisdom of the contemporary scholarly community is presented by Sangha and Pollay (1981).

Depth. The richness of advertising as a communication can only be captured to the extent that a procedure permits the coding of both art and copy and the recognition of both dominant and subordinate themes.

Inclusivity. Coding categories for all of the common advertising appeals should be included. The frequency with which these appeals occur will also determine the breadth or narrowness in the elaboration of coding categories. Some underutilized categories will no doubt persist, as advertising's cultural role may well be characterized by those values conspicuous in their absence. The coding scheme should also have concepts appropriate to the values attached to objects, self, and/or society, for all of these are used in advertising.

Reliability. The need for reliability suggests some parsimony in the length of the list, although, everything else being equal, reliability can be increased by making the coding task easier through a structural organization of the list into clear cognitive patterns and with consistency of definitions. The maximizing of reliability also calls for the careful training of coders and a procedure which minimizes coding fatigue.

Scale Development

Pilot testing on a sample of one hundred ads was performed using each of the schemes of Fowles, White, and Rokeach in the effort to develop a set of content categories which met these criteria. This process identified categories which were rarely utilized and which might be collapsed with little loss of information retrieval capacity. It also identified the desirability of partitioning some of the very frequently used categories into subcategories, such as the isolation of passive and active modalities of leisure or the delineation of the various kinds of practicality possessed by various products. The difficulty and apparent inexactness of coding of some ads suggested the need for additional categories not found on previous lists, categories like the valuation of products for their magical properties.

Colleagues in sociology, anthropology, and consumer behavior refined certain of the conceptual boundaries between categories and encouraged a crystallization of the concepts into dualistic pairs of naturally competitive values, for example, cheap versus dear, or practical versus ornamental. The application of the evolved sets of definitions to a large convenience sample of contemporary ads added further key words to the definitions and additional illustrations and examples that contemporary coders would be likely to recognize.

The final system of concepts, together with their definitions and occasional illustrative examples, can be seen in figure 8-1.

Testing Procedure

Two thousand magazine ads were drawn randomly from the best selling magazines of each decade from the turn of the century to contemporary times. This longitudinal sample was chosen to challenge the methodology with advertisements of diverse character. The coders, graduate students who had been coding these ads on other admittedly more mundane attributes, were trained for this task by an introductory session during which the concepts were introduced and discussed. As preparation for this session, the coders had read Hayakawa's (1964) "Poetry and Advertising."

They then rated an orientation sample of one hundred ads, attempting to identify primary, secondary, and tertiary themes and discussed with each other the challenges and clarifications they experienced. Difficulties with the division into three content levels led to a dominant/subordinate dichotomy. Clarifications to definitions and examples precipitated by this experience were checked to guarantee that they involved no misunderstanding of the core concepts. Since learning seemed to be continuing, the coders then independently rated a second orientation sample of fifty ads and the interrater consistency of this rating was discussed. All coding was carried out under the following instructions:

Dominant themes are those that are key elements of the ad's "gestalt," or first impression. They are manifest in illustrations and headings, titling,

Figure 8-1. Definition of Values

Belong (Belong)

Affiliation (Group)

to be accepted; liked by peers, colleagues, and community at large; to associate or gather with; to be social

to join, unite, or otherwise bond in friendship, fellowship, companionship, cooperation, reciprocity

to conform to social customs, have manners; social graces and decorum; tack and finesse

Note: Romantic affiliations code as *Sexuality* or **Family** based on context. Social dominance codes as **Status**.

Nurturance (Nurtur)

to give gifts, especially sympathy, help, love, charity, support, comfort, protection, nursing, consolation, or otherwise care for the weak, disabled, inexperienced, tired, young, elderly, etc.

Note: When given within the family, code under **Family**.

Succorance (Succor)

to receive expressions of love (all expressions except sexuality), gratitude, pats on the back

to feel deserving

Example: "You deserve a break today"

Note: The desire for marriage code under **Family** and for self-respect code under *Secure*.

Cheap (Cheap)

economical, inexpensive, bargain, cut-rate, penny-pinching, discounted, at cost, undervalued, a good value

Community (State)

relating to community, state, or national publics; public spiritedness; group unity; national identity; society; patriotism; civic and community organizations of other than social purpose

Family (Family)

nurturance within the family, having a home, being at home, family privacy, companionship of siblings, kinship

getting married

Note: References to ancestry code as **Traditional**.

Healthy (Fit)

> fitness, vim, vigor, vitality, strength, heartiness, to be active, athletic, robust, peppy, free from disease, illness, infection, or addiction

Leisure (Play)

> *Relaxation (Relax)*
>
> > rest, retire, retreat, loaf, contentment, be at ease, be laid-back, vacations, holidays, to observe
>
> *Enjoyment (Enjoy)*
>
> > to have fun, laugh, be happy, celebrate; to enjoy games, parties, feasts, and festivities; to participate

Magic (Magic)

> miracles, magic, mysticism, mystery, witchcraft, wizardry, superstition, occult sciences, mythic characters
>
> to mesmerize, astonish, bewitch, fill with wonder

Examples: "Bewitch Your Man With . . .", "Cleans like Magic."

Maturity (Mature)

> being adult, grown-up, middle-aged, senior, elderly; having associated insight, wisdom, mellowness, adjustment, respect

Example: "You're getting better with age."

Mild (Mild)

> *Safety (Safe)*
>
> > security (from external threats); carefulness; caution; stability; absence of hazards, potential injury or other risks
> >
> > guarantees, warrantees, and manufacturers reassurances

Example: "Be Sure With Allstate," "Contains no harmful ingredients."

> *Tamed (Tamed)*
>
> > docile, civilized, restrained, obedient, compliant, faithful, reliable, responsible, domesticated, sacrificing, self-denying
>
> *Morality (Moral)*
>
> > humane, just, fair, honest, ethical, reputable, principled, religious, devoted, spiritual
>
> *Modesty (Modest)*
>
> > being modest, naive, demure, innocent, inhibited, bashful, reserved, timid, coy, virtuous, pure, shy, virginal

Figure 8-1 *(continued)*

Humility (Humble)

unaffected, unassuming, unobtrusive, patient, fate-accepting, resigned, meek

Plain (Plain)

Unaffected, natural, prosaic, homespun, simple, artless, unpretentious, plain folk, down-to-earth

Frail (Frail)

delicate, frail, dainty, sensitive, tender, susceptible, vulnerable, soft, genteel

Modern (New)

contemporary, modern, new, improved, progressive, advanced

introducing, announcing . . .

Example: "Slightly ahead of our time."

Natural (Nature)

references to the elements, animals, vegetables, minerals, farming unadulterated, purity (of product), organic, grown, nutritious

Example: "Farm-Fresh."

Neat (Neat)

orderly; neat; precise; tidy; clean; spotless; unsoiled; sweet-smelling; bright; free from dirt, refuse, pests, vermin, stains, and smells; sanitary

Ornamental (Pretty)

beautiful, decorative, ornate, adorned, embellished, detailed, designed, styled

Popular (Common)

commonplace, customary, well-known, conventional, regular, usual, ordinary, normal, standard, typical, universal, general, everyday

Examples: "largest seller," the "ubiquitous comestible."

Practical (Pract)

Effective (Effect)

feasible, workable, useful, pragmatic, appropriate, functional, consistent, efficient, helpful, comfortable (clothes), tasty (food)

Note: Includes strength and longevity of effect.

Durable (Rugged)

long-lasting, permanent, stable, enduring, strong, powerful, hearty, tough

Convenient (Handy)

handy, time saving, quick, easy, suitable, accessible, versatile

Pride (Self)

Independence (Alone)

self-sufficiency, self-reliance, autonomy, unattached

to do it yourself, to do your own thing

original, unconventional, singular, nonconformist

Security (Secure)

confident; secure; possessing dignity, self-worth, self-esteem, self-respect, and peace of mind

Note: Freedom from external risk code as *Safety.*

Productivity (Work)

references to achievement, accomplishment, ambition, success, careers, self-development

being skilled, accomplished, proficient

pulling your weight, contributing, doing your share

Example: "Develop your potential," "Get ahead."

Note: Social recognition of achievement codes as **Status.**

Sexy (Sexy)

Vain (Vain)

having a socially desirable appearance; being beautiful, pretty, handsome; being fashionable, well-groomed, tailored, graceful, glamorous

Note: Generalized conceit may code as *Status.* Code beauty of obviously sexual nature or purpose as *Eros.*

Sexuality (Eros)

erotic relations: holding hands, kissing, embracing between lovers, dating, romance

intense sensuality, feeling sexual, erotic behavior, lust, earthiness, indecency

attractiveness of clearly sexual nature

Figure 8–1 *(continued)*

Status (Status)

envy, social status or competitiveness, conceit, boasting, prestige, power, dominance, exhibitionism, pride of ownership, wealth, trend-setting, to seek compliments

Example: "Keep up with (or ahead of) the Joneses."

Technological (Tech)

engineered, fabricated, formulated, manufactured, constructed, processed

resulting from science, invention, discovery, research

containing secret ingredients

Example: "Factory-Fresh," "includes XK–17."

Traditional (Old)

classic, historical, antique, old, legendary, time-honored, long-standing, venerable, nostalgic

Examples: "80 years of experience."

Unique (Unique)

Dear (Dear)

expensive, rich, valuable, highly regarded, costly, extravagant, exorbitant, luxurious, priceless

Distinctive (Rare)

rare, unique, unusual, scarce, infrequent, exclusive, tasteful, elegant, subtle, esoteric, hand-crafted

Examples: The "only . . . ," "the best . . . ," "At leading drug stores."

Wildness (Wild)

Adventure (Bold)

boldness, daring, bravery, courage

seeking adventure, thrill, or excitement

Example: "Go for the Gusto."

Notes: Code general confidence and psychological security as *Secure*. Sweepstakes, lotteries, etc., for which nothing is risked, code according to value of prizes.

Untamed (Untame)

primitive, untamed, fierce, coarse, rowdy, ribald, obscene, voracious, gluttonous, frenzied, uncontrolled, unreliable, corrupt, deceitful, savage

Example: "Go wild with Windsong."

Freedom (Free)

spontaneous, carefree, abandoned, indulgent, at liberty, uninhibited, passionate

Example: "X, for the Free Me."

Casual (Casual)

unkempt, disheveled, messy, disordered, untidy, ruffled, rumpled, sloppy, casual, irregular, noncompulsive, imperfect

Wisdom (Wisdom)

knowledge, education, awareness, intelligence, curiosity satisfaction, comprehension, sagacity, expertise, judgment, experience

Examples: "judge for yourself," "experts agree . . ."

Note: Detailed information, instructions, or recipes imply wisdom as at least a subsidiary theme.

Youth (Youth)

being young or rejuvenated, childlike, immature, undeveloped, junior, adolescent, resistant to aging

Example: "Feel young again."

---

and major captions. Code up to three thematic elements. Code all elements manifest in both illustration and key words. Code no more than one theme as dominant that is manifest in solely the illustration. Subsidiary themes are those additional themes manifest in the illustration, or embodied in the fine print of the body copy.

The procedure for this coding is as follows:

1. Look at the illustration and headings and code for dominant themes.
2. Read body copy and code subsidiary themes based on key words and phrases.
3. Examine illustration alone for any additional subsidiary themes manifest.
4. Review list of values as checklist for final cross-check of subsidiary themes.

It was felt that the best data for interpretive purposes would reflect a group consensus rather than a single individual's coding. Thus, independent ratings by two coders were subjected to an arbitration procedure. Any differences in the dominant categories identified by the two coders were detected and the conflict resolved by the author, thereby producing a single integrated rating reflecting the collective judgment of at least two of the three raters. About 10 percent of the ads required this adjudication.

Reliability

A test-retest reliability measure was calculated as the percent agreement in the repeated measure of fifty items imbedded in the larger sample of two thousand ads. Spuriously high reliability figures are sometimes reported when the reliability calculus incorporates all of the agreements as to properties not in evidence. Clearly such a statistic can be artificially inflated by adding multiple dimensions which are clearly able to be perceived as not applicable. To avoid this puffery, only the successful replication of identified dominant items are recognized as agreements. This produces a more stringent intrarater reliability score, measuring the internal consistency of each rater, and an interrater reliability score, measuring the commonality of perception and judgment between the two raters. A reliability measure was also calculated for the arbitrated codings, measuring the internal consistency of the adjudicated process.

The intrarater test-retest reliabilities were .75 and .85 for the two coders. The adjudicated process had a reliability coefficient of .79, representing 74 agreements out of 94 possible on a critical subsample of 50 ads. If the replication sample with 80 identified dominant themes is treated as the referent, the 74 agreements constitute a 93 percent score. These figures compare very favorably with Nunnally's (1967) acceptability criterion and with those studies cited by Peter (1979) who reports that, of the fewer than five percent of studies even measuring reliabilities, the vast majority had reliability measures of .7 or less. In comparison to the reliability scores obtained for other codings of the same sample by the same coders, however, these reliability statistics are modest. This is not surprising, since this task is far more complex in both the number and subtlety of concepts to be applied.

Sample

This measurement system was applied to a sample of two thousand magazine ads spanning the twentieth century to date. The sample includes two hundred and fifty ads from each of the first eight decades of the century and was drawn by randomly selecting five ads from one issue for each of five years from each of the ten largest circulation magazines within each decade. A mid-decade sample was selected, choosing the years 19×3 to 19×7 as the sample frame for each decade, e.g., 1953 to 1957. This sample of mass circulation magazines is characterized by general interest magazines, such as *Life, Look,* and the *Reader's Digest,* and by those with a more domestic focus, like *Better Homes and Gardens, Good Housekeeping,* and *Women's Home Companion.* It is also characterized by titles like the *Satur-*

day Evening Post, McCall's, and the *Ladies Home Journal,* each of which are included for at least seven of the eight decades. An analysis of the sampled media in the 1930s shows all of the magazines chosen to be midrange on a 9-point scale of cultural content developed by Morgan and Leahy (1934). The range of the full sample is indicated by the inclusion of the relatively sophisticated *National Geographic* and the more sensational confessional, *True Story,* both of which are in the sample for one decade.

Results

Due to space limitations, the results will be presented in tabular form without much discussion. Although this information provides excellent grist for the mills of historians, social critics, and perhaps even advertising strategists, the following brief discussion will not attempt such interpretations, but will seek to communicate general findings, facilitate interpretation of the tables, and suggest methodological modifications in light of the specific results.

Table 8–1 shows the mean number of values coded for each decade as dominant and subordinate. The average advertisement of today communicates two principal values. This double-barrelled emphasis has been characteristic of print ads since the 1920s, in contrast to the more spartan single-focus ads earlier in the century. The number of subordinate value appeals in the body of the text and fine print has been steadily declining since the 1930s, suggesting that the text of today's ad is more inclined to reinforce the main premises than to raise new value dimensions, at least more so than yesterday's ads.

Of course, not all values are utilized in advertising, because not all values are equally as easy to make commercial or to attach to mass market products. Similarly, not all values are as readily employed as heading and captions to attract attention and motivate readers. Some serve a reinforcing role in the text of an ad, providing additional rationale for the captured or motivated reader. Table 8–2 lists those value dimensions most commonly employed, including those occurring frequently as subordinate themes.

Table 8–1
Value Density By Decade

	1900s	*1910s*	*1920s*	*1930s*	*1940s*	*1950s*	*1960s*	*1970s*	*Total*
Dominant	1.6	1.6	1.9	2.1	2.0	2.2	2.0	2.0	1.9
Subordinate	2.9	3.1	3.2	3.3	2.9	2.6	2.0	1.8	2.7
Total	4.5	4.7	5.1	5.4	4.9	4.8	4.0	3.8	4.6

Table 8–2
Frequently Employed Values

| Variable | Proportion of Ads Employing Value | |
	As Central Theme	In Fine Print
Practical	44	41
Family	17	9
New	14	11
Cheap	13	19
Healthy	12	10
Sexy/Vain	12	4
Wisdom	11	27
Unique	10	23
Work	7	4
Status	6	7
Play	6	5
Neat	5	12
Mild/Safe	5	20
Pretty (Design)	5	4
Nature	3	13
Common	3	14
Technical	2	20

Tables in appendix 8–A show the relative frequencies with which all of the value variables were evidenced in the decades of the twentieth century to date. Three of these tables show the frequencies for dominant, subordinate, and total appeals to values, with the latter also presenting similar information for a sample of 250 television ads from the 1970s. A rank correlation of these frequencies for TV versus total print yields a Spearman coefficient of .89, suggesting that although TV ads are far less wordy and informational than print ads, they appeal to essentially the same values in much the same pattern of intensity. The value hierarchy of TV substantially matches that of print.

These tables report the date in a manner that aggregates certain of the original scales into collapsed cells with conceptual congruence. The last of the tables in appendix 8–A reports the character of the collapsed cells. Similar scales were combined in those instances when there were particularly low frequencies of utilization. Where possible, scales were also collapsed to preserve the dualism that exposes the inherent internal conflicts of any value system, a society's cultural contradictions. This dualism is also helpful in providing some structure to the concepts the raters must hold in mind during the rating task. This aids them in performing the ratings with greater accuracy and reliability.

Of course, the simple collapsing of cells reduces the net number of dimensions needing measurement, also simplifying the rating task and enhancing the potential for greater reliability and validity. This is particularly the case when similar dimensions are pooled, because it is the sometimes subtle discrimination between similar dimensions that most challenges reliability. If ads were rated along just the collapsed dimensions, the rating task would be reduced from a 42- to a 25-dimensional effort. While still presenting a nontrivial coding effort, partitioning this set according to its dualisms and whether the values relate to product attributes of consumer benefits provides a structure to the task so that the raters can operate as if they had just a dozen bipolar scales, some product-focused and some person-focused.

The choice of what scales to compress in this way depends, however, on the research purpose to which the study is addressed. It may be important for some studies to maintain the separable measures of component categories. Many studies, for example, might wish to preserve the decomposition of practicality along its component dimensions of performance, durability, and convenience. Measurement of component dimensions or the collapsing of cells involves the trade-off between detail of information and the likely reliability with which the coding task can be executed. Fewer dimensions improve reliability, but potentially at the risk of meaningfulness of results. The advantage of overly specified dimensions, as we witness here, is that they can be aggregated into more global dimensions. The reverse is not true. If the measured dimensions are too broad compared to the nature of later dimensions of curiosity and inquiry, these investigations will be frustrated.

Summary

Building on the work of White and Rokeach, a content analytic method was developed for the measurement of values specifically as manifest in advertising. Coding ads along 42 categories produced results with a stringent reliability measure of .79. Two thousand magazine ads spanning the twentieth century were measured using this method, with the results suggesting potential additional methodological modifications. Although undiscussed, the results also show the relative popularity of various value appeals for each decade of the century. In contrast to the ads from earlier in the century, today's print ads are more likely to assert two value themes in a strong way, but less likely to add as many subordinate themes to augment them. Thus, today's ads can be thought of as more focused, attempting fewer total value appeals, more forceful, and more successful at raising multiple appeals into dominance.

References

Andren, Gunnar, et al. *Rhetoric and Ideology in Advertising: A Content Analytic Study of American Advertising.* Stockholm: Liber Forlag, 1980.

Berger, Arthur Asa. Analyzing the Advertisement: A Methodology for Analyzing Advertising. In *Television as an Instrument of Terror; Essays on Media, Popular Culture and Everyday Life.* New Brunswick, N.J.: Transaction Books, 1980. Pp. 119–127.

Chamberlain, Neil W. *Remaking American Values: Challenge to a Business Society.* New York: Basic Books, 1977.

Churchill, Gilbert A., Jr. A Paradigm for Developing Better Measures of Marketing Constructs." *Journal of Marketing Research* 16 (February 1979):64–73.

Fowles, Jib. *Mass Advertising as Social Forecast: A Method for Futures Research.* Westport, Conn.: Greenwood Press, 1976.

Goffman, Erving. *Gender Advertisements.* Cambridge: Harvard University Press, 1979.

Greyser, Stephen. Advertising: Attacks And Counters. *Harvard Business Review* 50 (March 1972):22–28.

Hayakawa, S.I. Poetry and Advertising. In *Language in Thought and Action.* New York: Harcourt, Brace and World, 1964. Pp. 262–277.

Kaselow, Joe. TV-Takes along Madison Avenue. *Backstage* (November 1982).

Kassarjian, Hal. Content Analysis in Consumer Research. *Journal of Consumer Research* 4 (June 1977):8–18.

Kluckhohn, Clyde C. The Study of Values. In *Values in America,* edited by Donald N. Barrett. University of Notre Dame Press, 1961.

Levi-Strauss, Claude. *The Savage Mind.* London: Weiderfeld and Nicolson, 1966. Pp. 16–32.

Lucki, Deborah, and Richard W. Pollay. Content Analyses of Advertising: A Review of the Literature. Working Paper #799, Faculty of Commerce, U.B.C. Vancouver, B.C., 1981.

MacBride, Sean, et al. *Many Voices, One World.* New York: Unesco, 1980.

McCracken, Grant, and Richard W. Pollay. Anthropological Analyses of Advertising. Working Paper #815, Faculty of Commerce, U.B.C. Vancouver, B.C., 1981.

Morgan, Winona L., and Lice M. Leahy. The Cultural Content of General Interest Magazines." *Journal of Educational Psychology* 25 (1934): 530–534.

Munson, J.M., and S.H. McIntyre. Developing Practical Procedures for the Measurement of Personal Values in Cross-Cultural Marketing." *Journal of Marketing Research* 16 (February 1979):48–52.

Murray, Henry A. *Explorations in Personality.* New York: Oxford University Press, 1938.

Nunnally, J. *Psychometric Theory.* New York: McGraw-Hill Book Company, 1967.

Peter, J. Paul. Reliability: A Review of Psychometric Basics and Recent Marketing Practices.'' *Journal of Marketing Research* 16 (February 1979):6–17.

Potter, David M. *People of Plenty: Economic Abundance and the American Character.* Chicago: University of Chicago Press, 1954.

Price, Jonathan. *The Best Thing on TV: Commercials.* New York: Penguin Books, 1978.

Reynolds, Thomas J., and James P. Jolly. Measuring Personal Values: An Evaluation of Alternative Methods. *Journal of Marketing Research* 17 (November 1980):531–536.

Rokeach, Milton. *The Nature of Human Values.* New York: The Free Press, 1973.

Sangha, Mel S., and Richard W. Pollay. Advertising's Cultural Impact: A Review of Scholarly Conventional Wisdom. Working Paper #766, Faculty of Commerce, U.B.C. Vancouver, 1981.

Starch, Daniel. *Principles of Advertising.* New York: McGraw Hill, 1923.

White, Ralph K. *Value Analysis: Nature and Use of the Method.* Ann Arbor, Mich.: Society for the Psychological Study of Social Issues, 1951.

Appendix 8A
Distributions of Manifest
Values, 1900-1980

Table 8A-1
Dominant Argument Frequencies

	1900s	1910s	1920s	1930s	1940s	1950s	1960s	1970s	Total	Rank
Attributes										
Practical**	28	44	36	45	41	56	49	51	44	1
Pretty**	6	4	4	2	3	6	7	9	5	14
Cheap**	19	13	8	10	4	10	12	24	13	4
Unique**	9	6	12	6	6	12	14	14	10	8
Common	2	4	3	3	6	2	2	1	3	19
Old	2	—	3	1	2	2	2	4	2	21
New**	8	5	11	13	9	31	19	15	14	3
Nature	1	9	2	2	4	4	4	4	3	17
Technical	2	1	2	4	2	4	3	2	2	20
Benefits										
Wisdom*	6	9	11	16	11	14	12	9	11	7
Magic	0	1	0	1	2	2	0	2	1	24
Work**	13	6	10	4	8	4	4	7	7	9
Play	5	6	6	5	8	5	6	4	6	11
Mature	0	—	—	1	0	0	0	1	0	25
Youth	0	1	3	1	1	3	2	1	1	23
Healthy**	18	11	17	16	9	10	11	5	12	5
Neat**	0	3	6	9	6	7	7	4	5	12
Mild	6	5	7	7	4	4	6	4	5	13
Wild**	1	3	1	2	8	2	4	6	3	16
Sexy**	11	9	20	16	10	13	8	6	12	6
Self**	0	0	2	5	2	4	5	5	3	18
Belong	3	4	5	7	4	5	3	4	4	15
Status**	6	4	10	4	4	10	6	3	6	10
Family**	11	19	13	22	34	14	12	13	17	2
State	0	1	0	1	8	1	0	1	2	22

Note: Cell entries are percent of ads utilizing value out of 250/decade studied. * and ** indicate 5 percent and 1 percent levels, deviation from uniform distribution, across decades, where testable with two-tailed chi-squared test.

Table 8A-2
Values Utilized in Dominant Argument Components of Collapsed Cells

Variable	1900s	1910s	1920s	1930s	1940s	1950s	1960s	1970s	Totals
Practical									
Effect**	20	25	25	37	32	47	38	41	33
Rugged	0	5	1	2	2	1	2	2	2
Handy*	10	16	12	8	10	15	13	14	12
Unique									
Dear	—	—	2	—	—	1	—	1	—
Rare**	9	6	10	6	6	11	14	13	9
Play									
Relax	1	2	3	1	4	2	2	2	2
Enjoy	4	4	3	4	4	3	3	2	3
Sexy									
Vain**	10	9	17	14	6	10	4	4	9
Eros*	1	1	4	3	4	5	4	2	3
Mild									
Frail	—	—	—	—	—	—	—	—	—
Humble	—	—	—	—	—	—	—	1	—
Modest	—	—	—	—	—	—	—	—	—
Moral	—	1	—	—	—	—	1	—	1
Plain	—	—	—	—	—	—	—	—	—
Safe	5	4	4	6	2	4	5	3	4
Tamed	—	—	1	1	1	—	—	—	1
Wild									
Bold**	1	2	—	2	7	—	2	6	2
Casual	—	—	—	—	—	—	—	1	—
Free	—	—	—	—	—	1	1	—	—
Untamed	—	—	—	—	1	—	2	—	—
Self									
Alone	—	—	—	—	—	1	—	1	—
Secure**	—	—	—	—	2	4	5	4	3
Belong									
Group*	2	1	3	5	3	3	1	1	2
Nurture	1	3	2	2	2	2	2	2	2
Succor	—	—	—	—	—	—	—	1	—

Note: Cell entries are number of ads utilizing value out of 250/decade studied. Scores for larger concepts may *not* equal sum of components due to occasional ads scoring in more than one component category. * and ** indicate 5 percent and 1 percent levels, two-tailed chi-squared test against uniform distribution.

Table 8A–3
Supportive Argument Frequencies

	1900s	1910s	1920s	1930s	1940s	1950s	1960s	1970s	Total	Rank
Attributes										
Practical	47	47	50	46	42	34	33	27	41	1
Pretty	7	4	5	3	4	4	2	2	4	19.5
Cheap	20	22	20	28	20	19	15	8	19	6
Unique	30	31	19	26	26	23	—	17	23	3
Common	19	17	23	16	14	11	7	6	14	7
Old	6	13	12	10	6	6	7	4	8	13
New	12	10	13	11	12	12	11	7	11	10
Nature	11	20	14	15	12	14	12	6	13	8
Technical	11	14	24	34	20	27	16	14	20	4
Benefits										
Wisdom	26	31	31	32	30	25	17	23	27	2
Magic	2	—	3	2	3	6	2	1	2	23
Work	4	3	2	3	12	5	2	2	4	18
Play	4	4	5	5	6	6	3	6	5	17
Mature	—	—	—	—	—	1	—	—	—	25
Youth	2	2	8	7	1	1	2	2	3	22
Healthy	10	14	14	14	9	7	6	3	10	11
Neat	10	18	17	20	12	8	6	5	12	9
Mild	26	22	23	26	14	18	14	14	20	5
Wild	—	1	2	1	3	1	2	2	2	24
Sexy	3	2	6	4	3	4	3	4	4	19.5
Self	4	3	6	11	4	5	8	4	6	16
Belong	9	9	7	5	9	2	6	6	7	15
Status	10	7	8	6	6	7	5	6	7	14
Family	8	9	10	6	14	12	8	6	9	12
State	2	1	3	1	17	2	—	2	3	21

Note: Cell entries are percent of ads utilizing value out of 250/decade studied.

Table 8A–4
Total Argument Frequencies

	1900s	1910s	1920s	1930s	1940s	1950s	1960s	1970s	Total	Rank	Relative Usage as Dominant / Supportive		1970s TV
Attributes													
Practical	75	90	85	91	83	91	82	78	89	1	.52	/ .48	84
Pretty	13	9	9	5	6	9	9	10	9	19	.58	/ .42	3
Cheap	40	35	28	38	24	29	27	33	32	3	.39	/ .61	19
Unique	38	37	31	31	32	34	31	31	33	4	.30	/ .70	18
Common	21	20	26	20	20	14	9	8	17	11	.16	/ .84	5
Old	8	13	15	11	7	8	8	8	10	18	.19	/ .81	4
New	20	15	24	24	20	42	30	20	25	7	.55	/ .45	16
Nature	12	23	16	17	17	17	15	10	16	12	.18	/ .82	11
Technical	13	17	26	38	22	31	19	16	23	8	.11	/ .89	4
Benefits													
Wisdom	32	40	42	48	41	39	29	32	38	2	.29	/ .71	12
Magic	3	1	3	4	5	8	2	2	3	24	.28	/ .72	0
Work	18	9	12	7	19	9	6	8	11	15	.62	/ .38	2
Play	9	11	11	10	15	11	9	10	11	17	.52	/ .48	3
Mature	—	—	—	1	—	—	—	1	—	25	.87	/ .13	0
Youth	3	3	11	8	2	4	3	2	4	23	.33	/ .67	3
Healthy	28	25	32	31	18	17	17	8	22	9	.56	/ .44	6
Neat	10	22	23	29	19	15	12	9	17	10	.30	/ .70	11
Mild	32	27	30	33	17	22	20	18	25	6	.21	/ .79	8
Wild	2	4	3	3	11	3	6	8	5	21	.67	/ .33	2
Sexy	14	12	26	20	13	17	12	13	15	13	.76	/ .24	9
Self	5	3	7	16	6	9	13	8	8	20	.34	/ .66	2
Belong	12	13	12	12	13	7	9	11	11	16	.39	/ .61	6
Status	16	11	18	15	10	17	10	9	13	14	.48	/ .52	2
Family	20	28	23	28	47	25	19	19	26	5	.65	/ .35	18
State	2	2	3	2	25	2	1	3	5	22	.32	/ .68	1

Note: Cell entries are percent of ads utilizing value out of 250/decade studied.

Part III
The Influence of Values
on the Decision Process

Part III presents several alternative views of value influence on decision making. The chapters provide an applied discussion of the measurement and application of values as the basis of attitudes, detailed examinations of value and attribute relationships, and a challenge to the attitude-behavior link.

Ernest Dichter begins this section with a wide-ranging exposition on the attitude to value link and its measurement. He contends that knowing attitudes is necessary, but that one must ascertain the real attitudes and the values and subconscious factors which influence them.

In chapter 10, Prakash explores the impact of values on specific product attribute expectations for clothing and television. As with many of the studies in this book, the Rokeach value scale forms the basis for the study. Comparison between value and product expectations for blacks and whites is also presented.

Next, Reynolds and Gutman use a technique called *laddering* to construct means-end chains of values and product attributes. Unlike more frequently used mass survey techniques, laddering provides an in-depth examination of the decision process. Although even more complex than the repertory grid approach, laddering utilizes in-depth probing to uncover the higher-level meaning of value-attribute relationships. Unlike many approaches, however, laddering results are readily quantified and may be graphically portrayed.

In chapter 12, Sherrell, Hair, and Bush explore the manner in which values interact with the involvement construct in the evaluation of communications.

Finally, in chapter 13, the basic contention that the most frequently examined modification of values—attitudes—do in fact predict behavioral trends is questioned. Horn and Wells trace a number of attitudes and subsequent behavioral trends over a ten-year period. They conclude that to be predictive, attitudes must be specific and be enacted in only one way.

9 How Values Influence Attitudes

Ernest Dichter

Although attitudes rather than values are currently the most widely studied elements of consumer decision making, few really question the basis of attitude research. Attitudes, however, are subject to a variety of pressures and measurement problems. First, attitudes may not be verbally ascertainable. Really effective measurement of attitudes frequently requires techniques such as psychodrama or experimentation that can go beyond purely language-inhibited statements. Attitudes are also dynamic; they don't hold still. While subjects are being asked about their attitudes, they are often changing their minds. Further, attitudes have a cognitive and emotional level. In an highly emotional situation, I may answer one way but would really like to answer with as much rage as I really feel. Subconscious factors may distort my checkpoints, however. Attitudes also can be ambivalent. I am asked whether or not I like a certain politician and my real answer could be that I like him and I hate him at the same time. Finally, it is difficult to know what an attitude is and to distinguish between real ones and those hastily checked off on a list of possibilities. What we are looking for, or should be looking for, are the real attitudes and beliefs of consumers—not just those registered quickly in a research survey.

The examination of values provides a more meaningful and interpretative analysis of the underlying motives that structure attitudes and behavior. Almost everytime we are confronted with an attitude scale, we bring our values into play. The danger of wanting to appear intelligent when the real response should have been "I never really thought about it" is always present. Our research instruments have to be designed to take values and subconscious factors influencing our attitudes into consideration. Here are some possible safeguards to be considered.

Most of us prefer to rationalize our beliefs and to give intelligent and meaningful explanations for our behavior. At the same time, we are inclined to check off the most popular beliefs. When we are asked who is responsible for inflation or oil shortages and we have the choice of the large oil companies, the Arabs, the sheiks, and ourselves, we don't hesitate much to cast our indictment on the scapegoat targets, without thinking whether or not we are fair. We are expressing our political views and not necessarily our real attitudes.

This chapter is adapted from comments made by Ernest Dichter at the Consumer Psychology and Personal Value Conference at the University of Mississippi.

Many peace demonstrations and demands for a nuclear freeze produce similar results. How can one be against peace and motherhood? Often alternatives are not presented in their true relationship. Referendums on political, national, and local issues often have such pitfalls. No one will be against cutting taxes if no one points out the consequences of poorer roads or schools or less police protection. The respondent has to be encouraged to think about and admit possible unreasonable real attitudes and, at the same time, be guided step by step through appropriate techniques that permit the penetration to real beliefs.

Values have to be considered as preceding and coloring our attitudes. In order to achieve correct responses, new techniques have to be applied. They consist of getting the respondent to express his attitudes and beliefs, to become aware of his "value distortions," and to understand the possibility that he may not have been guided by reasons quite as lofty as those he has just checked off.

Here are a number of approaches that we have successfully tried. None of them take up much more space and time than a cut and dried checklist, but offer instead the possibility of coming much closer to a real understanding of the interplay between values and attitudes.

The Absolution Method. We asked doctors to tell us about their ethical attitudes. Every one, or nearly every one, asserted that he would never take kickbacks from pharmacists or other doctors. When we described these situations in novellas where another doctor or his wife had accepted such corruptive rewards—not calling them that, but softening them with statements like: "Things like that happen and are human"—the real attitudes came to the surface.

The Squeeze Method. We learned this approach from well-trained customs officials. When a traveler stated, "No. I have nothing to declare," the official repeated, with ever increasing urgency, "Are you absolutely sure, you have one more chance, I will let you off," and so forth. Three or more squeezes often produced enough pressure and the culprit came forth with the truth.

Psychodrama. Psychodrama permits a dramatic demonstration, in the true sense of the word, of the relationship between hidden values and expressed opinions.

We may ask the respondent to act out a buying situation, a belief, a product, and how he feels about it. By videotaping the "play," we have an absolutely irrefutable witness. More than once respondents have denied that they made a revealing movement or showed some significant body language. They had in a non-verbal fashion revealed important facets of their atti tudes. When they saw themselves on the screen, they often were shocked by the insight into their real actions.

In one case, we wanted to know about prejudice. Several white people were asked to shake hands with Moroccans with a darker skin and a different dress. A number of the white, well-dressed people wiped their hands unobtrusively after the handshake but were not aware of this unconscious gesture. Racial values had betrayed them.

Confrontation via Psychodrama with a Supposedly Rational Decision. One of the reasons so many opinion polls are wrong in their prediction of election results may well be that voters are not as determined in their opinion as they claim. In one approach we accepted at face value their answers as to which candidate would get their vote. Then we played a simulated record announcing that the candidate they had chosen had won by a landslide. Many more people than could have been expected were actually shocked by the realization that they had secretly hoped their candidate would not really win.

Making the Future Tridimensional. We also call it "taking someone through the paces." Suppose we want to know how an employee feels about the possibility of changing his job, becoming an entrepreneur, or moving up to a higher position. He can be administered an attitude scale. Of course he sees him as interested in making a career, being promoted, or making it on his own. It is one thing, however, to express an opinion about one's self and to be confronted with the real experience. Short of using simulators like the ones the astronauts are being put through one can 'play act' with the respondents the first day or week in the new situation, letting them feel emotionally all the pitfalls, fears, hopes, that may occur.

Developing an Attitude *ad absurdum*. While working for CBS on the problem of the atom bomb, we used the following research technique. We first asked people how they would solve the problem of the bomb. In this fashion we ascertained about seven or eight attitudes. These were in themselves interesting, but far removed from their roots. Copying some techniques used in clinical psychology, we took each one of the supposed solutions and carried it to its absurd conclusion. One opinion was that the atom bomb should be dropped on Russia. We accepted this solution at first, but then asked the respondents what the result would be. They answered: "unconditional surrender." (Of course, this was some time ago.) "What would happen next?" "We would have to occupy Russia," was the response we received. "Do you know how many soldiers we need to occupy Russia?" No. No one knew. We then produced the general who had been in charge of occupying

Germany. Bit by bit we then made it clear to the respondents, who had such firm opinions and solutions to the problem of the atom bomb, that at least ten times as many soldiers would be needed to occupy Russia. We carried this technique through to such a point that the proponent of this solution saw its absurdity.

Another solution, which had also been presented by a real group suggested that all atomic scientists be banned and put into a concentration camp. Again we tried to carry this opinion through to its absurd conclusion. We invited Einstein to participate—he was still alive then. He was reassured that the concentration camp would be located on a Pacific Island and then he countered with the question: "What would you do with my pupils? There are several thousands of them." The proponent who had offered the concentration camp solution was somewhat puzzled and stated: "Well, we would also put them on the island." "What would you do then," asked Einstein, "with all the writings on the atom bomb and atomic physics?" "We would have to burn them all." In any case we again carried the so-easily-offered attitude and solution to its absurd conclusion at which point it was rejected. In this fashion we approached all seven offered solutions. In the end, we pointed out that there was no easy solution and sent the respondents back to think about the problem of the atom bomb all over again. The moral or immoral values that had guided them became clear.

The Motivational Differential. The measurement of attitudes is important. It helps the advertiser, the manufacturer, and the politician to anticipate human behavior. However, a number of safeguards are necessary. First of all, there is the problem of feedback. If I have expressed one attitude, it may of necessity lead to two or three additional attitudes. They in turn, if I have thought them through, may exert their influence on the first expressed attitude. We are dealing here with the phenomenon of Gestalt. (The same nose placed in a different face has an entirely different meaning.) The same attitude placed in a different configuration together with other attitudes may change its original meaning. Our research has to be designed in such a way that attitudes are not listed in a linear fashion to be checked off, but rather grouped in their possible interrelationships.

When I am asked what the results of television viewing are going to be and am offered various choices that are all different degrees of convictions and values as to the positive or negative influence on our lives, the real answer may very well be that television sets and visual entertainment feed upon themselves. The more visual entertainment and visual education I receive, the more I am going to be interested in having our whole education changed and made more attractive. *Sesame Street* is not just a program for children but exerts its influence on dramatic changes in the whole field of communication. Being aware of such feedback may change my attitudes considerably.

Presenting Attitudes by Upper or Lower Limits. In modern psychology we have almost abandoned such concepts as the I.Q. Instead we have introduced the idea of wide bands. A person may find himself operating close to the upper limits of his band of potentialities or close to the lower limit of his potentialities or somewhere in the middle. An attitude can similarly be very close to its extreme intensity. We have to find means of expressing such emotional aspects and degrees of attitudes rather than presenting them to be checked off in a singular and atomistic fashion.

In sociometry we have an example of how the influence of values can be measured in an almost tridimensional and dynamic way. We design a field in which different individuals are placed in a random fashion. These individuals may be people working in an organization. In a similar way we can also represent products in a market. What we then do is draw arrows between the various individuals. The strength of the arrow and its direction indicate which way these relationships operate and their degree. In this way we can find out for management whether a person in a company is considered to be a star, attracting many relationships, or an "isolate," having little contact with people. We can gradually rearrange the real positions of these various individuals and bring about a better interrelationship. Something similar could be done to mirror values and attitudes, and show their relationship to products and events.

The Three-Dimensional Approach. Almost every opinion or attitude has at least three or four facets. There are various ways of expressing the same attitude. By presenting it in an almost three-dimensional fashion one can get a lot closer to the real attitude. After all, asking people to check off the appropriate answer on a checklist is really asking them in a psychological sense to identify themselves with a predetermined opinion. Identification is not, however, a one-way process. It can be changed and influenced by a number of factors. Peculiarly enough, we identify ourselves much more readily with a very concrete description, let us say, of a village, where the author states that one of the poplars was crooked and never could be straightened out. In this case we might think of another village where some other peculiarity exists and thus identify ourselves with the unique statement in the description of the unknown village. If instead the description is of a general nature, as in old-fashioned novels where authors went as far as talking about village X, much weaker identification takes place. Therefore, in measuring true attitudes and their value roots a lot will depend on whether or not they are presented in such a way that identification is facilitated.

Conclusion. Motivational research has to be used whenever we are interested in determining why people behave the way they do. An attitude scale can be purely descriptive, simply asking: "Are you spending more today then you did several years ago?'' ''How many suits or dresses do you own?'' or similar questions. We call this approach a descriptive one. It is much closer to bookkeeping than what I would call research. True research is interpretative and wants to find out what is really behind an attitude or human behavior and the role of values.

We feel that this is the true purpose of research because it is the only one that permits appropriate action. If we want to understand true attitudes in order to motivate human beings, whether it be for the purchase of a product, for better interrelationships in a company, or for the pursuit of politically or economically desirable goals, we cannot forego the analysis of moral, religious, and philosophical values. Human behavior is guided by many contradictions, positive and negative values, unconscious aspects, prejudices, hopes, and fears. Knowing what lies behind an expressed attitude can serve as a better guide in changing the basic values in our society.

10 Personal Values and Product Expectations

Ved Prakash

In recent years there has been an enormous growth of marketing research in personal values. Much of the research has supported the idea of market segmentation based on personal values (Scott and Lamont 1970; Vinson, Munson, and Nakaniski 1977; Vinson, Scott, and Lamont 1977; Henry 1976; Munson and McIntyre 1979). These findings have important implications for social class research, consumer satisfaction research, and advertising research. Values represent needs and perform functions similar to those served by attitudes (Rokeach 1973).

Most of the marketing studies in the area have used the Rokeach Value Survey consisting of 18 terminal values and 18 instrumental values. Terminal values (e.g., equality, salvation) are desired modes of existence and represent enduring sets of values. Instrumental values (e.g., ambitious, clean, honest) are desired modes of behavior helpful in the achievement of terminal values. Terminal values are more stable because they are acquired early in life, while instrumental values are more susceptible to changes in the socialization process.

There are two major trends in research dealing with the Rokeach Value Survey. The first trend deals with the influence of antecedent variables (e.g., ethnic background, age, sex, income, and education) on personal values. Rokeach maintains that while ethnic and cultural background is the predominant source of personal values, income, education, age, and sex should also be taken into consideration. Vinson, Munson, and Nakaniski (1977) and Ness and Stith (1983) support the role of ethnic background in accounting for differences in personal values. Crosby, Gill, and Lee (1983) show that age and life cycle contribute to differences in some personal values. Much of the research conducted by private industry is centered on the influence of lifestyle on value systems. Rokeach also raises the possibility of personality variables such as self-concept and locus of control impacting on personal values. But thus far, this aspect has not been researched in marketing.

The second major trend is in the area of measurement of values. Rokeach recommends ranking of terminal and instrumental values. Ranking procedure, however, yields ipsative (nonindependent) data and thus violates the assumption of independence among values. Rokeach refutes this criticism by pointing out that intercorrelations among values are so small that the assumption of independence is not seriously violated. The second problem with ranked data is that application of parametric statistics becomes inappropriate. Consequently, Munson and McIntyre (1979) recommend the use of Likert scales to measure the importance of values. Reynolds and Jolly (1980), on the other hand, support Rokeach's procedure by presenting empirical evidence to prove that Likert scales are significantly less reliable than rank ordering or paired comparison procedures. The controversy remains unresolved, but the evidence seems to be more in favor of the procedure recommended by Rokeach. Conceptually, values are relative to each other and not absolute, thus justifying the ranking process. Also, Rokeach (1973) presents evidence from Catell (1944) to show that ipsative measures can be employed to yield normative data, and Homant (1969) found that simple value rankings from 1 to 18 give essentially the same information as that obtained from complex semantic differential scales.

Research Gaps

There are many areas that offer potential for further research. Research thus far has focused on personal values as the dependent variable. There is now a need to examine personal values as the independent variable and study the variables that are caused by personal values. Rokeach maintains that values can influence satisfaction with oneself and also mold attitudes towards socio-political issues. In the field of marketing, it may be hypothesized that values determine product expectations, satisfaction with products, and the level of consumer discontent with the business system.

In the methodological area also there is a need for more research. Previous studies reduced values to a small set of factors. Rokeach (1973) reduced 36 values to 7 bipolar factors. Vinson, Munson, and Nakaniski (1977) reduced terminal values to 5 factors and instrumental values to 6 factors. None of the studies located by this author, however, further examined the impact of these factors on product-related expectations.

There are two advantages to the use of factor scales over the use of individual values. First, factor scales have the properties of interval scales, making it appropriate to apply parametric statistical techniques. Second, correlations between 36 values and product attribute expectations may not yield meaningful interpretation of analysis. For example, a significant correlation between the attribute of gas mileage for a car and the value of mature love may not make any sense. But a significant relationship between gas mileage and gratification of internal and external needs provides a meaningful understanding of consumer values.

Personal Values and Expectations

Rokeach has raised the possibility of causal relationship between personal values and satisfaction. Consumer research has shown that expectations and confirmation of expectations are important determinants of satisfaction (Oliver 1980; Prakash 1981). The causal sequence is: Expectations lead to confirmation of expectations, which leads to satisfaction. With the introduction of personal values in this relationship, the sequence can be modified: Personal values lead to expectations, which lead to confirmation of expectations, which leads to satisfaction. The important component in this sequence is the relationship between values and expectations, which is the focus of this chapter.

Personal values represent enduring needs and beliefs. Expectations represent standards and beliefs regarding product performance. Personal values are influenced by the cultural background of the consumer. Therefore, it may be hypothesized that because of personal values, consumers form different levels of product expectations. Vinson, Scott, and Lamont (1977) theorize that personal values impact domain-specific values; these domain-specific values are conceptualized to be expectations from manufacturers and expectations from products.

Research Objectives

There are two major objectives of this study. The first objective is to reduce the combination of 36 terminal and instrumental values to a small set of factors and to construct composite scales from these factors. The second purpose is to examine the significant correlations between value dimensions and ideal expectations from product attributes and to contrast this relationship for two different ethnic groups (whites and blacks). It is hypothesized that:

1.   There are significant relationships between value dimensions and product expectations
2.   The two ethnic groups emphasize different value dimensions in their expectations from product attributes

Research Method

Sample

The major antecedent variable in this study was ethnic background. Respondents were 106 whites and 100 blacks who were recruited from four census tracts based on the 1980 census. The data were collected in the summer of 1982. The census tracts were selected on the basis of equivalent rental and sales value of apartments and houses. Data were collected in the field using structured questionnaires and personal interviews. Interviewers were trained in data collection and were paid $6.00 for each completed questionnaire.

Values

The Rokeach Value Survey containing 18 terminal values and 18 instrumental values was chosen for obtaining data on personal values. Respondents were asked to rank values from 1 (most important) to 18 (least important).

Expectations

The literature on consumer satisfaction shows that there are three major types of expectations. *Predictive expectations* are expectations dealing with beliefs on the likelihood of the performance level. *Normative expectations* concern ideal standards about how a product should perform. *Comparative expectations* deal with performance of the brand compared to similar other brands. The literature further shows that normative expectations are the most appropriate determinants of satisfaction (Prakash 1981; Woodruff, Cadotte, and Jenkins 1981). For the purpose of this study, respondents were asked to indicate normative expectations on 5-point scales ranging from fair (1) to excellent (5). Products included in the study were clothing for social purposes and television sets. These products were chosen because of high customer involvement; consequently, the two ethnic groups are likely to have different expectations and values with regard to these products. On the basis of several focus group interviews, nine attributes of clothing and seven attributes of television sets were selected for evaluation of normative expectations.

Results

In order to reduce 36 values (terminal and instrumental) to a small number of meaningful dimensions, factor analysis was performed. The varimax factor rotation yielded 7 factors with eigenvalues greater than 1.0. Only those values with factor loadings greater than or equal to .30 were included in the interpretation of the factors. These factors account for 72.7 percent of the variance.

1. *Personal and Social Orientation.* This factor accounts for 19.9 percent of the variance. Personal orientation is represented by values of pleasure and true friendship. Social orientation is indicated by salvation, equality, and obedience values.
2. *Ethics and Social Achievement.* This factor accounts for 14.2 percent of the variance. The values showing ethical consideration are honesty and politeness. Social achievement is represented by values of capability, accomplishment, comfortable life, and ambition.
3. *Internal and External Gratification.* This factor accounts for 9.5 percent of the variance. Internal gratification is represented by wisdom, inner harmony, self-respect, and true friendship. External gratification is represented by comfortable life and exciting life values.
4. *Competence and Morality.* This factor accounts for 8.8 percent of the variance. Values representing competence are independent and intellectual. The morality aspect is shown by values of forgiveness and helpfulness.
5. *Aesthetic Value.* This factor is responsible for 7.4 percent of the variance. The two values in this dimension are world of beauty and world at peace.
6. *Social Safety and Personal Happiness.* This factor accounts for 6.7 percent of the variance. Social safety is shown by concern for national security and world peace. Personal happiness is shown by emphasis on a single value—happiness.
7. *Love.* This factor accounts for 6.6 percent of the variance and the two values included in this factor are loving and mature love.

In order to construct composite scales from these factors, the factor score coefficient of the value was multiplied by the normalized score of that value. This product was summed for the values in that factor to yield a composite scale. We obtained 7 composite factor scales or dimensions to be used for correlational analysis with normative expectations from product attributes.

In order to measure the relationship between value dimensions and product expectations, product moment correlation coefficients between value dimensions and expectations from product attributes were obtained. Only the significant correlation coefficients at $p < .05$ are shown in tables 10-1 and 10-2 for clothing and television sets, respectively. Separate correlational analyses were performed for whites and blacks.

With respect to clothing, the value dimension most frequently emphasized by whites is the aesthetic value and, secondly, the dimension of personal and social orientation. Blacks, on the other hand, mainly emphasize the dimension of competence and morality, thus wanting to obtain the fulfillment of these needs in the purchase of clothing. The attribute of brand

Table 10-1
Dimensions of Personal Values and Clothing Expectations

| | Dimensions of Personal Values—Significant Correlations[a] | | |
Clothing Attributes	Whites (N = 106)		Blacks (N = 98)	
Brand reputation	Personal and social orientation	(.19)		
	Inner and external gratification	(.18)	Inner and external gratification	(−.20)
Quality fabric	Personal and social orientation	(.21)		
	Aesthetic value	(−.24)		
Value fabric	Personal and social orientation	(.18)	Competence and morality	(.26)
	Aesthetic value	(−.20)		
	Social safety and happiness	(.17)		
Fitness	Personal and social orientation	(.30)	Competence and morality	(−.18)
	Aesthetic value	(−.31)		
Comfort	Aesthetic value	(−.17)	Competence and morality	(−.28)
	Social safety and happiness	(−.31)		
Ease of care	Aesthetic value	(−.39)	Competence and morality	(−.22)
Durability	Aesthetic value	(−.39)	Competence and morality	(−.21)
	Personal and social orientation	(.21)		
Contemporary fashion	Inner and external gratification	(.30)	Inner and external gratification	(−.24)
Style			Inner and external gratification	(−.24)
Ex (aggregate expectation)	Aesthetic value	(−.29)	Competence and morality	(−.18)
	Social safety and happiness	(−.26)		
	Personal and social orientation	(.22)		

[a]$p < .05$.

reputation is significantly related to internal and external gratification for both whites and blacks; in addition, whites emphasize personal and social orientation. In quality of fabric, whites find fulfillment of personal orientation and aesthetic value, while for blacks this attribute is not related to any value dimension. For whites, price is related to aesthetic value, personal orientation, social safety, and happiness dimensions. For blacks, price is related to the competence and morality dimension. In the case of whites, fitness, comfort, ease of care, and durability are primarily related to aesthetic value. For blacks, all these attributes are related to competence and morality. There is an agreement, however, between the two groups that the contemporary fashion attribute is related to the need for internal and external gratification. Overall, the motivation for the purchase of clothing among whites is the aesthetic value and secondarily it is because of personal and social orientation. For blacks this is largely a motivation for fulfillment of the competency and morality dimension. Whites are more diverse in their motivation, as compared to blacks. Whites may be putting a high emphasis on aesthetic value for clothing because of higher income levels.

Table 10–2 presents significant correlations between television attribute expectations and value dimensions. In the purchase of television sets, there are two main motivations among whites: (1) personal and social orientation and (2) internal and external gratification. For blacks, the predominant motivation is competence and morality. For whites, there are differences between the purchase of clothing and the purchase of a television set. In the purchase of clothing, the primary emphasis is on aesthetic value; in the purchase of a television set there is greater emphasis on internal and external gratification. The emphasis on personal orientation is common to the purchase of both products. For blacks, the primary motivation in the purchase of clothing is similar to the purchase of a television set, that is, to fulfill competency and morality needs.

With regard to specific television set attributes for brand reputation, among whites there is no particular motivation; for blacks, the motivation is the value of competence and morality. Price and warranty are important attributes to whites because of personal orientation and gratification dimensions, but to blacks these two product attributes are important because they fulfill competency- and morality-related values. There are no major differences between whites and blacks with respect to picture, size, and social prestige attributes, as the common motivations are personal and social orientation and internal and external gratification.

Discussion

The hypotheses proposed in this study are largely supported. We have found significant correlations between ideal expectations from product at-

Table 10-2
Dimensions of Personal Values and Television Set Expectations

Television Set Attributes	Dimensions of Personal Values—Significant Correlations[a]	
	Whites (N = 106)	Blacks (N = 98)
Brand reputation	Inner and external gratification (−.23)	Competence and morality (−.17)
Value of Price	Personal and social orientation (.20)	Competence and morality (−.31)
Warranty performance	Inner and external gratification (−.22)	Competence and morality (−.21)
Picture performance	Personal and social orientation (.31)	Personal and social orientation (.17)
Size performance	Personal and social orientation (.27)	Personal and social orientation (.19)
	Inner and external gratification (−.16)	Inner and external gratification (−.25)
	Aesthetic value (−.20)	
Social prestige	Inner and external gratification (−.18)	Inner and external gratification (−.32)
Overall performance	Personal and social orientation (.35)	Competence and morality (−.18)
	Competence and morality (−.20)	
Ex (aggregate expectation)	Personal and social orientation (.27)	Inner and external gratification (−.22)
	Inner and external gratification (−.23)	

[a]$p < .05$.

tributes and personal value dimensions. Also, we have seen that the two ethnic groups, whites and blacks, emphasize different value dimensions in the purchase of products. For whites, the predominant value dimension also varies from product to product. These findings have important implications for marketing research. They support the desirability of market segmentation on the basis of value dimensions and the design of advertising campaigns to appeal to the primary motivation for that value dimension. Also, the implication for satisfaction research is clear. Value dimensions have an important impact on satisfaction because of their significant association with product expectations. Therefore, values become antecedents to expectations (i.e., expectations are consequences of values). Future research should examine the impact of values on expectations from the marketing system and on consumer discontent with the business system. We are now involved in further research in exploring the interrelations between components in the complete model (cultural background leads to personal value dimensions, which lead to expectations, which lead to confirmation of expectations, which leads to satisfaction and dissatisfaction. These directions present enormous opportunities for researchers in personal values and consumer satisfaction.

References

Catell, R.B. Psychological Measurement: Normative, Ipsative, Interactive. *Psychological Review* 51 (1944):292-303.

Crosby, Lawrence A., James D. Gill, and Robert Lee. Life Status and Age as Surrogate Predictors of Value Orientation. Paper presented at the *Personal Values and Consumer Behavior Workshop*, University of Mississippi, 1983.

Guttman, Jonathan. A Means-End Chain Model Based on Consumer Categorization Process. *Journal of Marketing* 46 (1982):60-72.

Henry, Walter A. Cultural Values Do Correlate with Consumer Discontent. *Journal of Marketing Research* 13 (May 1976):121-127.

Homant, R. Semantic Differential Ratings and Rank Ordering of Values. *Educational and Psychological Measurement* 29 (1969):885-889.

Munson, Michael J., and Shelby H. McIntyre. Developing Practical Procedures for the Measurement of Personal Values in Cross-Cultural Marketing. *Journal of Marketing Research* 15 (February 1979):48-52.

Ness, Thomas E., and Mel Stith. Income and Race Effects on Value Structure. Paper presented at the *Personal Values and Consumer Behavior Workshop*, University of Mississippi, 1983.

Nie, R.E. et al. *Statistical Package for Social Sciences*. New York: McGraw-Hill, 1976.

Oliver, Richard L. A Cognitive Model of the Antecedents and Consequences of Consumer Satisfaction. *Journal of Marketing Research* 14 (November 1980):460.

Prakash, Ved. An Investigation of Predictive Brand Expectations as Determinant of Consumer Satisfaction. Unpublished doctoral dissertation, University of Tennessee, 1981.

Reynolds, Thomas J., and James P. Jolly. Measuring Personal Values: An Evaluation of Alternative Methods. *Journal of Marketing Research* 17 (November 1980):531–536.

Rokeach, Milton J. *The Nature of Human Values*. New York: Free Press, 1973.

Scott, Jerome E., and L.H. Lamont. Relating Consumer Values to Consumer Behavior: A Model and Method for Investigation. In *Increasing Marketing Productivity*, edited by Thomas V. Greer. Chicago: American Marketing Association, 1970, 283–288.

Vinson, Donald E., J. Michael Munson, and Masao Nakaniski. An Investigation of the Rokeach Value Survey for Consumer Research Applications. In *Advances in Consumer Research*, IV, edited by William D. Perrault. Provo, Utah: Association for Consumer Research, 1977, 247–252.

Vinson, Donald E., Jerome E. Scott, and Lawrence M. Lamont. The Role of Personal Values in Marketing and Consumer Behavior. *Journal of Marketing* 41 (April 1977):44–50.

Woodruff, Robert B., Ernest R. Cadotte, and Roger L. Jenkins. Understanding Consumer Expectation and Satisfaction Processes Using Experience Based Norms: A Modeling Approach. Working paper, Department of Marketing and Transportation, College of Business Administration, University of Tennessee, 1981.

11 Laddering: Extending the Repertory Grid Methodology to Construct Attribute-Consequence-Value Hierarchies

Thomas J. Reynolds and
Jonathan Gutman

Qualitative approaches[1] are used in a number of circumstances which include (Sampson 1972a):

1. problem definition (where nothing is known, formulating hypotheses for quantification)
2. to identify relevant attributes and behavior patterns for further research (perhaps as input for questionnaire rating scales or for use in multidimensional scaling studies)
3. conducting post-mortems to clarify quantitative findings
4. when the subject area precludes a straightforward approach using direct questioning

Of course, depending on the specific purposes, different qualitative approaches are more or less appropriate (focus groups, depth interviews, and projective techniques). However, central to all of the research needs outlined above is the overriding necessity to obtain responses in the true language of the consumer (Sampson 1972a). Secondarily, the concern for providing a framework to give more structure to the qualitative process, thereby minimizing the subjectivity of interpretation, also presents a major issue to researchers in this area (Jones 1981). Various techniques have been suggested to address these isues, probably the most systematic being the Repertory Grid (Kelly 1955). The Repertory Grid technique has been employed in market research because it was felt to be a much better way of locating attitude scale items or constructs from which scales for research could be devised (Sampson 1972a).

Repertory Grid

A review of the Repertory Grid approach has been undertaken elsewhere (Kelly 1955; Bannister 1965; Bannister and Mair 1968; Sampson 1972a).

The general procedure, however, can be described briefly as presenting a respondent with a list of stimuli typically ranging from 6 to 24. The choice of stimuli is not restricted, but most typically are products that have some relation to one another (in the same product class—i.e., cereals, drinks, cars, brand names, or product concepts).

To initiate the Repertory Grid, the respondent performs a series of triadic sorts; that is, the respondent is given a set of three stimuli and asked to state one way in which two of them are alike and yet different from the third. After identifying the perceptual construct that serves to discriminate among these three stimuli, the respondent is asked the same question with respect to the next triad of stimuli. This process is repeated until the respondent can state no further way in which the stimuli differ or until the predetermined set of triads is completed. After the perceptual constructs are obtained, an additional option involves obtaining a rating for each of the stimuli on each of the constructs. For example, if the construct obtained is "good mileage," the respondent would rate each of the stimuli, in this case automobiles, as to how well it is perceived to provide good mileage.

What one hopes to learn through the use of Repertory Grid triadic sorting process is what attributes or aspects of a stimulus are relevant and important enough to deserve following up with larger-scale surveys or experimental designs. It is also possible to produce a perceptual map of the stimuli and the content of the individual's beliefs and attitudes toward the specific stimuli using the language and concepts provided by the individual. This is accomplished by applying a data-reduction technique to the rating grid data, (i.e., factor analysis, multidimensional scaling, clustering). The results of these analytic methods provide an objective synthesis of what is essentially qualitative data. The problem, then, stems not only from the type of analysis selected, but also what interpretative frame or theoretical positioning is to be used to structure the interpretation.

Background

One view of the principles underlying the structure that a perceptual map might take can be found in the means-end chain literature (see Olson and Reynolds, 1983, for a completed review). A means-end chain is a model that seeks to explain how products or services, as means, are linked to ends, which are a person's values. Values have been defined as enduring beliefs that specific modes of conduct or end-states of existence are personally or socially preferable to opposite or converse modes of conduct or end-state of existence (Rokeach 1973, p. 5). Means-end chain models offer a view of how values guide behavior by formulating a model of how values, which are very general in nature, relate to consumer choice, which is very specific.

Several authors have put forth means-end chain models with differing components interposing between the means and the ends. For example, Vinson, Scott, and Lamont (1977) discuss centrality of beliefs in terms of global values, domain-specific values, and evaluative beliefs. Howard (1977) links terminal values to choice criteria, beliefs about the brand or product class, and then to attitudes toward the brand or product class. The means-end chain model used by the authors in extending the Repertory Grid procedure follows the scheme presented by Gutman (1982).

The centerpiece of the Gutman model is consequences which may be defined as any result (psychological or physiological) accruing (directly or indirectly) to the consumer (at some point in time) from his or her behavior. Consequences, in this framework, can be desirable (called benefits [Haley 1968; Myers 1976]) or undesirable. Marketers are interested in the benefits provided to consumers from using their products. They are also interested in which attributes in these products produce these benefits. An example of an attribute-benefit linkage (using cereals as an example) is: crunchy—"stays with me." Cereals having the attribute of crunchiness are thought to provide the benefit "stays with me." Thus, attribute-benefit linkages are important in making marketing decisions.

One also has to address the issue of why benefits are benefits or why certain outcomes are desirable and others are undesirable. In part, other than certain physiological responses, the values a person holds determine the evaluation of one's outcomes. In this sense, "stays with me" is a benefit, because it is linked through "helping me to avoid snacks," "aids weight loss," "improves my appearance," to "makes me feel better," and "am happier," at the values level. Thus, the second important linkage is the benefits-values linkage. However, because both linkages have a common terminus, the linkages in combination become the research focus. That is, the *attribute-benefit-value construct* contains both connections and all three types of content descriptors. It is this construct when considered as a totality that provides understanding of consumers, in terms of both their perceptual and evaluational process.

Problem

To be effective in explicating the content and structure of the consumer's cognitive map, the Repertory Grid technique (or any other approach) must draw out from consumers information about these important linkages. There are problems, however, with the Repertory Grid technique in uncovering these levels. The Repertory Grid task is inherently complex—it requires respondents to consider how stimuli that are the same differ and how stimuli that differ are the same. Clearly, some respondents are better able to cope with this task than are others.

For example, respondents who are divergent thinkers, as opposed to convergent thinkers, are more imaginative and able to construe more items (Sampson 1972b). Most respondents, due probably to the complexity of the task, respond at a low level of abstraction (Gutman and Reynolds 1979), providing descriptive responses relating directly to readily observable aspects of the stimuli comprising the Repertory Grid triads rather than evaluative responses which reflect consideration of the function and benefits delivered (Sampson 1972b). The nature of the task leads respondents to discriminate between stimuli more in terms of physical differences than in terms of benefits, experience, or value judgments. To the extent that this occurs, the Repertory Grid technique will have a low likelihood of generating material that is representative of the benefits or values level, but will be concentrated at the attribute level.

This shortcoming of the Repertory Grid technique is exacerbated by the fact that the Repertory Grid procedure was originally designed to be used with "important others" as stimuli. People as stimuli are far more complex and our interactions with them are far more involved than are those with consumer products. This lower level of involvement with most consumer products seems to lead to lower-level descriptive responses being given in response to triads. This reinforces the need for some procedure that can push respondents to respond beyond the superficial descriptive level. These higher-level responses, as well as the linkages between the lower-level descriptors and the high-level consequences and values are necessary if marketers are to develop a complete understanding of how consumers give meaning to the attributes and benefits inherent in products. The implication of this type of knowledge is to develop strategic positionings and advertising that link products to issues important to the consumer, thereby providing the function of differentiating products by making them more personally meaningful and involving.

Thus, the purpose of this article is to present a technique for enabling researchers to move beyond the surface properties or attributes inherent to products and brands to the consequences and values which provide the perceptual framework that gives meaning to these surface properties. As noted earlier, not only is it important to gain knowledge about these consequences and values, but it is also of importance to determine how these elements at their different levels are linked together. The focus of the rest of this chapter will be on the methodology for obtaining salient elements and determining the structure among these elements that comprise a hierarchical means-end-chain (or ladder).

Method

Laddering Procedure

An approach used by Gutman and Reynolds (1979) for deriving consequences- and values-level responses from respondents is modeled after a technique described by Hinkle (1965). Using the Repertory Grid triadic sorting as a starting point, the respondent is presented with a series of triads composed of brands or products within the domain of interest. For each triad, the perceptual construct elicited by the respondent has two components, a similarity and a contrast—which, in effect, is a dichotomous or binary distinction (Adams-Webber 1979, p. 5).

Respondents are asked which pole of their dichotomous distinction they most prefer. Then they are asked why that preferred aspect is important to them. The answer to the second question typically leads to distinctions involving product functions and consequences which result from using the product. These replies become the basis for generating still higher-level distinctions. The procedure is repeated until respondents can no longer answer the "Why?" question. Respondents often reach a level where they are responding at the values level (as indicated by comparing such responses to the Rokeach values inventory [Rokeach 1973]).

The laddering technique, then, refers to in-depth probing directed toward uncovering higher-level meanings. These meanings, both at a benefit and value level, provide the domain of information that one uses as the basis for information processing and decision making. Put simply, the means-end framework suggests that the relevance of any decision is translated first in terms of personal outcomes (consequences) which derive their meaning as to the degree they satisfy or modify self. Laddering seeks to uncover the key descriptors at all levels, as well as their connections or linkages that serve to provide the structure components of the cognitive network.

Interviewing Procedure

Twenty-six respondents, recruited (after screening for product familiarity) in an Eastern metropolitan area were invited to come to a central research location where all the interviewing took place.

Thirteen brands from several categories (breath aids, candy, toothpaste, and mouthwash) were used as stimuli (see figure 11–1). Fourteen triads were presented to each respondent (indicated by the circles in figure 11–1). They were systematically selected so as to represent the different subcategory interrelationships. Each respondent was presented with the fourteen triads and encouraged to provide a different response for each. The preferred pole of each construct was obtained. After completing all of the triads, the respondent was then asked to assign 0 or 1 ratings to each brand for each distinction they made, giving the brand a *1* if it possessed the attribute or lead to consequence or value indicated by the positive pole, and a *0* otherwise.

Then the respondents ranked their preferred poles with respect to overall importance. The positive poles of the six most important distinctions were each used as a starting point for laddering the respondents. Lastly,

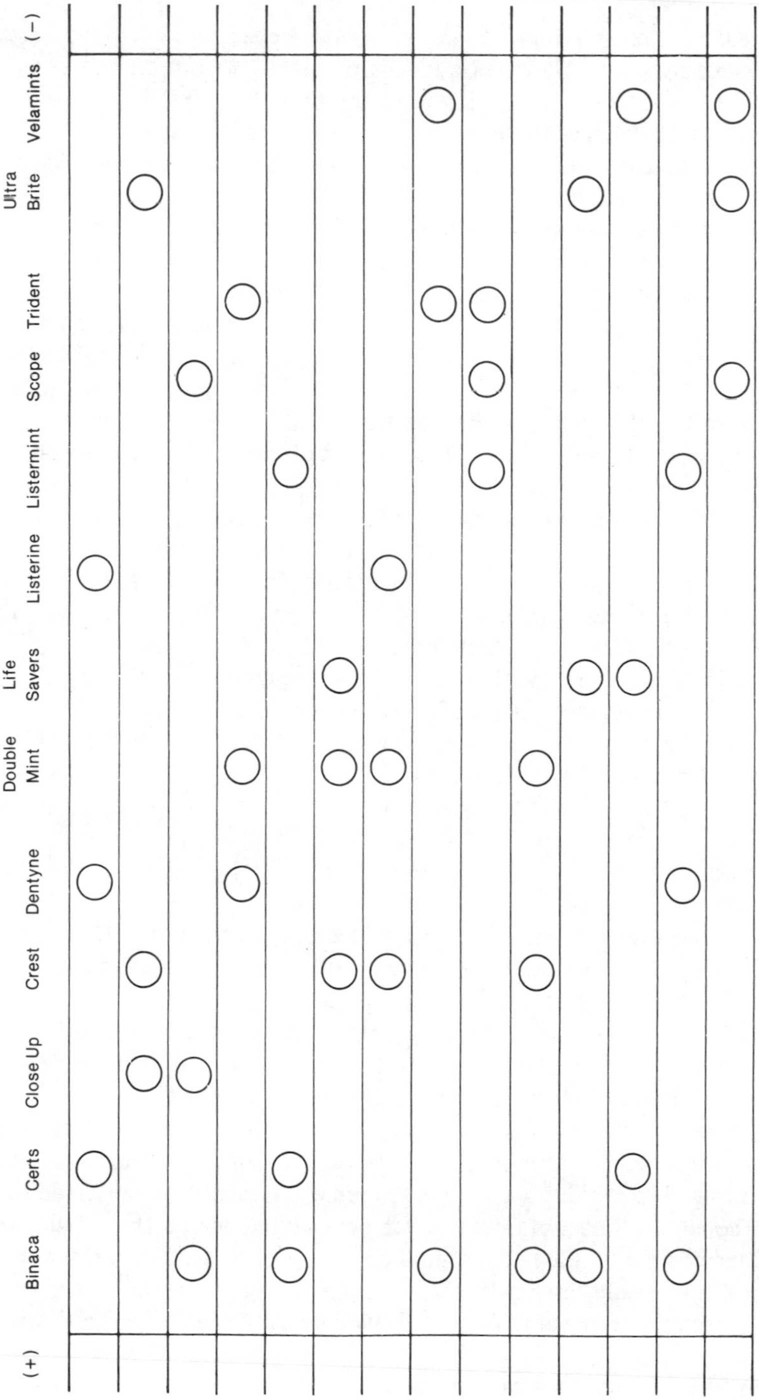

Figure 11-1. Repertory Grid

as a separate task, each respondent indicated the similarity-dissimilarity between all possible pairs of stimuli (13 × 12/2 = 78) using a 9-point scale.

Results

Relation of Triad Responses to Direct-Scaled Similarity Ratings

One of the major advantages of multidimensional scaling procedures is that they allow subjects complete freedom in determining the basis on which the pairs of stimuli are to be judged. This permits any degree of complexity respondents desire to bring to the task. The Repertory Grid task also allows a free response from the respondents' repertoire of possible responses. If the Repertory Grid is tapping distinctions which represent meaningful differences between stimuli, one would expect a significant correlation between the two sets of ratings.

To amplify, each triad can be considered to represent three unique pairs of products. The triadic act requires the respondent to select the pair that is most similar. The similarity-dissimilarity ratings permit us to correlate the similarity ratings of the stimulus pairs with the indications of which two stimuli are closest in each triad. (Each triad yields three pairs, one of which is coded *1* because the respondent judged the two stimuli as more similar than the other two pairs, which are coded *0*.) Biserial correlations obtained in previous work (Kehoe and Reynolds 1977) using psychological "important others" (in the clinical sense [see Kelly 1955]) as Repertory Grid stimuli yielded a median correlation of .35 across individuals with 26 of 31 individual grids being considered significantly related ($p < .05$). Following the same analytic format, the present research yielded a median correlation of .235 with only 6 of 26 intraindividual correlations significant ($p < .05$). This finding supports the primary contention that the Repertory Grid, when products are used as stimuli, provides perceptual constructs that are less representative of the underlying psychological dimensions that serve to differentiate products. It is this fundamental fact that requires the use of the additional methods to uncover the more determinant higher-order constructs.

Laddering

Table 11–1 shows the distinctions given by the 26 respondents in responding to the 14 triads. The table shows that the initial responses to the triads were

Table 11–1
Content Analysis of Positive Poles of Distinctions and Level at Which Distinctions Were Elicited

Positive Poles of Distinctions	Mentioned in Response to Triads	Mentioned Only as a Result of Laddering
Attributes		
Sugarless	Yes	
Fluoride	Yes	
Portable	Yes	
For morning	Yes	
Medicinal flavor	Yes	
Strong/Powerful	Yes	
Taste good/Pleasant flavor	Yes	
Minty taste	Yes	
Necessary conditions for use	Yes	
No extra calories		Yes
Consequences		
Fresh breath	Yes	
Clean/White teeth	Yes	
Long-Lasting	Yes	
Easy for me to use	Yes	
Cleans my mouth/Fights germs	Yes	
Prevents cavities	Yes	
Improves my health	Yes	
Eliminates mouth odor		Yes
Won't make me gain weight		Yes
Make me look better		Yes
Covers up (masks) odors		Yes
Helps me avoid embarrassment		Yes
Helps me be close to people		Yes
Helps me not offend others		Yes
Values		
Self-Confidence		Yes
Security		Yes
Feel good about self		Yes
Feel healthy		Yes

at the attribute level or were lower-level consequences directly produced by consuming or using the product. The consequences and values stemming from these immediate benefits from product use were elicited only as a result of the laddering procedure.

The object here is to build a common chart embracing all respondent's ladders which will serve as a reference point for defining important differences between respondents. What is important depends on:

1. to what ultimate values do the ladders connect
2. the linkages between attributes and higher-level consequences and values
3. the relation of products to the ladders, thereby providing implications for advertising strategy and product positioning

The twenty-six respondents produced 113 ladders. Forty-one percent of the ladders only had 2 steps (one beyond the initial response); 38 percent were 3 steps in length; and 21 percent of the ladders were at least 5 steps in length. As the level of a respondent's ladder reached higher, the responses shifted from being comprised of attributes to being comprised of consequences, and finally to consisting of values-level distinctions in most cases (see table 11–2).

The result of combining all the ladders into a single configuration is shown in figure 11–2 (see Olson and Reynolds, 1983, for a detailed description of method). This figure shows which attributes produce which consequences and how the consequences produce consequences closer and closer to the values level until a few key values-level distinctions are reached.

For purposes of interpretation, it should be noted that all respondents' ladders don't extend from one end to the other in the means-end hierarchy. Some start at the attribute level and end at the consequence level; some start at the consequence level and may or may not move beyond the consequence level to the values level. The linkages noted, then, are a representation of consistent patterns that are folded into a comprehensive structure representing a summary of this sample.

The overall map of the ladders (figure 11–2) has two major foci—"fresh breath" and "good for health." These relate, in turn, to internal needs relating to internal body states versus external needs stemming from favorable interactions with others. There is a crossover point ("look good") that links health-related consequences to socially produced consequences.

Table 11–2
Level of Distinction by Order of Elicitation

	Level of Elicitation (in percent)			
	1 (113)	2 (113)	3 (67)	4 (24)
Attributes	52	21	3	
Consequences	46	46	30	17
Values	2	33	67	83

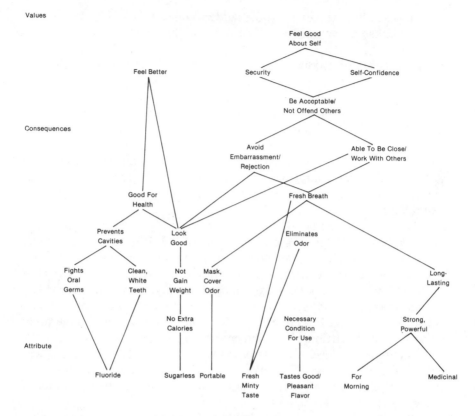

Figure 11-2.   Summary Map of Ladders

Discussion

The initial concerns of the authors about the low level of personal involvement of products leading to lower-level distinctions in response to Repertory Grid triads has been substantiated. The results have shown that the distinctions obtained tend to refer to product attributes or consequences directly produced by these attributes. That these lower-level considerations might not be tapping important aspects of products is further demonstrated by the relatively low biserial correlations between the direct similarity ratings and the triadic sorts which are obtained as part of the Repertory Grid process.

If laddering is to be used to elicit higher-level distinctions and to provide the linkages between the attribute-level distinctions and consequence- and values-level distinctions, the triadic sorting or alternative technique should be thought of as providing a highly involving situation. This is a necessary prerequisite to the in-depth probing process that laddering represents. Without these personalized constructs, in the respondents' own words, the probes became quite ineffective.

Direct Preference Distinctions

An alternative to utilizing triadic sorts as the foundation of the laddering process is to ask respondents to rate each product on a preference scale and on a usage scale. The respondent can then be asked for reasons why some products are used less or more than their preference ratings would indicate. Or, respondents can be asked about products which are highly preferred and used frequently, or products not preferred and used infrequently. Another approach is to have respondents rate products for appropriateness for use in various situations. They can then be queried as to why some products are appropriate in some situations and not others. The goal of these techniques is to increase respondent involvement in the measurement process, thereby increasing the meaningfulness of their responses.

Laddering Process

The laddering process described as stemming from triad distinctions consists of determining preferred poles and following up with questions about why that pole is preferred. Logically, one might expect the responses to be consistently at a higher level (more toward higher-level consequences and values) for each successive response. Quite frequently matters don't proceed in this way—respondents often provide responses that are explanations for previous responses or that provide the attributes on which the previously mentioned consequences depend. For example, the response "fresh breath" may be followed by "minty taste"—the respondent says he likes "fresh breath" because things that give you fresh breath have a minty taste. The interviewer may take the respondent directly back to fresh breath and then up to a higher level, or "minty taste" may lead to "eliminates odor" and then continue upward from there.

Sometimes, the respondent tells you why he doesn't like or use a product. Negative laddering can then be used to determine higher and higher-level negative consequences (for example, contains sugar leads to cavities leads to teeth will rot leads to bad for health and appearance leads to rejected by others). The process of laddering and of constructing maps of an individual's and ultimately a group's responses from the laddering responses cannot be rigidly specified. Clearly, like all qualitative research, it depends on who is doing the laddering and who is analyzing the content of the reasons. This is to suggest that the laddering process is potentially subject to the same degree of error common to similar qualitative analysis. However, the elaboration of the levels of abstraction criteria as the basis for coding provides a framework that has proved to be effective across a variety of product classes.

Moreover, unlike focus groups, depth interviews, or projective techniques, laddering does elicit specific responses from respondents that lead directly to qualitative models based on group maps (such as shown in figure 11–2). Thus, the authors feel that laddering procedures appear to bridge the gap between qualitative approaches that can't be quantified and the excessively quantitative models that lack depth of meaning. This is particularly important when higher-level constructs are hypothesized, such as for high-image product categories.

Notes

1. "Qualitative research involves finding out what people think and how they feel—or at any rate what they say they think and what they say they feel" (Bellenger and Greenberg 1978, p. 167). More specifically, there are those researchers who, through their use of projective techniques and interpretation of data, purport to know what consumers think and how they feel despite what they say (Dichter 1964). The interpretation of qualitative research inherent to the position just described is not the focus of this discussion. Rather, the primary area of interest to be addressed is qualitative approaches which are more objective in nature, namely, dependent on the face value of consumers' elicited responses.

2. The authors would like to thank the Young and Rubicam Research Department and, in particular, Joe Plummer for assistance in the development of this research effort. The senior author was Associate Research Director at Young and Rubicam at the time of the research.

References

Adams-Weber, J.R. *Personal Construct Theory.* Chichester, England: John Wiley & Sons, 1979.

Bannister, D. The Rationale and Clinical Relevance of Repertory Grid Technique. *British Journal of Psychiatry* 479 (1965):997–982.

Bannister, D., and J.M.M. Mair. *The Evaluation of Personal Constructs.* London: Academic Press, 1968.

Bellenger, D., and B.A. Greenberg. *Marketing Research.* Homewood, Ill.: Richard D. Irwin, 1978.

Dichter, E. *Handbook of Consumer Motivations: The Psychology of the World of Objects.* New York: McGraw-Hill, 1964.

Gutman, Jonathan. A Means-End Model Based on Consumer Categorization Processes. *Journal of Marketing* 46(2) (Spring 1982):60–72.

Gutman, J., and T.J. Reynolds. An Investigation of the Levels of Cognitive Abstraction Utilized by Consumers in Product Differentiation. In *Attitude Research Under the Sun,* edited by J. Eighmey. Chicago: American Marketing Association, 1979, 128–150.

Haley, R.I. Benefit Segmentation: A Decision Oriented Research Tool. *Journal of Marketing* 32 (July 1968):30–35.

Hinkle, D.N. *The Change of Personal Constructs from the Viewpoint of a Theory of Implications.* Unpublished doctoral thesis, Ohio State University, 1965.

Howard, J.A. *Consumer Behavior: Application and Theory.* New York: McGraw-Hill Book Company, 1977.

Jones, S. Listening to Complexity—Analyzing Qualitative Marketing Research Data. *Journal of the Market Research Society* 23(1) (1981): 27–39.

Kehoe, J., and T.J. Reynolds. Interactive Multidimensional Scaling of Cognitive Structure Underlying Person Perception. *Applied Psychological Measurement* 1(2) (1977):155–169.

Kelly, G. *The Psychology of Personal Constructs,* 2 volumes. New York: Norton, 1955.

Myers, J.H. Benefit Structure Analysis: A New Tool for Product Planning. *Journal of Marketing* 40 (October 1976):23–32.

Olson, J.C., and Reynolds, T.J. Understanding Consumer's Cognitive Structures: Implications for Advertising Strategy. In *Advertising and Consumer Psychology,* edited by Larry Percy and Arch Woodside. Lexington, Mass.: Lexington Books, 1983.

Rokeach, M.J. *Beliefs, Attitudes, and Values.* San Francisco: Jossey Bass, 1968.

Rokeach, M.J. *The Nature of Human Values.* New York: Free Press, 1973.

Sampson, P. Qualitative Research and Motivation Research. In *Consumer Market Research Handbook,* edited by R.M. Worcester. London: McGraw-Hill Book Company, 1972. Pp. 7–27.

Sampson, R. Using the Repertory Grid Test. *Journal of Marketing Research* IX (February 1972):78–81. (b)

Vinson, D.E., J.E. Scott, and L.M. Lamont. The Role of Personal Values in Marketing and Consumer Behavior. *Journal of Marketing* 41 (April 1977):44–50.

12 The Influence of Personal Values on Measures of Advertising Effectiveness: Interactions with Audience Involvement

Daniel L. Sherrell,
Joseph F. Hair, Jr., and
Robert P. Bush

Consumers' personal value systems have been recognized by researchers as a basic psychological construct with the potential for influencing a wide range of consumption-related behaviors (e.g., Nicosia and Glock 1968; Vinson 1978). Much of the research has examined the direct impact of personal values on the demarcation of market segments (Vinson and Munson 1976), differing perceptions of product attribute importance (Scott and Lamont 1974; Becker and Connor 1982), and self-reports on brand preference (Vinson, Munson, and Nakanishi 1977).

The use of research paradigms aimed at discovering the direct linkages between personal values and behaviors of interest would seem to run counter to the conceptual perspectives used in explanations of value theory. Rokeach (1968) defines values as enduring states of belief or knowledge with the power to affect other beliefs, attitudes, and behaviors. This inference of situational stability for values implies that some form of mediating psychological construct is required to actualize the influence of a value system for a specific situation. Consequently, a compatible research approach should be to investigate values and their interactions with other consumer psychological concepts in influencing behaviors of interest to marketers.

This chapter proposes a mediational linkage between consumer values and involvement. Values are posited to exhibit both a direct and an indirect influence on brand attitudes and purchase intentions. Using differences in values and the level of personal involvement as independent variables, measures of attitude toward the ad and brand purchase intention are analyzed in a 2 × 2 factorial design. The results have implications for marketers designing promotional communications for specific target markets, as well as offering refinements to the conceptual work on involvement.

Consumer Value Theory

Personal values seem to enjoy a rare implicit consensus among consumer researchers concerning conceptualization and definition. A predominant school of thought developed by Rokeach (1968; 1973) and others suggests that values are beliefs about types of conduct and desired terminal states. Values are seen as global beliefs that guide actions and inferences across specific objects and situations. No other approaches to value conceptualization (e.g, Allport and Veron 1931) have gained the degree of application of Rokeach's paradigm. Values seem to be one of the few accepted constructs in consumer psychology.

Only a few specific attempts have been made to explain the process by which values influence consumers behavior. Carman (1978) suggests that values are directly linked to an individual's lifestyle. Lifestyle is defined to be composed of activities, interests, opinions, and roles. These collections of factors, in turn, direct all consumption-related behavior. Thus, in Carman's formulation, values form a stable platform from which to direct the emergency of an individual's lifestyle and, consequently, his consumption behavior.

Howard and Sheth (1969) suggest that the values in a culture affect consumption motives which, in turn, partially set the choice criteria used by individual consumers. Attitudes with respect to choice alternatives are also assumed to be affected by values, as is brand comprehension. Howard and Sheth's perspective partially masks the enduring nature of values suggested by Rokeach and Carman in that Howard and Sheth's model implies that the influence of values for each purchase situation will be different, as will the effects on attitude towards brand alternatives and brand comprehension. Indeed, it is the enduring nature of values and their influence that have attracted consumer researchers. The ability to generalize successfully inferences about behaviors across situations is woefully lacking in many consumer psychological constructs.

Vinson, Scott, and Lamont (1977), expanding work reported earlier by Scott and Lamont (1974), give values a more active role in the consumer behavior decision process. Since Rokeach defined values as stable, superordinate beliefs, Vinson, Scott, and Lamont suggest that both global values and those values that are specific to the behavioral domain of interest combine to influence the type and nature of evaluative beliefs formed in the expectancy-value model of attitude formation.

A common implication of the theoretical frameworks discussed so far is the proposition that those values which are more centrally held (i.e., more important) or those values which possess more linkages with the individual's knowledge base, will exert more influence on behaviors. Either the concerned value(s) will be a powerful determinant of specific behaviors (e.g., the value or belief that it is wrong to take a life) or the concerned value(s) will be seen to exert lesser influence over a wide range of behaviors, which have in common the value base that is being affected.

There is a trade-off to be made at the conceptual as well as the operational level at this point. A value of central importance or with many connecting linkages to an individual's knowledge base is likely to be definable only in very broad, global terms. Consequently, measurement of such a variable and its influence is likely to be difficult to operationalize for a study in a specific situation. The level of specificity designed into a value measurement instrument is a critical component. Measures that are too general may not indicate strong relationships to behaviors of interest. Conversely, measures that are too specific may be measuring some other psychological construct besides values.

Empirical Values Research

Market segmentation has been a frequently studied variable in values research. Vinson and Munson (1976) used students and their parents as subjects, expecting and finding differences in value structures, as well as differing perceptions of automobile attributes between the two groups. Henry (1976) found significant correlates between ownership of generic auto categories and various value dimensions, providing early suggestions of market segmentation potential. Belch (1978) found significant relationships between a taxonomy of different types of belief systems and a variety of purchase intentions for twelve products ranging from deodorant to country club membership.

Scott and Lamont (1974) linked values to attribute importance perceptions via a multiset factor analysis. Becker and Connor (1982) reported that subjects classified according to degrees of professed price sensitivity exhibited differing instrumental value structures as well as price conscious store patronage behavior. Bozinoff and Cohen (1982) found that inclusion of situational factors along with personal values doubled the amount of explained variation of attribute importance for cars, stereo speakers, and libraries. It must be noted, however, that the level of total variation explained in the data was below 20 percent.

Becker and Connor (1981) reported a values hierarchy which differed among heavy users of different mass media. Heavy television viewers exhibited more traditional, religious value systems and were less concerned with achieving success when compared to heavy magazine readers.

Given the empirical evidence for the influence of values on such constructs as attribute importance, patronage behavior, and media usage, the possibility certainly exists that values have gone unmeasured in their own right and have instead been labeled with such terms as involvement, attitude, commitment, etc. Becker and Connor (1982) suggest that in many studies where media behavior has been correlated with other psychological constructs, relationships have been found that are really dependent on the behavior of some underlying variables. Personal value hierarchies are a good example of such underlying variables. Indeed, many such studies may have been examining the influence of values when the researchers thought they were investigating something different.

The Relationship Between Value Systems and Involvement

One of the attractive features of the construct of personal values is that values are broadly defined at a highly abstract level and research has demonstrated their influence across a variety of situations and behaviors. A kindred concept, albeit more specifically bounded, is that of involvement. Numerous articles point to the confusion concerning the proper definition of involvement and the lack of consistent empirical results arising from such a situation (e.g., Mitchell 1979, 1981; Leavitt, Greenwald, and Obermiller 1981; Sherrell and Shimp 1982). As the discussion below points out, involvement shares a common base with values. Perhaps one of the difficulties with coming to grips with involvement is the requirement of separating it from the construct of values.

Sherif and Cantril (1947) describe ego-involved attitudes as attitudes that have been learned, primarily as social values, with which the individual identifies. Krugman (1965, 1967) defines involvement as the number of personal connections made per minute between the viewer and the televised message. Ostrom and Brock (1968) devised a cognitive model of involvement energized by the degree to which the concerned values are central to the individual and/or the number of values affected. Kassarjian (1981) discusses high and low involvement in terms of personalities or tendencies, as well as decision processes. In short, much of the foundation literature on involvement links values into the conceptual framework in some manner.

Some of the recent information processing perspectives on involvement (e.g., Mitchell 1979, 1981) focus more on the symptoms of involvement (e.g., arousal, excitement, etc.). However, Mitchell (1981) does relate involvement to the goals of the individual. Houston and Rothschild (1978) discuss situational involvement, which is dependent on the individual's prior experience in the situation and/or the strength of the values which are relevant to the particular situation. For the purposes of this chapter, the definition offered by Mitchell (1979) is most appropriate. Involvement is viewed as a state variable instead of a process at the individual level, indicative of the level of arousal, interest, or drive induced by a particular stimulus or situation.

The activation of the involvement mechanism is accomplished by the connection(s) of the particular stimulus situation to the individual's value hierarchy. For those situations where the values affected are either not central to the person or there are not that many values affected, the individual will not exhibit symptoms of high involvement. The thesis of this chapter is that the decision to label a situation or stimulus as high or low involvement should come from an inspection of the centrality or the number of the values affected by the situation or the stimulus, not the observed level of arousal. Assessing the involvement level of a situation or stimulus by determining the level of arousal is analogous to diagnosing the nature of a disease by the level of a patient's fever. Such a practice is occasionally effective, but yields no clear understanding of the illness.

The empirical research on the effects of involvement are primarily couched in the terminology of persuasive communications. Swan and Trawick (1980) found that low involvement products resulted in fewer evaluations than high involvement products. Bloch (1982) suggests that important (highly involving) products are more likely to affect attitudes and behaviors than less important, low involvement products. Bowen and Chaffee (1974) present empirical evidence that highly involved consumers make different prepurchase judgments than do low involved consumers. Highly involved individuals appear to display more positive ad evaluations and intentions to buy in the relevant product class.

The question of interest to the present effort is this: Does an individual's value structure influence the cognitive processes entirely through the mechanism of involvement, or do values have some direct effect upon attention, perception, comprehension, recall, retrieval, attitude, and intention formation? If the process is of a mediational nature, operated entirely through involvement, empirical data supporting such a connection should provide valuable knowledge on how to include value items on scales to measure involvement. If the value structure is directly involved in the mental processes, measurement of value hierarchies should enhance the understanding of the consumption processes, with the possibility of generalizing across situations. In addition, since the very nature of values is less idiosyncratic, measurement development for values should be less difficult.

Method

The research objectives in the study were to assess the relationship between values systems and levels of subject involvement. The dependent measures of attitude toward the ad and product purchase intentions should be affected by differences in subjects' value systems. No main effect was expected for the involvement level of the subjects. There was however, the expectation of an interaction effect between the subject's relevant values and involvement.

An attempt was made to secure two groups of subjects with different value hierarchies. Since the focus of this paper was exploratory, a convenience sample of students was used. The students offered the added advantage of potentially possessing homogenous value structures. The results are intended for use in further theoretical development and as such, generalization to other populations of interest was not a primary concern (i.e., Calder, Phillips, and Tybout, 1981).

Since value structures are related to age, education, and maturity level, it was decided to use undergraduate and graduate students as the two groups with differing value structures. Groups of subjects were needed which could be assumed to differ significantly in value structures, but which would possess homogeneous characteristics on most other critical dimensions, such as intelligence, maturity, etc. In effect, age and education levels were used to assure differences in values systems.

Given the problematic nature of the concept of involvement and its diverse operationalizations in many studies, the simple expedient of selecting high and low involvement products was used. Stereo cassette decks and aspirin were chosen as the high and low involvement products, respectively. Informative ads were selected for each product and pretests using students indicated the products were indeed perceived differently and that the ads were primarily neutral in emotional content or connotation.

Rokeach's (1973) global terminal and instrumental value scales were used to measure subjects' value structures. Subjects indicated the importance of each value on a 7-point Likert-type scale with the end-points labeled "extremely important to me" and "extremely unimportant to me." There is some disagreement in the values research literature over the benefits of this scaling variation on Rokeach's original ranking procedure. However, researchers (e.g., Vinson, Munson, and Nakanishi 1977; Schuchman 1974) have reported reliabilities and factor analysis results showing rated values data essentially equivalent to ranked data in terms of structure. Consequently, it was decided to use the scale rating procedure. Vinson, Scott, and Lamont (1977) have developed and tested a set of scale items which they suggest taps a consumption value domain of the respondent. A decision was made to utilize their scale in the present research. An inspection of the research indicated that several items in the domain-specific scale loaded together in factor analysis results. The authors had some concern over the demands placed on the respondents by the length of the instrument. Consequently, the duplicate items were eliminated from the current version of the scale, leaving a total of 17 items.

In addition, the consumption values were also formatted so that respondents could indicate how well the ad they were exposed to represented the list of consumption values on a 7-point scale, with the end-points labeled "not well at all" and "extremely well." The intent was to assess respondents' perceptions of the level of fit between their own value system and the particular ad. A four-item Likert-type attitude scale was included to assess subject's attitude toward the end.

Given the difficulty of defining and measuring involvement, an indirect assessment of the existence of involvement was attempted by measuring the association between subjects' reported consumption value importance ratings and their evaluations of how well the ad represented those values. Those subjects showing a high degree of fit between the values engendered by the ad and their own value structures could be defined to have the potential to exhibit higher involvement under Ostrom and Brock's (1968) theoretical framework. Attitude toward the ad was used as a dependent measure, since persons with values more closely represented by the ad would be likely to develop stronger measures of affect. Shimp (1982) indicates that attitude toward the ad is one component of an individual's overall attitude toward the product and the act of purchasing it. Purchasing intentions for the respective products were also utilized as dependent measures of interest. Finally, demographic information was collected from each respondent.

Procedure

Subjects were initially handed the value scales measuring global and consumption values. Both scales asked subjects to record their perceptions of how important each of the scale items were to them. Following the completion of the value scales, subjects were shown either the ad for the bottle of aspirin or the cassette deck, depending on the condition to which they had been randomly assigned. Undergraduate subjects saw either the aspirin or the stereo ad, as did the graduate students. The research design was a between subjects 2 × 2 factorial design.

After subjects had been exposed to the ad for 3 minutes, the slide was turned off, and respondents were asked to fill out the scale asking how well they thought the ad they had seen represented the list of consumption values. Subjects then recorded their attitude toward the particular ad, their likelihood of purchasing the respective product, and provided demographic information. A total of 99 subjects, 57 undergraduate and 42 graduate students, were used in the survey. Following the completion of the questionnaire, subjects were told the purpose of the study and any questions they had were answered.

Results

Both the global and consumption value scales were analyzed via a principal components analysis using a varimax rotation. The objective was to ascertain the degree to which subjects perceived the scales as measuring separate entities. Table 12-1 displays the primary output of the analysis.

There were nineteen factors whose eigenvalues were greater than or equal to one. However, the first two factors accounted for the majority of the 77 percent explained variance. The scale items for the global values loaded on separate scales from the consumption value scale items. In no instance did the scale items load on factors other than with their own type of items. The results suggest that the scales are indeed measuring separate constructs.

Reliabilities were calculated for the overall global and consumption value scales, as well as for the subscales of terminal and instrumental values. The coefficient alpha values are reported at the bottom of table 12-1. All reliability figures indicated a strong level of internal consistency, even the consumption values which were selectively chosen from the larger scale by Scott and Lamont (1974).

Table 12-1
Primary Results of Factor Analysis of Value Scales[a]

Factor	Item Description[b]	Percent of Explained Variance[c]
1	Happiness, mature love, national security, pleasure, true friendship, wisdom, cheerful, clean, courageous, forgiving, helpful, honest, loving, obedient, polite, responsible, self-controlled	.24
2	Durable, dependable, guaranteed to work as advertised, responsive to true needs of consumer, supplies clear and accurate information on product, cares about the needs of individual consumer, does not lie or deceive in advertising, does not misrepresent product	.09
3	Ambitious, broad-minded, capable, imaginative, intellectual, logical	.05
4	Safe products, environmentally sound	.05
5[d]	Fairly reasonably priced, inexpensive to use, easy to repair, maintains lowest price possible	.04

[a]A total of nineteen factors with eigenvalues greater than one were elicited from the data. The five factors shown here represent the factors explaining the greatest portion of the data variance.

[b]All items shown displayed factor loadings of .50 or better.

[c]Total explained variance with the nineteen factors was 77 percent.

[d]All factors past this point consisted of either one or two item factors explaining less than 3 percent of the variance.

Cronbach's alpha for summed global scale = .95; alpha for summed global terminal subscale = .90; alpha for summed global instrumental subscale = .91.

Cronbach's alpha for summed consumption scale = .89; alpha for summed consumption terminal subscale = .82; alpha for summed consumption instrumental subscale = .84.

The items' means from the global and consumptions value scales were compared to determine if the two subject groups possessed different value structures. Tables 12-2 and 12-3 show the results of those comparisons. Seven of the eighteen global terminal values were not significantly different at the .10 level or better. Only three of the global instrumental values showed no significant differences.

Table 12-2

Comparison of Global Value Means Across Subject Groups

Scale Item	Group 1	Group 2	t value	p
	(N = 63)	(N = 37)		
A Comfortable Life	6.21(1.00)	5.65(1.44)	2.08	.04
An Exciting Life	6.12(0.92)	5.84(1.04)	1.44	.15
A Sense of Accomplishment	6.19(0.98)	5.13(1.13)	0.26	.80
A World at Peace	5.65(1.36)	5.54(1.39)	0.39	.69
A World of Beauty	5.46(1.34)	4.83(1.14)	2.46	.02
Equality	5.25(1.31)	5.08(1.52)	0.60	.55
Family Security	6.41(0.93)	5.94(1.20)	2.03	.05
Freedom	6.54(0.78)	6.16(1.09)	1.84	.07
Happiness	6.65(0.65)	6.16(1.26)	2.19	.03
Inner Harmony	6.33(0.90)	5.86(1.16)	2.11	.04
Mature Love	6.54(0.67)	5.92(1.18)	2.92	.01
National Security	5.97(1.23)	5.38(1.67)	1.87	.07
Pleasure	6.04(0.92)	5.59(1.30)	1.86	.07
Salvation	5.78(1.47)	5.19(1.81)	1.77	.08
Self-Respect	6.52(0.61)	6.38(0.79)	0.95	.34
Social Recognition	5.63(1.25)	5.43(1.32)	0.75	.45
True Friendship	6.41(0.87)	6.03(0.98)	1.96	.05
Wisdom	5.90(1.13)	5.51(1.44)	1.41	.16
Summed Global Terminal Values	109.63(10.50)	102.65(13.64)	2.68	.01
Ambitious	6.16(0.97)	5.35(1.23)	3.42	.001
Broadminded	6.01(1.00)	5.46(1.32)	2.21	.03
Capable	6.21(0.92)	5.54(1.17)	2.97	.004
Cheerful	6.01(1.02)	5.40(1.23)	2.66	.01
Clean	5.65(1.33)	4.84(1.40)	2.88	.01
Courageous	5.98(0.97)	5.41(1.23)	2.44	.02
Forgiving	5.94(0.96)	5.19(1.10)	3.55	.001
Helpful	5.52(1.43)	4.97(1.26)	1.93	.06
Honest	6.17(1.01)	5.49(1.24)	3.02	.003
Imaginative	5.32(1.19)	5.30(0.99)	0.08	.93
Independent	6.14(1.04)	6.11(0.77)	0.18	.85
Intellectual	6.05(0.91)	5.73(1.15)	1.44	.15
Logical	5.97(0.99)	5.13(1.29)	3.37	.001
Loving	6.19(1.21)	5.49(1.24)	2.77	.01
Obedient	5.32(1.34)	4.11(1.52)	4.14	.001
Polite	5.87(1.10)	5.00(1.43)	3.19	.002
Responsible	6.38(0.81)	5.89(1.02)	2.64	.01
Self-Controlled	5.87(1.20)	5.03(1.26)	3.35	.001
Summed Global Instrumental Values	106.78(11.83)	95.43(13.22)	4.31	.0001
Summed Global Values	216.41(21.19)	198.08(25.05)	3.69	.0005

Table 12–3 shows the results of the comparisons of the two subject groups for the consumption values. The majority (7 out of 10) of the so-called terminal consumption values were not significantly different between the two subject groups. The summed terminal consumption value score was significantly different at the .10 level. The instrumental consumption values revealed that 4 of the 7 value items were not significantly different between subject groups. Both the summed consumption instrumental and the total consumption value score were significantly different between the undergraduate and graduate subject groups. Overall, the graduate subjects rated the value items as more important than did the undergraduate subjects, with the exception of two values, indicated by the negative t value in the table. The two groups did exhibit distinctively different value structures.

Next, the subjects' perceptions of how well the particular ad represented the consumption value items were correlated with the same subjects' report of how important the consumption values were to them. Rank order correlations were calculated by subject group between each corresponding pair

Table 12–3
Comparison of Consumption Value Means Across Subject Groups

Scale Item	Group 1	Group 2	t value	p
	(N = 63)	(N = 37)		
Durable, Long-Lasting	6.11(0.90)	5.57(1.17)	2.44	.02
Reasonably Priced	5.46(1.07)	5.59(1.04)	−0.61	.54
Safe	5.97(1.13)	5.59(1.16)	1.57	.12
Inexpensive to Use	4.86(1.33)	4.81(1.51)	0.16	.87
Exciting, Stylish	5.24(1.32)	4.86(1.31)	1.37	.17
Easy to Use	5.22(1.17)	5.03(1.34)	0.76	.45
Dependable, Trustworthy	6.38(0.75)	6.05(0.99)	1.73	.09
Beautiful, Attractive	5.16(1.28)	5.00(1.18)	0.61	.54
Easy to Repair	5.19(1.43)	4.78(1.58)	1.32	.19
Comfortable, Secure	5.71(1.07)	5.08(1.29)	2.64	.01
Summed Consumption Terminal Values	55.30(6.71)	52.38(8.24)	1.83	.07
Guarantees Product to Work as Advertised	6.19(1.04)	5.35(1.25)	3.60	.001
Responsive to True Needs of Consumer	5.98(0.97)	5.32(1.41)	2.51	.01
Supplies Clear, Accurate Information on Product	5.82(1.14)	5.43(1.28)	1.59	.12
Cares About Needs of Individual Consumer	5.70(1.14)	5.11(1.24)	2.41	.02
Does Not Lie or Deceive In Advertising	6.24(1.10)	6.08(1.01)	0.71	.48
Maintains Lowest Price Possible	4.95(1.45)	5.03(1.44)	−0.25	.80
Does Not Misrepresent the Product	6.24(1.01)	6.03(1.07)	0.99	.32
Summed Consumption Instrumental Values	41.12(5.09)	38.35(6.85)	2.14	.04
Summed Consumption Values	96.43(10.36)	90.73(14.16)	1.13	.04

of consumption values, as well as for the summed consumption scales. Table 12–4 shows the results of the correlation analysis. The undergraduate subject groups evidenced no significant associations between their perceptions of the importance of the consumption value items and the degree to which the particular ad they were exposed to represented those values. Segmenting the data on the basis of the product ads used produced the same pattern of results.

In the graduate student group, the summated consumption value scale produced a correlation of .45, with the subscales of terminal and instrumental consumption values showing coefficients of .29 and .35, respectively. These coefficients were all significant at the .05 level or better. The individual items demonstrated weak levels of association with 2 terminal and 2 instrumental scale items displaying significant coefficients. In summary, the attempt to select ads which were differentially related to subjects' value structures was only partially successful. The strength of the conclusions which can be drawn from the study suffer as a result.

Table 12–4
Rank Order Correlations Between Consumption Values and Perceptions of Ad/Value Fit

Scale Items	Group 1	Group 2
	(N = 63)	(N = 37)
Durable, Long-Lasting	.01	−.15
Reasonably Priced	.02	−.08
Safe	.09	.33*
Inexpensive to Use	.13	−.15
Exciting, Stylish	.17	.23
Easy to Use	−.19	.20
Dependable, Trustworthy	−.07	.33*
Beautiful, Attractive	.14	.06
Easy to Repair	−.08	.18
Comfortable, Secure	.12	.15
Summed Consumption Terminal Values	.11	.29*
Guarantees Product to Work as Advertised	−.18	−.01
Responsive to True Needs of Consumer	−.04	.43**
Supplies Clear, Accurate Information on Product	−.05	.14
Cares About Needs of Individual Consumer	−.01	.34*
Does Not Lie or Deceive in Advertising	−.13	.01
Maintains Lowest Price Possible	.12	.11
Does Not Misrepresent the Product	.20	.12
Summed Consumption Instrumental Values	−.19	.35*
Summed Consumption Values	−.02	.45*

*$p \leq .05$.
**$p \leq .01$.

An analysis of variance model was used to test the expectations of value influence and involvement-value interactions on the dependent measures. Attitude toward the ad and the subject's professed purchase intentions were the dependent measures. The summated global value scale, the summated consumption value scale, the involvement (i.e., product) condition, and the subject group were all used as independent variables and all possible two-way interactions were included. Group medians for the summated global and consumption value scores were used to break the subjects into high and low groups, respectively. The subject group (i.e., undergraduate/graduate) was included as a treatment variable to block for any systematic bias attributable to sources other than the value structure differences. Table 12–5 displays the results of the analysis.

The model for the attitude toward the ad was significant at the .08 level. The variance accounted for the model was 16 percent. The summated value measures, both global and consumption, were significant as main effects, with the only interaction effect being between consumption values and the subject's involvement level. Such a result was predicted, since the consumption values are more situation-specific and serve as a guide to behavior in particular situations. The model for the product purchase intentions was not significant. One reason for this was the lack of variability in the dependent variable. Subjects almost uniformly indicated that they bought or were slightly likely to buy the brand of aspirin indicated in the ad. The converse was true of the purchase intention measure for the cassette deck, with very low likelihood of purchase being indicated.

Table 12–5
ANOVA Results for Attitude Toward the Ad Measure

Source	df	SS	Mean Square	F ratio	p > F	R^2
Model	10	44.43	4.43	1.75	.08	.16
Error	89	225.83	2.54			
Total	99	270.26				

Source	df	SS	Mean Square	F ratio	p > F
Global Values	1	9.40	9.40	3.71	.06
Consumption Values	1	15.05	15.05	5.93	.02
Product	1	2.27	2.27	0.90	.35
Group	1	4.88	4.88	1.92	.17
Global X Product	1	0.01	0.01	0.00	.97
Consumption X Product	1	7.78	7.78	3.07	.08
Global X Group	1	0.41	0.41	0.16	.69
Consumption X Group	1	0.38	0.38	0.15	.70
Product X Group	1	3.53	3.53	1.39	.24
Global X Consumption	1	0.55	0.55	0.22	.64

Overall, the results indicate differences in value structures between the groups used in the study. The data showed that the value scales used as instruments were perceived as separate constructs by subjects. The attempt to use ads which were closer to one groups' value structure than the other was only partially successful, as evidenced by the correlation analysis. Such a result makes the findings of the ANOVA model difficult to interpret. The value structures did make a difference in the subjects' response to the ads, and there was a significant interaction effect between the consumption value structure and the type of product used. However, the suggestion that involvement was the conceptual mechanism concerned cannot be made with any great confidence. The results do suggest that further examination of the link between value structures and involvement would prove fruitful.

Discussion

The study results suggest the potential of individual value systems for influencing attitudinal reaction to persuasive communications. Although a direct linkage with the involvement mechanism was not firmly established, the possibility of such a relationship is still a strong one. Subjects were shown to differ on both global and consumption-related value measures. These differences were related to significant main effects on respondents' attitudes toward the advertisements used in the study. In addition, the use of high and low involvement products exhibited a mediating effect on the influence of consumption value structures for the attitude toward the ad measure.

The previous conceptual discussion suggested that the involvement mechanism is activated for those situations in which the stimulus information is seen to be instrumental to some goal the individual has or possess some intrinsic importance for the person due to the particular value structure in force. The more central the value affected by the incoming information is to the person, the more that value or set of values will influence the person's cognitive and behavioral actions. The number of values affected also represent a possible operationalization of the influence procedure. Ostrom and Brock (1968) have proposed such a definition, but never tied their framework to the established work in value research.

The appearance of the interaction of consumption values and product type (an indirect manipulation of involvement) suggest that the values touched on by each type of ad were different and produced differential associations with professed attitudes toward the ads. The absence of interactive effects between the product type and the global values is expected, since global values are defined and operationalized to work at a more abstract level. Consequently, their influence on attitudes in specific situations is more general. Evidence concerning the influence of global values would be more profitably collected by inspection of attitudinal data over a series of situations. The intent would be to look for patterns of response indicating the general influence of a particular set of values.

The inability to draw stronger conclusions from the study findings stems from the lack of fit between the ads used and the subjects' value structures. It was expected that selecting two homogeneous groups that would vary in value systems would allow one or the other of the groups to display a better fit between perceptions of value importance and the values represented by the ads. In this manner, the group exhibiting the closer fit could be said to be more involved and would therefore be expected to have more favorable attitudes toward the ad and higher purchase intentions for the product. The lack of fit does not permit the claim that involvement was the mechanism associated with the interaction effect between consumption values and product type. However, the conceptual framework remains sound and future testing with cognitive response variables, as well as attitudinal variables, should prove beneficial.

The inclusion of values in involvement research provides the energizing force behind the mechanism of involvement activation that has always been lacking. The explanation of why involvement is present for some situations and not for others usually has been accounted for by appeals to the concepts of importance, salience, etc. These semantic variations for involvement only added confusion to definitional efforts in this area. With values as the foundation, involvement may be more clearly defined as the mechanism of arousal for information assimilation. The particular value structure that is operant provides the basis for inferences of instrumentality for a given situation.

The empirical evidence of value structure stability across different dependent measures and situations can provide researchers with the ability to generalize involvement findings across similar situations. Previously, if involvement was not manipulated successfully in a study, the reasons for the failure were not clear. Now, the possibility of inefficient appeals to a set of related values is an alternative explanation.

The use of values also provides the ability to develop more parsimonious measures of involvement. Researchers might not need to include the questions calling for inferences about involvement on the subjects' part. The existence of robust value scales would permit studies of the convergent and discriminant validity of the two constructs for particular situations. Indeed, value scale development appears to be more advanced than the scale research in many other areas of consumer behavior.

Practitioners might be able to use knowledge of the relationships between values and involvement to more precisely target advertising for low or high involvement product decision processes. Making sure the product ads appeal to salient or powerful values for a particular market segment seems to be one way of enhancing the effectiveness of the message. Rokeach's (1979) work on value modification through behavioral confrontational inconsistencies suggests that persuasive attempts at consumption value modification might be an effective strategy. The paradigms of labeling and behavioral influence might prove useful in such a context. Comparative ads utilizing such a format could be a vehicle for these attempts.

Finally, the mediational role of values in influencing many consumer psychological constructs needs to be studied. Since values, especially global values, are conceptualized to operate at an abstract level, some type of intervening variable is needed to adapt the influence of global values to a specific situation. While the use of consumption values is an example of one type of intervening variable, there should others. Possible candidates might include the differential selection of decision scripts or heuristics, the distortions in the perceptional or attributional processes for specific situations, or other such constructs.

This chapter explores the nature of the linkage between values, both global and domain-specific, and involvement. Many of the attempts to define involvement have used values as the conceptual base to drive the process of involvement. However, none of the research has addressed the empirical relationship between involvement and values. The findings reported in this study hint at the nature of this relationship. However, the implications of such a linkage are many and would seem to warrant the continuation of further efforts in this area.

References

Allport, G., and D.E. Vcron. A Test for Personal Values. *Journal of Abnormal and Social Psychology* 48 (1931):233.

Becker, B.W., and P.E. Connor. Differences in the Personal Values of the Heavy User of Mass Media. *Journal of Advertising Research* 21 (1981):37–43.

Becker, B.W., and P.E. Connor. The Influence of Personal Values on Attitude and Store Choice Behavior. In *An Assessment of Marketing Thought and Practice*, edited by B.J. Walker, W.O. Bearden, W.R. Darden, P.E. Murphy, J.R. Nevin, J.C. Olson, and B.A. Weitz. Chicago: American Marketing Association, 1982.

Belch, G.E. Belief Systems and the Differential Role of the Self Concept. In *Advances in Consumer Research*, edited by H.K. Hunt. Ann Arbor, Mich.: Association for Consumer Research, 1978.

Bloch, P.H. Involvement Beyond the Purchase Process: Conceptual Issues and Empirical Investigation. In *Advances in Consumer Research*, IX, edited by A.A. Mitchell. Ann Arbor, Mich.: Association for Consumer Research, 1982.

Bozinoff, L., and R. Cohen. The Effects of Personal Values and Usage Situations on Product Attribute Importance. In *An Assessment of Marketing Thought and Practice*, edited by B.J. Walker, W.O. Bearden, W.R. Darden, P.E. Murphy, J.R. Nevin, J.C. Olson, and B.A. Weitz. Chicago: American Marketing Association, 1982.

Bowen, L., and S.H. Chaffee. Product Involvement and Pertinent Advertising Appeals. *Journalism Quarterly* 51 (1974):613–621.

Calder, B.J., L.W. Phillips and A.M. Tybout. Designing Research for Application. *Journal of Consumer Research* 8 (1981):197–207.

Carman, J. Values and Consumption Patterns: A Closed Loop. In *Advances in Consumer Research*, V, edited by H.K. Hunt. Ann Arbor, Mich.: Association for Consumer Research, 1978.

Henry, W.A. Cultural Values do Correlate with Consumer Behavior. *Journal of Marketing Research* 13 (1976):121–127.

Houston, M.J., and M.J. Rothschild. Conceptual and Methodological Foundations of Involvement. In *Research Frontiers in Marketing: Dialogues and Directions*, edited by S.C. Jain. Chicago: American Marketing Association, 1978.

Howard, J.A., and J.N. Sheth. *The Theory of Buyer Behavior*. New York: John Wiley & Sons, Inc., 1969.

Kassarjian, H.H. Low Involvement: A Second Look. In *Advances in Consumer Research*, VIII, edited by K.B. Monroe. Ann Arbor, Mich.: Association for Consumer Research, 1981.

Krugman, H.E. The Impact of Television Advertising: Learning Without Involvement. *Public Opinion Quarterly* 29 (1965):349–356.

Krugman, H.E. The Measurement of Advertising Involvement. *Public Opinion Quarterly* 30 (1967):583–596.

Leavitt, C., A.G. Greenwald, and C. Obermiller. What Is Low Involvement Low In? In *Advances in Consumer Research*, VIII, edited by K.B. Monroe. Ann Arbor, Mich.: Association for Consumer Research, 1981.

Mitchell, A.A. Involvement: A Potentially Important Mediator of Consumer Behavior. In *Advances in Consumer Research*, VI, edited by W.L. Wilkie. Ann Arbor, Mich.: Association for Consumer Research, 1979.

Mitchell, A.A. The Dimension of Advertising Involvement. In *Advances in Consumer Research*, VIII, edited by K.B. Monroe. Ann Arbor, Mich.: Association for Consumer Research, 1981.

Nicosia, F.M., and C.Y. Glock. Marketing and Affluence: A Research Perspective. In *1968 Fall Conference Proceedings*, edited by F.W. Webster. Chicago: American Marketing Association, 1968.

Ostrom, T.M., and T.C. Brock. A Cognitive Model of Attitudinal Involvement. In *Theories of Cognitive Consistency: A Sourcebook*, edited by R.P. Abelson, E. Aronson, W.J. McGuire, T.M. Newcomb, M.J. Rosenberg, and P.H. Tannenbaum. Rand-McNally Co., 1968.

Rokeach, M.J. *Beliefs, Attitudes and Values*. San Francisco: Jossey-Bass, 1968.

Rokeach, M.J. *The Nature of Human Values*. New York: Free Press, 1973.

Rokeach, M.J. *Understanding Human Values: Individual and Societal*. New York: Free Press, 1979.

Schuchman, F.K. *Personal Values and Consumer Behavior*. Unpublished doctoral dissertation, University of Colorado, 1974.

Scott, J.E., and L.E. Lamont. Relating Consumer Values to Consumer Behavior: A Model and Method for Investigation. In *Increasing Marketing Productivity*, edited by T.V. Greer. Chicago: American Marketing Association, 1974.

Sherif, M., and H. Cantril. *The Psychology of Ego-Involvement*. New York: John Wiley & Sons, Inc., 1947.

Sherrell, D.L., and T.A. Shimp. Consumer Involvement in a Laboratory Setting. In *An Assessment of Marketing Thought and Practice*, edited by B.J. Walker, W.O. Bearden, W.R. Darden, P.E. Murphy, J.R. Nevin, J.C. Olson, and B.A. Weitz. American Marketing Association, 1982.

Shimp, T.A. Attitude Toward the Brand as a Mediator of Consumer Brand Choice. *Journal of Advertising* 10 (1982):9–15.

Steele, R.G.D., and J.H. Torie. *Principles and Procedures of Statistics*. New York: McGraw-Hill Book Company, 1960.

Swan, J.E., and I.F. Trawick. Satisfaction Related to Predictive vs. Desired Expectations. In *Proceedings of Fourth Annual Conference on Consumer Satisfaction*, edited by H.K. Hunt and R.L. Day. Bloomington, Ind.: Indiana University, 1980.

Vinson, D.E. Human Values and the Marketing Function. In *Avoiding Social Catastrophes and Maximizing Social Opportunities: The General Systems Challenge*, edited by R. Ericson. Washington: Society for General Systems Research, 1978.

Vinson, D.E., and J.M. Munson. Personal Values: An Approach to Market Segmentation. In *Marketing: 1776–1976 and Beyond*, edited by K.L. Bernhardt. Chicago: American Marketing Association, 1976.

Vinson, D.E., J.M. Munson, M. Nakanishi. An Investigation of the Rokeach Value Survey for Consumer Research Applications. In *Advances in Consumer Research*, edited by W.D. Perreault. Atlanta: Association for Consumer Research, 1977.

Vinson, D.E., J.E. Scott, and L.E. Lamont. The Role of Personal Values in Marketing and Consumer Behavior. *Journal of Marketing* 41 (1977): 44–50.

13 Do Trends in Attitudes Predict Trends in Behavior?

Martin I. Horn and
William D. Wells

Consider the following examples which typify thinking about attitude trends and their behavioral consequences. The examples are distilled from a variety of sources. Each reflected a truism at the time it was popular.

> People are becoming increasingly concerned about physical exercise and sound nutrition. There seems to be a growing obsession in this country with a slim figure and a healthy heart. Jogging is a national sport and health spas will proliferate and prosper.

> Use of certain products will be curtailed as they become symbols of antisocial feelings and outmoded behavior. Among them are aerosols, tobacco, gas-guzzling cars, and drugs.

> The 1980s will extend the "Me Decade" mentality of the 1970s. As a result, there will be an increased use of tobacco, caffeine, alcohol, and drugs.

> With gasoline prices increasing, family trips in the car will be planned more carefully, and the car itself will be more appreciated. New products will spring up to keep the car better looking and in better running condition.

These examples have two elements in common: (1) they observe or infer a general attitude; and (2) they predict a specific behavior from this attitude: more products to take care of the car, more health spas, less use of aerosols, less use of drugs, more use of drugs, less use of tobacco, more use of tobacco, and so on.

Is it reasonable to believe that general attitudes can predict specific behaviors? That question is the topic of this chapter. In addressing this question, we will not refer to cross-sectional prediction—for example, people who like a product buy more of it than those who don't. That sort of prediction usually works very well. Nor will we challenge the validity of the attitude trends and behaviors implied in the examples given above. Rather, we will examine how well trends in specific behaviors can be predicted from trends in general attitudes at the aggregate level.

187

We will use the word *predict* liberally in the discussion. Predictions will include all those occasions in which trends in attitudes and trends in behavior seem to agree. Likewise, the term *attitude* will be used liberally and will include intentions and opinions, as well as more general attitudes. Our usage of predict and attitude is generous, but not uncommon.

Method

The data to be reported are from a lifestyle survey conducted annually since 1975 by Needham, Harper & Steers. This survey collects information on approximately 200 attitudes, interests, and opinions; the purchase of 300 products and services; and respondent participation in about 90 activities. Respondents' media use also is obtained.

Each year, self-administered questionnaires are mailed to a nationally representative sample of 2,000 married men and 2,000 married women who are members of a consumer mail panel. The men and women are not from the same household. (The study is cross-sectional, not longitudinal.) The sample is balanced according to U.S. census figures. The questionnaire return rate is about 85 percent. Because the survey is not specifically designed to address questions about relationships between attitudes and behavior, many of the attitude items have no behavioral counterparts. However, there is enough overlap to allow examination of when attitudes and behavior concur and when they do not.

Conclusions

In examining the wide range of attitudes and behaviors collected through the lifestyle study over the past nine years, we come to three conclusions.

Conclusion 1: There are many ways to enact an attitude.

Conclusion 2: Many factors can come between an attitude and a behavior.

Conclusion 3: Behaviors related to the same attitude can interact, sometimes reinforcing each other, sometimes canceling each other out.

The findings in this paper illustrate these conclusions.

Conclusion 1

The first conclusion is that *there are many ways to enact an attitude.* The first three examples of this observation are positive ones in which behaviors closely follow—or at least closely agree with—the attitudes. The fourth example demonstrates how trends in attitudes and behavior do not always follow the same path.

Figure 13–1 shows the trend in intention to purchase and actual ownership of digital watches among males in the sample. (The trend among females is similar.) The trend in both purchase intention and ownership marches steadily upward from 1976—when the question was first asked—through 1983. There were pauses between 1979 and 1980 and unprecedented increases between 1982 and 1983.

Figure 13–2 shows another example in which intentions and ownership rise and fall together. Citizen band (CB) radios enjoyed their greatest popularity in the early and mid-1970s. In the late '70s, sales began to fall off and have been relatively flat through the present, although 1983 shows a very slight upturn.

Thus far, specific purchase intentions (attitude) have tracked fairly well with actual purchases (behavior) for these two consumer durables. An

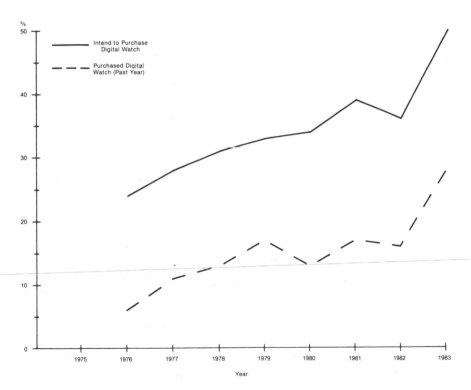

Figure 13–1. Digital Watches (Males)

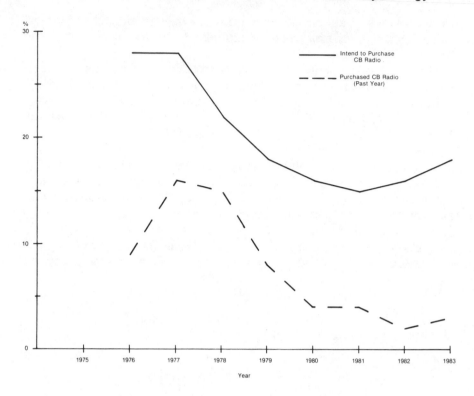

Figure 13-2.   CB Radios (Males)

optimist might even say that purchases were carried out just as intentions would predict. Other data, such as the University of Michigan's indicators of consumer behavior (Curtin 1982) show much the same pattern—specific intentions are often congruent with specific behaviors.

The next example includes a more general attitude than purchase intent. Figure 13-3 shows the percent of men in the lifestyle study who agree with the statement, "Most big companies are just out for themselves." It shows an ominous trend from 1977 through 1982. If 1983 is any indication, adverse attitudes toward big business may be easing. Several predictions can be made from this trend, including, perhaps, a growing disaffection with well-known brand names. Indeed, reported purchase of branded items is declining.

Again, attitudes and behavior track pretty well. As general attitudes toward large corporations become more unfavorable, reported use of well-known brand names declines. While year-to-year movement of attitudes and behavior may not always follow the exact same direction, the overall

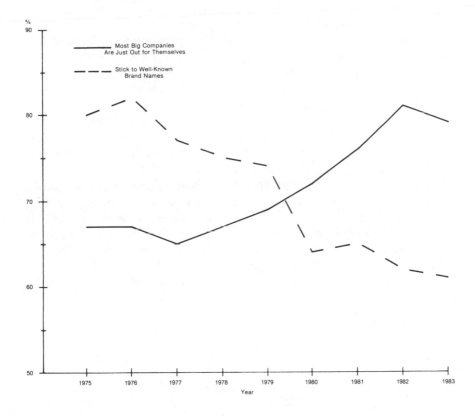

Figure 13-3. Big Business and Brand Names (Males)

trends closely coincide. As mentioned earlier, attitudes toward big business improved slightly in 1983. Given this improvement, one would probably predict a rise in the reported use of branded goods. But, as figure 13-3 shows, this prediction would be incorrect. Use of well-known brand names continues to decline despite more favorable views toward big business.

This example brings up two related points: (1) It is difficult to predict a behavior from an attitude at any one point in time, and (2) a behavior may not track with the attitude even if it had done so in the past. And, as the above example shows, trying to predict behavior can be further complicated because there may be an unforeseen change in the attitude trend itself!

While it is only speculation, one reason that attitudes toward large businesses and brand name use did not follow the traditional pattern in 1983 may be greater consumer acceptance of, and satisfaction with, nonbranded items during previous years. Consumers began to see some nonbranded (generics, "no frills") products as acceptable alternatives to brand name goods, even as their attitudes toward companies that manufacture well-known brands became more favorable. In other words, mediating circumstances may have wedged themselves between the attitude and the behavior. The effect of mediating circumstances on attitudes and behaviors will be examined further when discussing conclusion 2.

Continuing with conclusion 1, the fourth example illustrates conflicting trends between a general attitude and possible consequent behaviors. The solid line in figure 13-4 represents agreement among women with the statement, "I like to feel attractive to members of the opposite sex." Agreement is high and steady. Observing the strength and stability of this attitude, one might predict that various cosmetic aids, such as hair care products, would continue to have strong and steady use over an extended period of time. But, as figure 13-4 demonstrates, product success is mixed. Women's use of hair color has faded since the mid-1970s and only recently has its use begun to creep upward. Even so, reported usage levels in 1983 are far from what they were in 1975. The steady downward trend and current use levels would not have been predicted by the general attitude portrayed above. Nor would the gradual, steady increase in use of home permanents shown in figure 13-4.

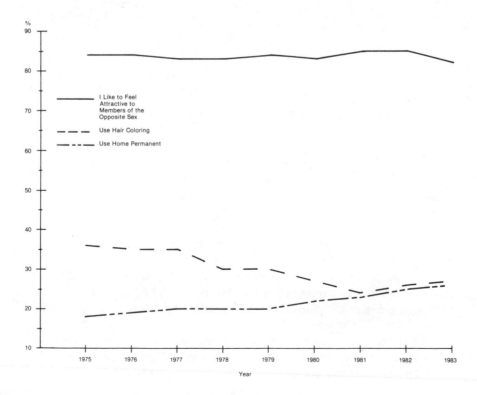

Figure 13-4. Cosmetics (Females)

These contradictory findings may not seem startling if the obvious conclusion is drawn: women can do many things to feel attractive to the opposite sex. They do not have to use hair coloring. They may prefer to use home permanents. This conclusion is correct—and it also mirrors conclusion 1: there are many ways in which consumers can enact attitudes.

Conclusion 2

Conclusion 2 states that *many factors can come between an attitude and behavior*. Without knowing what those factors are, predicting the behavioral outcome of an attitude becomes difficult, if not impossible. For example, more and more women in the lifestyle survey feel that meal preparation should take as little time as possible. This trend reflects, in part, the increase in the number of working women and the greater demands being placed on busy homemakers. While the trend line is not monotonic, the overall direction is clear. As such, one reasonable prediction from this attitude toward meal preparation would be increased use of convenience foods. Use of various types of convenience foods, however, does not follow the attitudinal trend, contrary to the prediction. Purchases of frozen pizza vary from year to year, while consumption of the traditional TV dinner has declined. See figures 13–5 and 13–6.

Consumer use of frozen vegetables is of particular interest. Figure 13–7 shows a sharp decrease in frequent consumption of frozen vegetables in the face of an attitude change that would have predicted the opposite. This apparent paradox is a good example of the second observation: many things can interfere between an attitude and behavior. One thing that happened to frozen vegetables can be explained by price. Frozen vegetable use dropped when relative prices in the category increased. Note that frozen vegetables are finding their way back to more dinner plates in the past two years as their relative price has begun to moderate (Consumer Price Index, 1977–1983).

Further examples of conclusion 2, and perhaps conclusion 1 as well, arise in the dessert category. While fewer women agree with the statement "dinner isn't complete without dessert," canned frosting and whipped topping, to name a few items, have had uninterrupted success since the end of the 1970s. See figure 13–8. There are a number of possible explanations for these contradictory trends. For example, the traditional dessert occasion (i.e., after dinner) may be losing some of its appeal, but dessert products may not be; they simply are being eaten at different times of the day. Or, there could be greater reliance on more convenient dessert and baking items as the pressures of meal preparation mount (see figures 13–5 through 13–7). Yet again, innovative homemakers might be discovering untraditional (nondessert) uses for these products. Whatever the exact reason (and in all

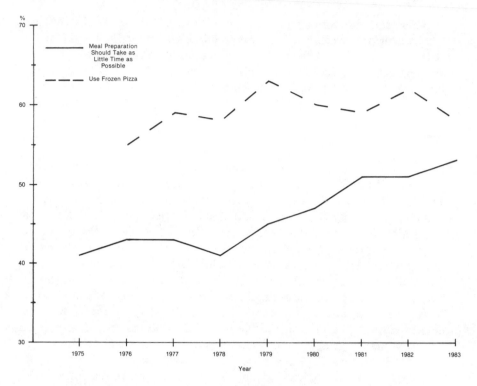

Figure 13-5. Meal Preparation and Frozen Pizza (Females)

likelihood it is a combination of reasons), the important point is that circumstances impinge on specific behaviors—circumstances which make
predicting these behaviors from an attitude alone rather risky.

Conclusion 3

Disposable income and shopping behavior exemplify the third conclusion:
*behaviors related to the same attitude can interact, sometimes reinforcing
each other, sometimes canceling each other out.* The trend in "No matter
how fast our income goes up, we never seem to get ahead" is shown in
figure 13-9.

Clearly, consumers are concerned about the economy and feel that increased earnings may not help them cope. This feeling was most prominent
during the peak inflation years of the late '70s. As inflation has cooled, so
have consumer concerns about making ends meet, the current recession not-
withstanding. Consumers are feeling more optimistic about an economic

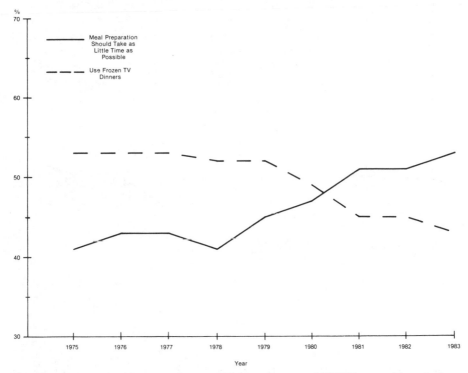

Figure 13–6. Meal Preparation and Frozen Prepared TV Dinners (Females)

recovery, feelings recently corroborated by Roper (1983). From this trend, it might be expected that there would be more use of coupons and more shopping for specials during the time in which consumers were feeling most financially pinched. As figure 13–9 shows, use of coupons did increase as consumers worried about the economy, and has trailed off slightly as worries recede. But, according to the reports of the respondents, shopping around for specials has declined slightly throughout the entire nine-year period. Did use of coupons begin to replace shopping for specials as manufacturers deluged shoppers with more and more coupons and as shopping trips became more expensive? It is difficult to know for sure, and hard to tell from these trends, but the relationships point once again to the hazards of predicting consumer behavior from trends in attitudes.

Discussion

What implications can be drawn from these examples? First, the examples do not show that attitudes and behavior are unrelated. Attitude trends often

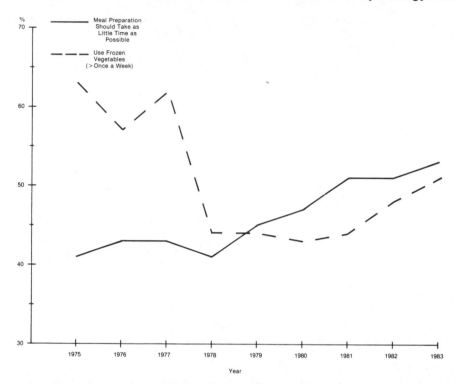

Figure 13-7. Meal Preparation and Frozen Vegetables (Females)

are related to behavior trends when the attitude takes the form of a specific intention that can be enacted in only one way. The digital watch and CB radio examples are good illustrations. But, even when intentions are specific, behaviors do not always follow immediately from them. Behaviors may interact with each other, as may have been the case between use of coupons and shopping for specials. Or, forces in the environment may interfere between attitudes and behavior, such as the effect of price on frozen vegetable consumption.

It should be emphasized that an unanticipated behavior does not invalidate the attitude on which the prediction was made. Likewise, the behavior is not invalid because it does not directly follow from the attitude. Rather, it simply suggests that the relationship between the attitude and behavior is weak, or more likely, that a host of other factors interfere with the relationship. The problem arises when predictive leaps are made from an attitude to a behavior without fully understanding the environment in which the attitude and behavior occurred. An understanding of that environment is critical to marketing and advertising planners.

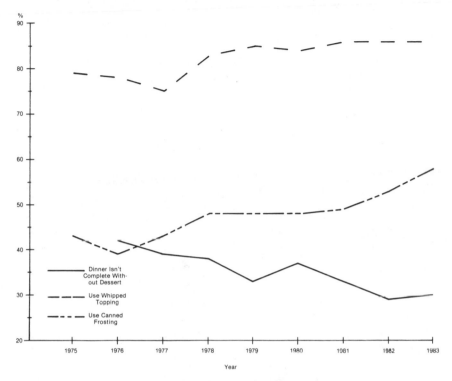

Figure 13-8.   Desserts (Females)

Here is an example. If we know why a decline in the belief that "dinner isn't complete without dessert" can coexist with increased use of dessert-related items, we may decide to shift dessert strategies from after-dinner use to broader use occasions. In this case, as in many others, the principal benefit of the attitude—behavior relationship is *not* prediction—it's a *lack* of prediction, which in turn leads us to press for fuller understanding. Examples of this kind lead to the somewhat surprising, and therefore previously unlisted, conclusion 4: cases in which attitudes and behavior don't agree often are more interesting than the cases in which the relationships are direct. Disagreements between expectations and behavior often precipitate to scramble to understand the reasons why the relationship has broken down. This scramble, in turn, often produces a deeper analysis of the situation. For marketing practitioners, this analysis can improve the chances of taking the right strategic direction. When you know what's happening, you can sometimes figure out what to do!

The other part of conclusion 4, also derived from the first three conclusions, is equally clear: attitudes are least likely to be useful when one at-

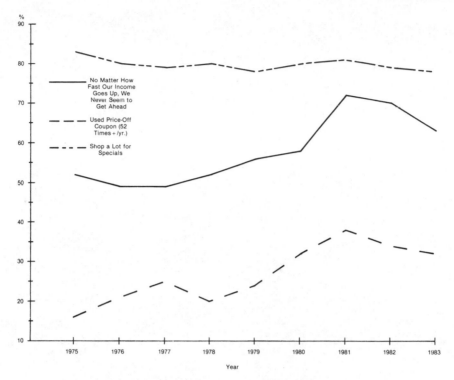

Figure 13-9.   Income and Shopping (Females)

tempts to predict specific behaviors from broad, general attitudes, simply because attempts at such prediction usually do not succeed. When they do succeed, they often succeed only in retrospect, or only by chance. While these conclusions may seem obvious in light of what has long been known about attitudes and behavior, a glance back at the predictions listed in the introduction of this chapter will serve as a reminder that such predictions are continually being made. And these predictions often are listened to attentively.

References

Curtin, Richard T. Indicators of Consumer Behavior: The University of Michigan Surveys of Consumers. *Public Opinion Quarterly* 46 (1982):340–352.

The Roper Organization, Inc. *Roper Reports*, 1983 (3), 218–223.

U.S. Department of Labor, Bureau of Labor Statistics. *Consumer Price Index*, December, 1977–February, 1983.

Part IV
Cultural and
Subcultural Basis
of Values and
Their Formation

In part IV the cultural and subcultural foundation of personal values is explored. Life states, age, ethnic and geographic factors, and social class are the basis for the first three chapters. A final chapter provides insight into the importance of education in values formation.

Life states and age influences on value orientation are examined by Crosby, Gill, and Lee in chapter 14. Age and life status are each shown to have a unique effect on individual values.

Powell and Valencia address subcultural and geographic relationships in a study of Hispanic value orientation in New York, Miami, San Antonio, and Los Angeles. The authors found significant economic and age effects, but little differences between respondents for the four cities examined. Further, they interpret the value profiles to indicate a strong desire for assimilation.

Chapter 16 explores black versus white profiles using a matched socioeconomic sample methodology. Ness and Stith found that the middle-class blacks and whites in the study both espouse basic middle-class values. Middle-class blacks, however, tended to embrace these values even more strongly than whites.

Chapter 17 is an examination of education influence in value formation. Kramer suggests that higher education by its concentrated cognitive and behavioral elements is, in fact, a major influence on personal values. He suggests a methodology for examining the role of college education and self-evaluation.

14 Life Status and Age as Predictors of Value Orientation

Lawrence A. Crosby,
James D. Gill, and
Robert E. Lee

Marketing practitioners today are investing considerable sums of money in an effort to understand the changing values orientation of the consuming public. Corporations and consulting organizations[1] are undertaking large-scale national studies of consumer values with two purposes in mind. One is to track the direction and velocity of values change in the aggregate population. The second is to segment the population into groups defined on the basis of their predominant values orientation. Findings from applied studies such as these are being used to make critical decisions with respect to marketing strategy and mix programming.[2]

Much of the pioneering work on consumer values has its origin in industry and not academe. In fact, this may be a classic example of technology leading science (O'Shaughnessy and Ryan 1979). Only in recent years has the topic of values begun to appear in the consumer behavior literature.[3] It seems that these academics, in their self-appointed role as the guardian of marketing knowledge and the conscience of marketing research, have maintained a healthy skepticism about the values construct. This is understandable given the limited contribution of personality level concepts, including psychographics, to the development of consumer behavior theory (Kassarjian 1971).

The major contribution of the published literature has been to add a needed dose of theory and scientific discipline to the study of consumer values. In addition to articles which investigate the empirical relationship between values and consumer behavior (Henry 1976; Darden et al. 1980; Becker and Connor 1982; Bozinoff and Cohen 1982), there are thoughtful discussions about the content and conceptual nature of values (Clawson and Vinson 1978; Kanter 1978), issues involved in measuring values (Vinson, Munson, and Nakanishi 1977; Reynolds and Jolly 1980), and the role of values in the consumer decision-making model (Vinson, Scott, and Lamont 1977; Carman 1978). These efforts reflect the goals of scientific inquiry which include "the organization and classification of knowledge on the basis of explanatory principles obtained through the application of the scientific method" (O'Shaughnessy and Ryan 1979, p. 579). Practitioners profit from these efforts to ground technology in the findings of science through improvements in the reliability of goal attainment (Bunge 1972).

There is, however, one area of noticeable gap in the consumer behavior literature on values. It appears that little research has been done for the express purpose of identifying value antecedents. Knowledge of these antecedents is important to marketing management for two reasons. First, forecasts regarding the future course of demand can be made more accurate by taking these antecedents into account, since they are also the source of values change. Second, antecedents may provide a better means for identifying values segments, thus making the segments more accessible to marketing communications.

Value Antecedents

A value has been defined as an enduring belief that a specific mode of conduct (instrumental value) or end-state of existence (terminal value) is personally or socially preferable to other modes of conduct or end-states of existence (Rokeach 1968; 1973). Like attitudes, values have cognitive, affective, and behavioral components. Unlike attitudes, they transcend objects and situations. Antecedents of human values are traceable to the socialization process as it occurs in various cultures and societies (Rokeach 1973). Values represent an important conceptual link between the social structure and personality (Bengston and Lovejoy 1973).

Cross-cultural value differences have been studied in consumer research and the implications for international marketing examined (Munson and McIntyre 1978). Within cultures, four major predictors of value priorities have been posited: socioeconomic status, education, generation, and life-cycle stage (Inglehart 1977).[4] Consumer researchers investigating the linkage with socioeconomic status have found some strata differences, but the results generally support the concept of a mass society (Darden, Darden, and Carlson 1980). Researchers in other fields have also found only weak support for the hypothesis that value orientations vary by position in the social structure (Bengston and Lovejoy 1973). A study in political science incorporated all four major predictors in a multiple regression analysis and found that generation, life-cycle, and education variables were related to values but not to income (Dalton 1977). A closer examination of two of these hypothesized antecedents, namely generation and life cycle, appears in the sections below.

Age-Related Differences

Substantial age group differences in values are assumed to exist by many marketers and form the basis of innovative marketing strategies (see e.g.,

Engel and Blackwell 1982, pp. 202-214). However, the extent to which this assumption is based on empirical data that actually measure values rather than attitudes is not entirely clear. Studies in other fields have produced results which are inconsistent with and, in some cases, contradict this assumption. In part, these inconsistent results may be explained by a diversity of theoretical perspectives, choice of values constructs, and measurement methods (Antonucci et al. 1979). Likewise, there is considerable variability in study design, ranging from periodic studies of college students' views (Morris and Small 1971; Hoge 1976), to studies of different generations of related individuals (Penn 1977), to large cross-sectional studies of household heads (Christensen 1977). Nevertheless, based on their review of this diverse literature, the authors of one study concluded: "there does appear justification for a proposition regarding contrasts or changes between age groups in conceptions of the desirable. However, the differences may be less than the current 'generation gap' debate warrants" (Bengston and Lovejoy 1973).

Based on the notion of core values in a culture or society, an argument can be made that age group differences in values should be fairly modest. The stability of a culture is premised on the maintenance of a delicately balanced system of values (Williams 1970). Dominant values serve as the "glue" which binds society together. The role of the older generation is to carry these dominant values and transmit them to the younger generation. Only in the case of severe social tension tearing at the very fabric of the culture would there be large value cleavages across age groups.

When age group differences in values are detected, of any magnitude, there remains a problem of interpretation. Age itself can only be interpreted as a surrogate variable. A cohort explanation of age group differences focuses on the economic condition (Inglehart 1971), historical events (e.g., wars, technological developments, etc.), and deprivations experienced by each age group during its period of socialization and values programming (Massey 1975). Table 14-1 relates the 1982 chronological age of consumers to their period of values programming and associated conditions and events.

A rival explanation is that differences in values reflect differences in the life-cycle positions of the age groups (Payne et al. 1973; Mason et al. 1973; Ike 1973; Jennings 1976). It is argued, for example, that with the increasing responsibilities of adulthood, youthful values shift away from liberalism-humanitarianism to conservatism (Glenn 1974). Therefore, as the cohort ages, its values preferences come to resemble those which the older cohorts now display (Dalton 1977). A third possible explanation is maturational; age group differences in values are taken as indicators of stages in personality development (Erikson 1950). Maturational influences, however, are probably of secondary importance in determining values priorities.

Table 14–1
Cohort-Historical Influences on Consumer Values

1982 Age	Year Born	Period of Values Programming	Important Conditions and Events
65 +	1917	1920s or earlier	World War I, Roaring 20s, cars, airplanes, radio
60	1922	1930s	Great Depression, New Deal,
55	1927	1930s	World War II
50	1932	1940s	
45	1937	1940s	
40	1942	1950s	Affluence, fall-out shelters,
35	1947	1950s	television, rock and roll,
30	1952	1960s (early)	JFK, Vietnam
25	1957	1960s (late)	Drugs, protests, space flights,
20	1962	1970s	computers, Watergate, inflation
18	1967	1970s	

Adapted from Massey (1975).

To Untangle the Influences

The rival cohort-historical versus life-cycle hypotheses pose a difficult research problem to the extent that these effects are confounded in empirical data. Still, it is important for marketers to know whether separate effects exist, because each has particular implications in terms of marketing strategy and information requirements.[5] If age group differences are found to depend on historical experience, this suggests a very dynamic marketplace where the number, size, and orientation of the values segments continues to change depending on the unique conditions and events surrounding each period of socialization. Obviously, this is a situation calling for continuous values monitoring. If values differences are found to depend on life-cycle position, this suggests that marketers must pay particular attention to trends in family structure. Key questions then become: what are becoming the predominant life-cycle stages (life status categories)? What is the associated values orientation? What portion of the population is in each life status? How are these proportions likely to change?

Life Stage Versus Life Status

It appears that recent demographic changes have partially invalidated the traditional family life-cycle concept (Murphy and Staples 1979). More heterogeneity now exists as to the sequence of stages and the velocity at which families and individuals pass through them. We observe, for example, delays in both family formation and child-bearing among certain segments of the population. Families have become smaller, thus shortening the "full nest" periods, and more couples are choosing not to have children at all. With rising divorce rates, there is also a higher incidence of single parent families. These trends have contributed to a significant degree of divergence from the traditional family life-cycle path. This divergence appears sufficient that use of the terms *cycle* and *stage* in this connection may no longer be appropriate. Better terminology reflecting multiple, alternative paths might be *life-status category*.

One consequence of this increased heterogeneity in family patterns is that the life-status and age variables have become less confounded. Within a given age category, there is now more variability in terms of life status. This is not to suggest that the variables are independent, but only that they are less correlated.

Causal Model and Hypotheses

The model in figure 14-1 represents our interpretation of the relationship between age related variables and values. In this diagram, age is shown

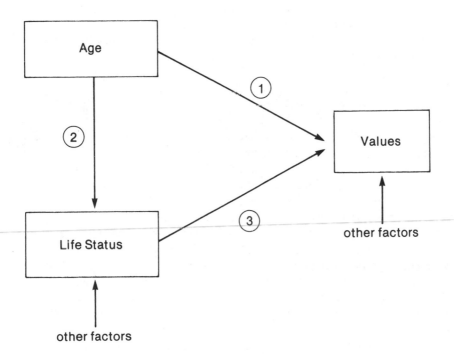

Figure 14-1. Assumed Causal Influences

as having both direct (path 1) and indirect (paths 2 plus 3) influences on values orientation. Path 1 is assumed to represent both cohort-historical and maturational influences on values. Elaborate forecasts and theories exist which have as their premise historically driven changes in consumer values (see e.g., Mitchell 1981; Yankelovich 1981). Without attempting to review all these arguments, suffice it to say there is sufficient justification for expecting cohort-historical influences on values. Path 2 depicts the relationships between age and life status. Despite recent demographic changes, there are certain biological and economic constraints which limit the range of life-status alternatives available to a given age group. Therefore, it seems doubtful that age and life status could ever be entirely independent. Path 3 represents the influence of life status on values orientation. As an example of this relationship, one might expect to find an increase in the value importance of family security with the onset of parenthood. Parenthood and other major changes in a person's life require psychological adaptation manifest, perhaps, in a shift in values priorities from those laid down early in life (Bengston and Lovejoy 1973).

Hypotheses follow directly from figure 14-1 and the foregoing discussion:

1. Controlling for age, significant differences exist in consumer values across life-status categories.
2. Controlling for life status, significant differences exist in consumer values across age-groups.

Analytic Approach

To test the hypotheses, an appropriate method is needed for partitioning the variance in values that acknowledges the high intercorrelation of the age and life-status variables. Value ratings may be employed as multiple dependent variables. Incremental partitioning is the procedure recommended for a three-construct model of the form in figure 14-1 (Pedhazur 1982, p. 182). This involves calculating the portion variance in values accounted for by age and the portion of variance in values accounted for by life status after age has been taken into account, for example, the increment in the portion of variance accounted for that is due to life status. It is expected that life status will contribute a statistically significant explained variance increment given the heterogeneity in life-cycle paths that now exist in American society. Using this method, a positive result for the life-status variable would clearly support hypothesis 1.

The drawback in this procedure is that all of the explained variance shared by age and life status is allocated to age. Therefore, assuming a significant age effect, it would be appropriate to reverse the procedure and enter life status first. If age then contributes a statistically significant explained variance increment, hypothesis 2 would be supported, providing evidence of cohort-historical and/or maturational effects.

Sample

The data for this analysis are from a larger study of consumer/voter behavior on bottle bills. These bills appeared on the November 2, 1982 ballots in California and Colorado. A quota sample of consumer panel households in these states was supplied by National Family Opinion, Inc. Households were selected for inclusion by matching household characteristics with known census data for each state. A random selection procedure was then used to select an eligible adult voter within each household. The questionnaire, preceded by a prealert postcard, was mailed to five hundred panel members in each state. A standard inducement was offered to panel respondents. A total of six hundred sixty-five completed surveys were returned (66.5 percent response rate).

Values Measurement

Respondents' terminal and instrumental values were measured using the value survey developed by Rokeach (1973). This method requires subjects to rank order two alphabetically listed series of 18 terminal and instrumental values. Unfortunately, this procedure yields a variable that is only ordinal in scale and not suitable as input to MANOVA. It does have the advantage of requiring respondents to evaluate thoroughly their values priorities and make relatively fine importance distinctions.

An alternative to the ranking procedure suggested by Rokeach is a Likert-scale rating approach. The merits of this approach have been discussed by Vinson, Munson, and Nakanishi (1977). While rating is a less cognitively demanding task than ranking (sometimes an important property in mail surveys) and has the added advantage of approximating an interval scale, there is concern that respondents may complete the items in an undifferentiated manner.

To overcome these problems, a compromise solution was attempted of having respondents first rank then rate the values items. Both tasks were completed on the same questionnaire page, making it possible for respondents to consult their rankings when checking the rating scales. It was hoped the dual procedure would have the advantages of both ratings and rankings. The added effort required by the dual procedure did not appear to be a problem in this study as suggested by the relatively high response rate.

Life-Status and Age Assignment

Life-status categories were created by crossing the variables of marital status, work force membership/nonmembership, and the presence and age of children within the household. Consideration was also given to the presence of a "significant other" in the household (cohabitation), with regard to the unmarried. However, as Murphy and Staples (1979) also found, an insignificant number of such relationships were detected and the variable was removed.

An analysis of respondent characteristics revealed twelve life-status categories containing a reasonable number of sample members. These life-status categories are described in table 14–2.

To test the influence of age on values, respondents were grouped into four age categories (18 to 29, 30 to 44, 45 to 64, and 65 years and older).

Table 14–2
Age and Lifestyle Respondent Characteristics[a]

	Age			
	18–29	30–44	45–64	65 and over
Life-Status Group[b]	(N)	(N)	(N)	(N)
Never married, outside work force, no children (e.g., students)	27	8	2	3
Never married, in work force, no children	15	13	6	0
Married, in work force, youngest child under 6 yrs.	40	52	0	0
Married, in work force, youngest child 6–17 yrs.	14	81	24	0
Married, in work force, youngest child 18 yrs. or older	12	15	41	2
Married, in work force, no children in nest	18	10	64	16
Divorced, outside work force, children present (e.g., alimony and child support recipients)	12	19	6	0
Divorced, in work force, no children	1	11	10	1
Divorced, outside work force, no children (e.g., alimony recipients)	1	3	7	2
Married, retired, youngest child 18 yrs. or older	12	15	41	2
Married, retired, no children in nest	2	0	25	52
Alone, outside work force, no children (e.g., solitary survivors)	0	0	8	13

[a]Lambda (asymmetric) = .22 with life status dependent on age.
[b]N = 646 (19 respondents were not classified).

These category ranges were selected to reflect distinct historical conditions and events affecting various generations (as indicated in table 14–1). The age groupings also appeared to provide a sensitive measure of maturational influences on values.

Respondent age and life-status characteristics are cross-tabulated in table 14–2. A moderate degree of correlation between life-status and age categories was indicated by the Lambda (asymmetric) statistic (.22 with life status dependent on age).

Results

The MANOVA results lend support to both hypothesis 1 and hypothesis 2. As shown in table 14–3 and table 14–4, a significant life-status effect on terminal ($p = .001$) and instrumental values ($p = .03$) was found despite the previous inclusion of age in the relevant models. These life-status effects were also not confounded by an age by life-status interaction ($p = $ ns). However, separate univariate tests of life-status influence on 18 terminal and instrumental values revealed significant differences for only 3 terminal values and 1 instrumental value.

Similarly, a significant age effect on terminal ($p = .001$) and instrumental values ($p = .04$) was found after the influence of life status was removed. As noted earlier, no significant interactions occurred. Univariate test results identified significant age differences for only 1 terminal and no instrumental values.

It should be noted that a very conservative test of the significance of each univariate effect was applied. The approach involved the Bonferroni F procedure, which controls for any inflation of the alpha level (Type 1 error rate) due to dependent variable correlations. The method requires that the F statistic for each test exceed a substantially increased critical value level, in comparison to the levels found in traditional F tables. Of course, an argument could be made that such a stringent approach is unnecessary, given Rokeach's (1973) position that each value in his values survey is distinct. Indeed, when traditional F table critical values are applied, significant life-status differences for 7 terminal and 3 instrumental values are realized ($p = .05$). Similarly, significant age differences exist for five terminal and two instrumental values ($p = .05$).

Discussion

Our study confirms previous findings that indeed there are age group differences in values. Recognizing that age is a surrogate predictor and that it

Table 14-3
Multivariate and Univariate Analysis of Variance of Age and Life Status on Terminal Value Scores

Analysis	Dependent Variable	Source of Variation	MS	U^{-a} Statistic	df	F	Significance [b] Level
Multivariate	Vector	Age by Life Status		.46127	414,7542	1.02	ns
		Life Status		.58576	198,4989	1.47	.001
		Age		.72359	54,1568	3.33	.001
Univariate	Comfortable Life	Life Status	2.10676		11,543	1.05	ns
	Exciting Life		6.10518		11,543	2.45	ns
	Accomplishment		1.84064		11,543	1.07	ns
	World at Peace		1.72979		11,543	.92	ns
	World of Beauty		1.77983		11,543	.84	ns
	Equality		4.68680		11,543	2.06	ns
	Family Security		4.18864		11,543	4.92	.01
	Freedom		.78026		11,543	.81	ns
	Happiness		.99841		11,543	1.01	ns
	Inner Harmony		1.96677		11,543	1.22	ns
	Mature Love		2.21484		11,543	1.11	ns
	National Security		3.64739		11,543	1.80	ns
	Pleasure		3.79736		11,543	1.81	ns
	Salvation		13.82983		11,543	3.14	.01
	Self-Respect		1.40372		11,543	1.32	ns
	Social Recognition		7.48211		11,543	2.83	.05
	True Friendship		1.51696		11,543	.99	ns
	Wisdom		.68077		11,543	.45	ns
Multivariate	Vector	Age by Life Status		.46127	414,7542	1.02	ns
		Age		.81598	54,1568	2.05	.001
		Life Status		.51910	198,4989	1.81	.001
Univariate	Comfortable Life	Age	.76669		3,543	.38	ns
	Exciting Life		5.53039		3,543	2.22	ns
	Accomplishment		1.04874		3,543	.61	ns
	World at Peace		8.64378		3,543	4.64	ns
	World at Beauty		4.93276		3,543	2.34	ns

Equality	3.66138	3,543	1.61	ns
Family Security	1.08540	3,543	1.28	ns
Freedom	.73135	3,543	.76	ns
Happiness	.93242	3,543	.94	ns
Inner Harmony	5.05250	3,543	3.12	ns
Mature Love	1.18760	3,543	.59	ns
National Security	15.28992	3,543	7.57	.01
Pleasure	3.16602	3,543	1.51	ns
Salvation	16.68618	3,543	3.79	ns
Self-Respect	2.81116	3,543	2.64	ns
Social Recognition	2.81247	3,543	1.06	ns
True Friendship	.74244	3,543	.49	ns
Wisdom	2.81904	3,543	1.89	ns

[a]Wilks' lambda statistic.

[b]Univariate tests of significance were based on Bonferroni's procedure in which nearest F critical values for a family-wise alpha of .01 are $F_{11,543} = F_{3,543} = 5.93$; for family-wise alpha of .05 they are $F_{11,543} = 2.65$ and $F_{3,543} = 4.76$ (Huitema 1980).

Table 14-4
Multivariate and Univariate Analysis of Variance of Age and Life Status on Instrumental Values

Analysis	Dependent Variable	Source of Variation	U-[a] Statistic	MS	df	F	Significance[b] Level
Multivariate	Vector	Age by Life Status	.49967		432,7907	.90	ns
		Life Status	.65208		198,5149	1.21	.03
		Age	.81051		54,1618	2.31	.001
Univariate	Ambitious	Life Status		5.54269	1,560	1.41	ns
	Broad-Minded			.89751	1,560	1.77	ns
	Capable			1.61049	1,560	1.01	ns
	Cheerful			2.38695	1,560	1.37	ns
	Clean			12.69056	1,560	1.15	ns
	Courageous			1.68491	1,560	.83	ns
	Forgiving			.26964	1,560	3.41	.01
	Helpful			.93139	1,560	1.47	ns
	Honest			.41001	1,560	.91	ns
	Imaginative			10.11064	1,560	2.03	ns
	Independent			2.95308	1,560	1.63	ns
	Intellectual			.84880	1,560	1.73	ns
	Logical			5.06748	1,560	.63	ns
	Loving			1.93787	1,560	1.19	ns
	Obedient			4.78982	1,560	1.52	ns
	Polite			1.09550	1,560	1.66	ns
	Responsible			.41447	1,560	.73	ns
	Self-Controlled			4.01733	1,560	.85	ns
Multivariate	Vector	Age by Life Status	.49967		432,7907	.90	ns
		Age	.87374		54,1618	1.39	.04
		Life Status	.59780		198,5149	1.46	.001
Univariate	Ambitious	Age		3.35069	3,560	1.86	ns
	Broad-Minded			3.01431	3,560	.08	ns
	Capable			1.30477	3,560	1.22	ns
	Cheerful			2.02114	3,560	1.08	ns
	Clean			4.33625	3,560	2.48	ns

Courageous	1.52267	3,560	.61	ns
Forgiving	4.36910	3,560	2.13	ns
Helpful	1.86547	3,560	1.08	ns
Honest	.41553	3,560	1.07	ns
Imaginative	5.61831	3,560	2.05	ns
Independent	2.67937	3,560	1.64	ns
Intellectual	3.16245	3,560	.84	ns
Logical	1.33118	3,560	2.43	ns
Loving	1.84830	3,560	.23	ns
Obedient	4.03454	3,560	2.00	ns
Polite	2.60259	3,560	1.25	ns
Responsible	.44976	3,560	.94	ns
Self-Controlled	2.03750	3,560	1.01	ns

[a]Wilks' lambda statistic.

[b]Univariate tests of significance were based on Bonferoni's procedure in which nearest F critical values for a family-wise alpha of .01 are $F_{11,560}$ = 3.05, and $F_{3,560}$ = 5.93; for family-wise alpha of .05 they are $F_{11,560}$ = 2.65 and $F_{3,560}$ = 4.75 (Huitema 1980).

accounts for a unique portion of the variance in values over and above life status, we conclude that cohort-historical, maturational, or some other age-related influence on values is present. This would seem to have implications for the direction of future research in both the basic and applied social science fields (e.g., psychology and marketing).

Of theoretical interest in psychology might be the question of how to conceptualize personality development in adulthood. In fact, some stage-type variable is needed to test whether maturational influences are present. While adult stage theories do exist in the literature, they have neither empirically established validity nor general acceptance. Furthermore, the causal priorities are unclear. Do values changes contribute to or follow from personality changes or are they different manifestations of the same underlying phenomenon? It might be noted, however, that research on values and personality maturation would be an extremely expensive proposition requiring years of longitudinal data. Cross-sectional designs such as the present study employed can only establish values differences, not values changes.

Assuming the existence of cohort-historical influences, psychological theory is also needed to better explain the process by which these effects occur. For example, many subscribe to a deprivation theory of values formation which assumes that needs not satisfied during socialization come to be represented as important values later in life (e.g., adults raised during the depression and World War II tend to attach greater importance to national security). While having intuitive appeal, we note that deprivation/satiation theories are somewhat out of vogue in motivational psychology. It might be useful to compare predictions based on deprivation/satiation theory with those derived from a different viewpoint. An attribution theorist might argue, for example, that the environment largely determines the opportunities for reinforcement and, consequently, behavior. People then examine their externally defined behavior and make inferences about their personal values. Thus, the increased isolation of the individual in society may account for the current values subscriptions of the "Me Generation."

In the applied field of marketing, evidence as to cohort-historical influences also has important research implications. To predict the path of values evolution, marketers need to understand what classes of historical conditions and events have the most profound impact on values. Certain theorists tend to stress one type of influence over another based largely on their own training and discipline orientation. Marketers, on the other hand, cannot afford to be so arbitrarily selective. A preoccupation with economic determinants (as reflected in the works of Inglehart 1971, 1977; and Dalton 1977) could lead to an underestimation of other values-shaping forces such as trends in technology. It might be predicted, for example, that as interpersonal relationships are replaced by man-machine relationships, consumer priorities attached to personal values will shift dramatically. This, in turn, could alter consumers' preferences for "high (personal) touch" versus "high technology" approaches to marketing and distribution.

Insight as to what types of conditions or events are most important is also a requisite for detecting such effects. This is seen most clearly with reference to table 14-1, where the hypothesized causal influences are used to identify age cohorts (a categorization of the age variable). It is assumed that value priorities will be more homogeneous within and more heterogeneous between the age groupings. If the wrong categories are selected, it is quite possible that no differences in values would be detected, even when large differences actually exist.

We take little solace in the fact that life status accounts for a unique portion of the variance in values over and above age. Other writers have argued, on occasion, that too much is made of cohort values differences since these differences tend to diminish as the cohort ages. This might be reassuring if everyone followed the same life-cycle path, but as Murphy and Staples (1979) have shown, this is no longer the case. Our data reveal that this diversity in life status is coupled with a diversity in values and we seriously question whether the values of individuals exposed to such radically different life experiences will ever converge. The implication is clear that marketers of goods and services may find themselves facing increasingly heterogeneous markets and the need to devote a larger portion of their research budgets to values monitoring.

One cautionary note, however, should be offered lest too much be made of the effects noted in this study. In examining the percentage of values response variability explained by the combination of age and life status, we found that a statistically significant yet small amount of the variance had been accounted for. We are reminded, therefore, of a comment attributed to an unknown source that the pace of values change is truly "glacial."

Notes

1. Leaders in this field appear to be Yankelovich, Skelly, and White, Inc. and SRI International, Inc.

2. In the channels area, for example, values changes have contributed to a polarization of the retail marketplace. The strategy implication is that outlets should be either high service/high price or low service/low price, but not in between.

3. Other social science fields, however, have a rich literature on the topic of personal values.

4. There is also sporadic evidence of differences across subcultures (Christenson 1977) and by sex (Antonucci, Gillett, and Joyer 1979).

5. With intercorrelated independent variables there is little chance of ever being able to unambiguously partition the variance so that statements can be made about relative importance of the effects (Pedhazur 1982). Techniques do exist, however, for testing the significance of effects as long as the causal model can be explicated.

References

Antonucci, T., N. Gillett, and F.W. Hoyer. Values and Self-Esteem in Three Generations of Men and Women. *Journal of Gerontology* 34 (May 1979):415–422.

Becker, B.W., and P.E. Connor. The Influence of Personal Values on Attitude and Store Choice Behavior. In *Educators' Proceedings,* edited by Bruce J. Walker et al. Chicago: American Marketing Association, 1982, 21–24.

Bengston, V.L., and M.C. Lovejoy. Values, Personality, and Social Structure. *American Behavioral Scientist.* 16 (July/August 1973):880–912.

Bozinoff, L., and R. Cohen. The Effects of Personal Values and Usage Situations on Product Attribute Importance. In *Educators' Proceedings,* edited by Bruce J. Walker et al. Chicago: American Marketing Association, 1982, 25–29.

Bunge, M. Toward a Philosophy of Technology. In *Philosophy and Technology,* edited by C. Mitcham and R. Mackey. New York: The Free Press, 1972.

Carman, J.M. Values and Consumption Patterns: A Closed Loop. In *Advances in Consumer Research,* edited by H. Keith Hunt. Provo, Utah: Association for Consumer Research, 1978, 403–407.

Christensen, J.A. Generational Value Differences. *The Gerontologist* 17 (1977):367–374.

Clawson, C.J., and D.E. Vinson. Human Values: An Historical and Interdisciplinary Analysis. In *Advances in Consumer Research,* V, edited by H. Keith Hunt. Provo, Utah: Association for Consumer Research, 1978, 396–402.

Dalton, R.J. Was There a Revolution? A Note on Generational Versus Life Cycle Explanations of Values Differences. *Comparative Political Studies* 9 (January 1977):459–473.

Darden, D., W. Darden, and M. Carlson. *Social Class and Values.* Paper presented to the Mid-South Sociological Association, 1980.

Darden, W.R., O. Erdem, D.K. Darden, and R. Howell. Consumer Values and Shopping Orientations. *Proceedings Southwestern Marketing Association.* San Antonio, Texas, 1979.

Engel, J.F., and R.D. Blackwell. *Consumer Behavior.* Hinsdale, Ill.: The Dryden Press, 1982.

Erikson, E.H. *Childhood and Society.* New York: W.W. Norton, 1950.

Glenn, N.D. Aging and Conservatism. *Annals of American Academy of Political and Social Science* 415 (September 1974):176–186.

Henry, W.A. Cultural Values do Correlate with Consumer Behavior. *Journal of Marketing Research* 13 (May 1976):121–127.

Hoge, D.R. Changes in College Students' Value Patterns in the 1950's, 1960's, and 1970's. *Sociology of Education* 49 (April 1976):155–163.

Huitema, B.E. *The Analysis of Covariance and Alternatives.* New York: John Wiley and Sons, 1980.

Ike, N. Economic Growth and Intergenerational Change in Japan. *American Political Science Review* 67 (December 1973):1194–1203.

Inglehart, R. The Silent Revolution in Europe: Intergenerational Change in Post-Industrial Societies. *American Political Science Review* 65 (12) (1971):991–1017.

Inglehart, R. *The Silent Revolution: Changing Values and Political Styles Among Western Publics.* Princeton, N.J.: Princeton University Press, 1977.

Jennings, M.K. The Variable Nature of Generational Conflict. *Comparative Political Studies.* 9 (2) (1976):171–188.

Kanter, D.L. The Europeanizing of America: A Study in Changing Values. In *Advances in Consumer Research,* V, edited by H. Keith Hunt. Provo, Utah: Association for Consumer Research, 1978, 408–410.

Kassarjian, H.H. Personality and Consumer Behavior: A Review. *Journal of Marketing Research* 8 (November 1971):409–418.

Mason, K.O., W.M. Mason, H.H. Winsborough, and W.K. Poole. Some Methodological Issues in Cohort Analysis of Archival Data. *American Sociological Review* 38 (April 1973):242–258.

Massey, M. *What You Are Is Where You Were When* (video program). Farmington Hills, Mich.: Magnetic Video Library, 1975.

Mitchell, A. *Consumer Values: A Typology.* Menlo Park, Calif.: SRI, 1981.

Morris, C., and L. Small. Changes in Conceptions of the Good Life by American College Students from 1950 to 1970. *Journal of Personality and Social Psychology* 20 (2) (1971):254–260.

Munson, J.M., and S.H. McIntyre. Personal Values: A Cross Cultural Assessment of Self Values and Values Attributed to a Distant Cultural Stereotype. In *Advances in Consumer Research,* V, edited by H. Keith Hunt. Provo, Utah: Association for Consumer Research, 1978, 160–166.

Murphy, P.E., and W.A. Staples. A Modernized Family Life Cycle. *Journal of Consumer Research* 6 (June 1979):12–22.

O'Shaughnessy, J., and M.J. Ryan. Marketing, Science, and Technology. In *Conceptual and Theoretical Developments in Marketing,* edited by O.C. Ferrell et al. Chicago: American Marketing Association, 1979, 577–589.

Payne, S., D. Summers, and T.R. Stewart. Value Differences Across Three Generations. *Sociometry* 36 (1) (1973):20–30.

Pedhazur, E.J. *Multiple Regression in Behavioral Research.* New York: Holt, Rinehart, and Winston, 1982.

Penn, J.R. Measuring Intergenerational Value Differences. *Social Science Quarterly* 58 (2) (1977):293–301.

Reynolds, T.J., and J.P. Jolly. Measuring Personal Values: An Evaluation of Alternative Methods. *Journal of Marketing Research* 17 (November 1980):531–536.

Rokeach, M.J. *Beliefs, Attitudes, and Values.* San Francisco: Jossey Bass, 1968.

Rokeach, M.J. *The Nature of Human Values.* New York: The Free Press, 1973.

Vinson, D.E., J.M. Munson and M. Nakanishi. An Investigation of the Rokeach Value Survey for Consumer Research Applications. In *Advances in Consumer Research,* IV, edited by W.D. Perreault, Jr. Provo, Utah: Association for Consumer Research, 1977, 247–252.

Vinson, D.E., J.E. Scott, and L.M. Lamont. The Role of Personal Values in Marketing and Consumer Behavior. *Journal of Marketing* 41 (April 1977):44–50.

Williams, R.M., Jr. *American Society.* New York: Knopf, 1970.

Yankelovich, D. *New Rules.* New York: Random House, 1981.

15

An Examination of Hispanic Subcultural and Regional Value Orientations

Terry E. Powell and
Humberto Valencia

Much of the research in the area of Hispanic/Anglo consumer differences has focused on overt behaviors (Bellenger and Valencia 1982; Boone et al. 1974). This research has also treated Hispanics and Anglos as aggregate groups, without examination of regional or subcultural groupings. However, an important determinant of consumer behavior—values—has not been considered. The purpose of this chapter is to report the results of a study examining cultural value differences across Hispanic/Anglo groups in New York, Miami, San Antonio, and Los Angeles.

Culture and Values

Cultural influences on consumer behavior are pervasive, last from birth to death (Barnhill 1967), and are the most enduring influences (Kotler 1972). Barnhill (1967) describes this influence.

> Consumptive behavior starts at the breast, or the bottle, or whatever is the culturally accepted mode of feeding a newborn child. Consumptive behavior is modified as the human organism develops and as physical, social and psychic values change. Moreover, and at all times, the consumer is within a culture and in every case the kind of consumer activities in which people engage are culturally determined.

Duesenberry (1949), for instance, has conceptualized the relationships between culture and consumer behavior. He suggests that cultural heritage partially explains consumption differences between culturally different groups because many of the activities in which people participate are culturally based. Further, marketplace behaviors are directed at either providing physical comfort or facilitating those activities that define one's culture.

In any case, there is a general agreement that culture affects consumer behavior. The concept of culture has been related to consumer behavior through values. According to Howard and Sheth (1969), values affect consumption motives and, therefore, individual choice criteria. Furthermore,

Darden (1979) posits terminal and instrumental values as having direct and indirect influences on shopping orientations.

Henry (1976), Omura (1980), and Barnhill (1967) have provided empirical support to the general notion that value systems are an underlying determinant of some aspects of consumer behavior. Henry and Omura found significant correlations between cultural orientation values and the ownership of generic automobile categories (i.e., full-size and intermediate-size cars). Barnhill found a positive association between food preferences and cultural values for three generations of Japanese-Americans.

Robinson and Shaver (1971) present five categories of values used in axiology, the study of values. These categories are: (1) telic, referring to means and ends; (2) ethical, referring to good and evil; (3) aesthetic, dealing with beauty; (4) epistemological, the search for truth; and (5) economic, the evaluation of worth. Within the telic value category, the work of Milton Rokeach (1973) is most widely known.

According to Rokeach (1973), when we say one has a value, this means that one has a long-term belief that one mode of conduct (instrumental value) or end-state of existence (terminal value) is chosen by the individual over other modes of conduct or end-states of existence. In his work *The Nature of Human Values* (1973), Rokeach addresses the relationship of values and consumer behavior. Different value structures were found between owners of various brands of automobiles. Rokeach, however, listed these findings under the heading *unconsequential attitudes*.

Vinson and Munson (1976) have proposed values as a market segmentation device. They demonstrated that consumer groups (undergraduate students and their parents) segmented on the basis of personal values, evaluated product attributes differently, and had dissimilar product preferences. They also found that age is highly related to values.

It is also generally accepted that cross-cultural value differences exist. Munson and McIntyre (1979) examined cross-cultural differences in value systems among Anglos, Thais, and Mexican-Americans and found empirical support for this notion. Their sample was, however, limited to a convenience sample of Los Angeles respondents.

Since cultural values lie at the core of culture, a prerequisite for examining the effects of culture on consumer behavior differences is to demonstrate differences in value orientations between cultures. Otherwise, the conclusions would be unfounded.

In other research, Vinson, Scott, and Lamont (1977) found regional value differences between samples of college students at a western university and a southern university. These authors conclude that value orientation could be expected to vary geographically, and that orientations could further be expected to vary by age, education, income, and other demographics. Thus values have been used to measure cultural differences and have also been found to differ between groups on the basis of age and region.

The approach presented by Rokeach is particularly well suited to measure values. As mentioned previously, this approach distinguishes between terminal values and instrumental values. Within each type, Rokeach developed eighteen values for a total of 36 items in the paradigm. Vinson, Munson, and Nakanishi (1977) have proposed a viable alternative to the original ranking procedure because of two major limitations of this measurement approach: (1) subjects are forced to make trade-offs when actually two or more values may be of equal importance and (2) the large number of values in each group (18) may exceed the respondents' ability to process the information accurately. Instead, Likert scale measurement is recommended, and the authors concluded that this approach offers marketers many advantages. This new approach is very well suited to mail questionnaires.

The Study

Interest in studying the Hispanic market in the United States is growing. The phenomenal growth and expanding purchasing power of this minority have augmented the need for research on Hispanics. Between 1970 and 1980, the Spanish origin population grew from 9 million to 14.6 million (U.S. Department of Commerce, 1981). Currently, about 7 percent of the United States population is Hispanic and is expected to grow to about 10 percent by 1990 (Watanabe 1981). Furthermore, Hispanics tend to concentrate in large metropolitan areas (e.g., New York, Los Angeles) which makes them more accessible to marketers.

Much of the research to date has concentrated on aggregate measures of demographic and purchase differences between Anglos and Hispanics, without consideration of possible age, region, and social-class differences. Sturdivant (1973) has presented the following criticisms of subcultural studies:

> In recent years increasing attention has been given to race, ethnicity, and poverty as determinants of unique attitudes and behavior . . . Too many questions remain unanswered. Is the behavior which is described attributable to the fact that the subjects are black or is it because they are poor, or Southern, or urban, or young? . . . In sum, because of the methodological problems, including the failure to isolate the presumed causal factor, heavy reliance on survey data, and almost complete absence of comparative analysis, marketing literature on subcultures presents a largely confused picture—a trait that it shares with much of the literature in the behavioral sciences.

It is likely that the influences of these factors have been underestimated.

This study recognizes these methodological issues and has attempted to isolate the ethnic values by controlling for the effect of age, socioeconomic status, and region. Socioeconomic status was measured using Duncan's Updated Socioeconomic Index for All Occupations (Siegel 1971). This index uses combined information on educational and income levels. Age was measured directly.

The Sample

Since it is likely that people living in the same city may not be exposed to the same or even similar experiences due to influences such as city size, intercity variations, and unique marketplace factors, it is necessary to select a more homogeneous sample within each population. For this reason, the data collection approach sampled Anglos and Hispanics from the same census tracts.

Within the selected census tracts, a random sample of Spanish surname and non-Spanish surname households was chosen as an initial sampling step. Respondents were asked to self-report their ethnic origin for classification purposes. This approach was used to eliminate blacks and other ethnic minorities, and to insure proper identification of the two ethnic groups. The sample cities were New York, Miami, San Antonio, and Los Angeles. These cities were selected to represent the four major Hispanic groups within the United States—Puerto Ricans, Cubans, Tex-Mex, and Cal-Mex. These four cities account for nearly one half of the U.S. Hispanic population.

A total of 467 responses was obtained from the mail survey. After editing for missing items, usable replies from 150 Hispanics and 253 Anglos were analyzed.

The Instrument

The instrument gathered a variety of information, including age, socioeconomic status, ethnic origin, and both terminal and instrumental values identified by Rokeach. Since many Hispanics are either not literate or do not feel comfortable in English, the questionnaire was translated into Spanish and verified using the back-translation and committee methods. Briefly, the approach involved translating the questionnaire into the target (Spanish) language and then independently back-translating the questionnaire into the source language (English). Any differences were then resolved using a committee of bilinguals to obtain consensus on the final form. For this study, one of the researchers who was bilingual translated the instrument into Spanish. Then, four independent translators (a Cuban, a Mexican-American, a Puerto Rican, and an American fluent in Spanish) back-translated this Spanish version to English. Differences were resolved by modifying the item or filtering. Bilingual representatives from the major Hispanic subgroups were used to ensure idiomatic consistency. Table 15-1 presents the Spanish version of the Rokeach value scale. The resulting instrument was pretested on both Hispanics and Anglo groups and was found to be acceptable.

Results

To test for the effects of ethnicity and region on both terminal and instrumental values, the MANOVA model was used. This test took the form of a 2 × 4 design with covariates for age and socioeconomic status. Terminal values and instrumental values were tested separately. This approach uses tests for within-cells regression and then adjusts cell means for these effects. Following this, factor effects are adjusted for all other remaining treatments.

Table 15-2 presents the results of the terminal value tests. First, the findings indicate an overall significant relationship between the covariates (age, SES) and the terminal values. Examination of the univariate tests provides further support for the findings of Vinson et al. (1977) on age. In that study, constructs developed from the terminal values were tested. One of the constructs showing significant difference between age groups contained three of the five terminal values (a world at peace, national security, and salvation) found significant in this study. Therefore, this study supports the use of these covariates.

The absence of any interaction effects between city and ethnicity suggest that terminal values are independently influenced by ethnic and regional differences directly rather than by the interaction of the factors.

The city effects were shown to be significant overall, but only three value dimensions were different. A closer examination of the univariate results and the group means shows that freedom is highly evaluated by Miamians and inner harmony and salvation are rated lower by New Yorkers. It is likely that since many of the Cubans in Miami are recent immigrants from a communist homeland, their desire for freedom has resulted in an increased overall awareness in the Anglo and Hispanic communities.

The striking differences, however, were on the ethnic factor. The overall test was significant ($p < .001$) and a majority (14 out of 18) of the value dimensions were significantly different between Anglos and Hispanics.

Table 15-3 presents the results of the test of instrumental values. First, the covariates were overall significant ($p < .05$). This confirms the use of these covariates to control for possible confounding effects prior to examination of the treatments. Four (clean, obedient, polite, and self-

Table 15-1
Spanish Language Rokeach Scale

LO SIGUIENTE SON DOS LISTAS DE VALORES PERSONALES, POR FAVOR INDIQUE LA RELATIVA IMPORTANCIA DE ESTOS VALORES PARA USTED, PARA LA PRIMERA LISTA,
POR FAVOR INDIQUE LA IMPORTANCIA DE ESTOS VALORES PARA USTED COMO OBJECTIVOS EN LA VIDA

	SIN IMPORTANCIA	*MENOS IMPORTANTE QUE EL PROMEDIO*	*DE IMPORTANCIA PROMEDIO*	*QUE EL PROMEDIO MUY IMPORTANTE*
1. Una vida cómoda (una vida próspera)	1	2	3	4	5
2. Una vida excitante (una vida activa, estimulante)	1	2	3	4	5
3. Un sentido de realización personal (contribución que perdura)	1	2	3	4	5
4. Un mundo en paz (libre de guerra y conflicto)	1	2	3	4	5
5. Un mundo de belleza (belleza de la naturaleza y del arte)	1	2	3	4	5
6. Igualdad (hermandad, igual oportunidad para todos)	1	2	3	4	5
7. Seguridad familiar (cuidado para los seres queridos)	1	2	3	4	5
8. Libertad (independencia, libre de escojer)	1	2	3	4	5
9. Felicidad (contento)	1	2	3	4	5
10. Armonía interna (libre de conflictos int ernos)	1	2	3	4	5
11. Amor adulto (armonía sexual y espiritual)	1	2	3	4	5
12. Seguridad nacional (protección de ataque)	1	2	3	4	5
13. Placer (una vida agradable, comodidad)	1	2	3	4	5
14. Salvación (una vida eterna, salvado)	1	2	3	4	5
15. Respeto de sí mismo (aprecio personal)	1	2	3	4	5
16. Reconocimiento social (respeto, admiración de otros)	1	2	3	4	5
17. Amistad verdadera (compañerismo fraterno)	1	2	3	4	5
18. Sabiduría (un entendimiento maduro de la vida, prudencia)	1	2	3	4	5

PARA LA SIGUIENTE LISTA, POR FAVOR INDIQUE LA IMPORTANCIA DE ESTOS VALORES COMO PRINCIPIOS PARA GUIAR LAS ACTIVIDADES DIARIAS

19. Ambicioso (trabajador fuerte, que aspira ser)	1	2	3	4	5
20. Tolerante de otras ideas (de mentalidad abierta)	1	2	3	4	5

21. Capaz (competente, eficaz)	1	2	3	4	5
22. Alegre (de buen humor, despreocupado)	1	2	3	4	5
23. Limpio (ordenado, pulcro)	1	2	3	4	5
24. Valeroso (defensor de tus creencias)	1	2	3	4	5
25. Perdonador (dispuesto a perdonar a otros)	1	2	3	4	5
26. Ayudador (útil, trabajar para el bienestar de otros)	1	2	3	4	5
27. Honesto (sincero, verdadero)	1	2	3	4	5
28. Imaginativo (emprendedor, creativo)	1	2	3	4	5
29. Independiente (con confianza en sí mismo, capaz de sostenerse)	1	2	3	4	5
30. Intelectual (inteligente, reflexivo)	1	2	3	4	5
31. Lógico (consistente, racional)	1	2	3	4	5
32. Cariñoso (afectuoso, tierno)	1	2	3	4	5
33. Obediente (respetuoso, sumiso)	1	2	3	4	5
34. Cortés (de buenas maneras, benévolo)	1	2	3	4	5
35. Responsable (digno de confianza)	1	2	3	4	5
36. Con control de sí mismo (con refreno de sí mismo, auto-disciplina)	1	2	3	4	5

Table 15–2
Terminal Value MANOVA Results[a]

I. Covariates (Age, SES)

A. Overall	Rao's F (df)	p <
Root 1–2	2.53 (36,752)	.001
Root 2–2	1.07 (17,376.5)	n.s.

B. Univariate	F (2,393)	p <
An exciting life	6.481	.002
A world at peace	6.358	.002
Mature love	3.587	.029
National security	16.715	.001
Salvation	3.873	.022

II. Interaction (city × ethnicity)

A. Overall	Rao's F (df)	p <
Root 1–3	.707 (54,1121)	n.s.
Root 2–3	.494 (34,753)	n.s.
Root 3–3	.390 (16,377)	n.s.

B. Univariate	F (3,393)	p <

No variable significant at .05 or less

III. City

A. Overall	Rao's F (df)	p <
Root 1–3	1.486 (54,1121)	.014
Root 2–3	1.302 (34,753)	n.s.
Root 3–3	1.294 (16,377)	n.s.

B. Univariate	F (3,393)	p <
Freedom	2.892	.035
Inner harmony	2.684	.046
Salvation	3.209	.023

IV. Ethnicity

A. Overall	Rao's F (df)	p <
Root 1	4.001 (18,376)	.001

B. Univariate	F (1,393)	p <
A comfortable life	8.351	.004
A sense of accomplishment	3.932	.048
A world of beauty	12.342	.001
Equality	29.123	.001
Family security	19.829	.001
Freedom	14.807	.001
Happiness	8.974	.003
Inner harmony	20.004	.001
Nation of security	10.282	.001
Pleasure	11.801	.001
Salvation	16.019	.001
Self-Respect	7.190	.008
Social recognition	10.811	.001
Wisdom	9.463	.002

[a]Only results significant at $p < .05$ are reported.

Table 15–3
Instrumental Value MANOVA Results[a]

I. Covariates (Age, SES)

A. Overall	Rao's F (df)	p <
Root 1–2	2.721 (36,752)	.001
Root 2–2	2.053 (17,377)	.003
B. Univariate	F (2,393)	p <
Clean	4.439	.012
Imaginative	3.941	.020
Intellectual	3.405	.034
Loyal	6.000	.003
Obedient	3.444	.033
Polite	5.417	.005
Self-controlled	8.693	.001

II. Interaction (city × ethnicity)

A. Overall	Rao's F (df)	p <
Root 1–3	1.300 (54,1121)	n.s.
Root 2–3	.692 (34,753)	n.s.
Root 3–3	.363 (16,377)	n.s.
B. Univariate	F (3,393)	p <
Imaginative	5.087	.002

III. City

A. Overall	Rao's F (df)	p <
Root 1–3	1.466 (54,1121)	.017
Root 2–3	1.302 (34,753)	n.s.
Root 3–3	.819 (16,377)	n.s.
B. Univariate	F (3,393)	p <
Obedient	5.644	.001

IV. Test of Ethnicity

A. Overall	Rao's F (df)	p <
Root 1–1	4.375 (18,376)	.001
B. Univariate	F (1,393)	p <
Ambitions	5.578	.009
Broad-minded	2.242	.079
Cheerful	3.232	.045
Clean	25.286	.001
Courageous	7.277	.001
Forgiving	7.033	.003
Helpful	23.069	.001
Honest	2.667	.008
Imaginative	14.983	.001
Independent	6.207	.001
Intellectual	4.313	.016
Loyal	9.666	.001
Obedient	16.369	.001
Polite	10.573	.001
Responsible	5.247	.001
Self-Controlled	13.361	.001

[a]Only results significant at $p < .05$ are reported.

controlled) of the seven significant univariate results are consistent with the results obtained by Vinson et al. (1977).

No overall interaction effect was present, and only one instrumental value (imaginative) was significant. Analysis of means reveals that Hispanics residing in Miami rate this value much higher than any other combination. One plausible explanation for this finding might be in the requirements placed on the recent immigrant by the acculturation process.

City effects were overall significant, but only one value (obedient) seems to account for most of the differences.

Once again, the big differences were on the ethnic factor. The overall test was significant ($p < .001$) and nearly all of the univariate tests (16 out of 18) showed value differences between the two ethnic groups.

Implications

Based on the findings of this study, three major implications can be stated. First, partial support for Sturdivant's critical recommendations (1973) is substantiated. Second, regional/city effects on subcultures may not be as pervasive as previously believed. Finally, the high mean ratings for Hispanics may reflect the desire for assimilation.

Sturdivant called for the use of controlling factors in subcultural/cross-cultural research. This study has shown that age and socioeconomic status were important confounding variables. Thus, future subcultural/cross-cultural research should make use of such controlling factors to avoid misleading and possibly incorrect conclusions.

The lack of significant interaction effects poses two issues. First, the effect of city or region on subcultures may be less influential than previously suspected. Second, it further suggests that Hispanic culture is a far more important determinant of values than differences between the subcultures (i.e., Cubans, Puerto Ricans, Tex-Mex, Cal-Mex). Therefore, one might conclude that future cross-cultural studies between Hispanics and Anglos need not be as concerned with these subcultural groupings.

The final implication of this study can provide important insights for marketing managers. Hispanics, in most cases, rated the values higher than Anglos. This may well be due to their desire to assimilate into mainstream culture. The phenomenon of increased value orientations is not unique and was first reported by Rokeach (1973) in studies among blacks. It is hypothesized that the desire to assimilate may result in increased role aspirations on the part of Hispanics. Alternatively, this desire could also be an effect of the immigration self-selection process, where individuals with high achievement needs are most likely to migrate. In a pragmatic sense, this orientation may result in a greater awareness and use of prestige products and well-known brands.

In conclusion, Hispanics have been shown to differ from Anglos on most values. This provides evidence for using a segmented marketing approach based on ethnicity for marketers aiming to sell products and services to Hispanics. Future research should be conducted to test the influence of these value differences on specific evaluations of marketing attributes. For this purpose, conceptualizations such as those presented by Vinson, Scott, and Lamont (1977) or Darden (1979) would provide an effective framework.

References

Barnhill, J. Allison. Marketing Cultural Anthropology: A Conceptual Relationship. *University of Washington Business Review* 27 (1) (1967).

Bellenger, Danny N., and Humberto Valencia. Understanding the Hispanic Market. *Business Horizons* 25 (3) (1982).

Boone, Lovis G., David L. Kurtz, James C. Johnson, and John A. Bonna. City Shoppers and Urban Identification: Revisited. *Journal of Marketing* 38 (3) (1974).

Darden, William R. A Patronage Model of Consumer Behavior. 1979 American Marketing Association Special Symposium on Department Stores, 1979.

Duesenberry, J. *Income, Savings, and the Theory of Consumer Behavior.* Cambridge, Massachusetts: Harvard Business Press, 1949.

Henry, Walter A. Cultural Values Do Correlate with Consumer Behavior. *Journal of Marketing Research* 13 (1976).

Howard, John A., and Jagdish N. Sheth. *The Theory of Buyer Behavior.* New York: John Wiley & Sons, Inc., 1969.

Kotler, Philip. *Marketing Management: Analysis, Planning, and Control.* 2d Ed. Englewood Cliffs, N.J.: Prentice-Hall, 1972.

Munson, J. Michael, and Shelby H. McIntyre. Developing Practical Procedures of the Measurement of Personal Values in Cross-Cultural Marketing. *Journal of Marketing Research* 16 (1979).

Omura, Glenn S. Cultural Values as an Aid in Understanding Domestic Versus Foreign Car Ownership. In *Evolving Marketing Thought for 1980,* edited by J.H. Summey and R.D. Taylor. Carbondale, Ill.: Southern Marketing Association, 1980.

Robinson, J.P., and P.R. Shaver (Eds.) *Measures of Social Psychological Attitudes.* Ann Arbor, Mich.: Institute for Social Research, 1971.

Rokeach, Milton J. *The Nature of Human Values.* New York: Free Press, 1973.

Siegel, Paul M. *Prestige in the American Occupational Structure.* Unpublished doctoral dissertation, University of Chicago, 1971.

Sturdivant, Frederick D. Subculture Theory: Poverty, Minorities, and Marketing. *Consumer Behavior: Theoretical Sources.* Englewood Cliffs, N.J.: Prentice-Hall, 1973.

U.S. Department of Commerce *Commerce News,* (February 1981).

Vinson, D.E., and J.M. Munson. Personal Values: An Approach to Marketing Segmentation. In *Marketing: 1776–1976 and Beyond,* edited by K.L. Bernhardt. Chicago: American Marketing Association, 1976.

Vinson, D.E., J.M. Munson, and M. Nakanishi. An Investigation of the Rokeach Value Survey for Consumer Research Applications. In *Advances in Consumer Research,* edited by W.O. Perreault. Proceedings of the Association for Consumer Research, 1977.

Vinson, D.E., J.E. Scott., and C.M. Lamont. The Role of Personal Values in Marketing and Consumer Behavior. *Journal of Marketing* 41 (1977).

Watanabe, Marc. Hispanic Marketing: A Profile Grows to New Heights. *Advertising Age* (April 1981).

16 Middle-Class Values in Blacks and Whites

Thomas E. Ness and
Melvin T. Stith

The marketing literature concerning black and white consumers has generally focused attention on differences in consumption without controlling
for socioeconomic variables (Fisk 1963; Mock 1964; Bauer 1966). In many
of these studies, the black consumers were predominantly from the lower-
income groups, while the whites were more likely to be from the middle-
class category. Sexton (1972), in fact, has pointed out that income may explain many of the differences attributed to race. More recent marketing
research (Henry 1976) has suggested that when socioeconomic status is controlled, blacks exhibit characteristics similar to whites. Middle-class blacks
may embrace middle-class American values even more strongly than do
whites (Frazier 1957; Darden 1977).

Many studies of the black consumer date from the 1960s and 1970s.
Past purchasing habits of blacks were greatly affected by the socioeconomic
conditions of loss of educational opportunities, discrimination, and occupational and social deprivation. However, these conditions have, to a large
extent, been altered by recent legal, social, and economic changes. New
segments of the black consumer are emerging. The freedom to move and
have access to housing, travel, and employment awakens the desire for
material goods, which represent well-being and status for white Americans
(Bauer and Cunningham 1970). These values are increasingly reflected in
black spending for education, travel, housing, and household furnishings
(U.S. Department of Commerce, 1975).

Black middle-class families are increasing in numbers. In the North and
West, black husband-and-wife families headed by a person under age 35
earned 101 percent of comparable white income if both husband and wife
were income earners in 1972. Median income of black husband-and-wife working families in the North and West was $12,300. The figure for white families
with husband-and-wife earners was $12,170 (U.S. Bureau of Census, 1976).

With the growth in black purchasing power, additional information
concerning the black consumer is needed. As the Department of Commerce
document indicates, blacks are now climbing the social mobility ladder in
record numbers. Thus, a major question arises for marketers: Is there a
similar value system operating for blacks and whites given relative levels of
income, occupation, and education, or is there really a culture of poverty
among blacks, as earlier advocated by Moynihan (1967)?

231

This study is an attempt to address issues raised by this question via a comparative analysis of the values of middle-class blacks and whites. As stated above, much of the research concerning the black consumer has been written from the low-income perspective (Alexis 1962; Sturdivant and Wilhelm 1968; Stith 1980). The research concerning the black middle-class consumer has focused on purchasing habits (Ginzberg 1967; Bullock 1959, 1961a, 1961b). Little of the previous research has attempted to understand the psychological field of the black middle-class consumer as compared to his white counterpart. This study is intended to help fill this void in the marketing literature by focusing on the middle-class consumer. Successful marketing programs can occur only when the marketing mix of the product is matched with the values of the consumer.

Method

The data for this study were gathered using a self-administered questionnaire that was personally delivered to each respondent and then returned by mail to preserve anonymity.

The convenience sample included 25 black professionals and a like number of whites in similar positions. All were faculty and staff members at the same large urban university. One questionnaire from a white respondent was incomplete and not used in the analysis.

The questionnaire was pretested, both as a face-to-face and as a self-administered instrument. Minor revisions were made during pretesting.

The respondents were asked to rate the importance of each item from Rokeach's (1968) terminal and instrumental values on a scale of 1 (of little importance) to 7 (of great importance). Although the Rokeach values were not designed for marketing applications, there is precedence in the field (Vinson, Scott, and Lamont 1977). In addition to values, the repondents also rated the importance of a number of general product attributes and several attributes specifically related to automobiles, nearly identical to those used by Vinson, Scott, and Lamont (1977), as well as their agreement with six fashion-awareness items previously used by Rich (1963). Demographics and other respondent characteristics were obtained as well.

The ratings of the value items for blacks were compared to the ratings for whites using the mean, median, and mode. The significance of differences between the racial groups was evaluated using the Mann-Whitney U test, the Kolmogorov-Smirnov two-sample test, contingency table analysis, and (with the assumption the measurement scales could be considered internal) a two-tail t test.

Results

First, the black and white subsamples were compared in terms of age, income, and education. The two groups were found to be quite similar. As shown in table 16-1, the mean age for black respondents was 36.8; for whites, 36.5; the median income for blacks was $28,500; for whites, $31,700; the mean number of years of college for blacks was 6.0; for whites, 6.5.

The black and white subsamples were compared using means and medians to determine the differences in averages. The Mann-Whitney U test was chosen as the appropriate nonparametric technique since it was anticipated there would be a large number of ties. The results of the Mann-Whitney and t tests were nearly identical. On both of these tests, six of the 18 terminal values and 6 of the 18 instrumental values were significantly different at the .10 level. Furthermore, 8 items were significantly different at the .05 level on both tests. These items are noted in table 16-2.

Using contingency table analysis to compare the distributions of the two groups, significant differences (.10 level) were found between middle-class blacks and middle-class whites on 7 of 18 terminal values and on 8 of 18 instrumental values. Table 16-2 exhibits the items which had significantly different response patterns for the two groups. It should be noted that response codes 1 through 5 were collapsed into a single category for this analysis.

The Kolmogorov-Smirnov two-sample test is sensitive to any kind of differences in the distributions from which the two racial samples were drawn (i.e., location, dispersion, skewness, etc. [Siegel 1956, p. 127]). The two groups were found to differ significantly (.02 level) on 2 terminal values and 2 instrumental values as indicated in table 16-2.

Table 16-2 also includes the mean, median, and mode for each value item for each group, and an indication of which group rated the item most important (regardless of whether the item significantly discriminated between the groups or not). Blacks rated 14 of the 18 terminal value items and 17 of the 18 instrumental value items more important than whites.

Table 16-1
Characteristics of Blacks and Whites in Sample

	Mean Age	Median Household Income	Mean Years of College
Blacks	36.8 yrs.	$28,500	6.0
Whites	36.5 yrs.	$31,700	6.5

Table 16-2
Comparison of Value Ratings for Black and White Respondents

Terminal Values	Mean B	Mean W	Median B	Median W	Mode B	Mode W	Group with High Score	Test with[a] Sign. Diff.
1. A comfortable life (a prosperous life)	6.0	5.5	6.2	5.5	7	5	B	C
2. An exciting life (a stimulating, active life)	5.8	5.3	5.9	5.6	7	6	B	M,*t
3. A world at peace (free of war and conflict)	6.1	6.5	6.4	6.8	7	7	W	M,t,C
4. Equality (brotherhood, equal opportunity for all)	6.7	5.8	6.9	6.5	7	7	B	M,t,C
5. Freedom (independence, free choice)	6.8	6.3	6.9	6.6	7	7	B	C
6. Happiness (contentedness)	6.6	6.3	6.8	6.6	7	7	B	—
7. National security (protection from attack)	6.1	5.9	6.5	6.3	7	6	B	—
8. Pleasure (an enjoyable, leisurely life)	5.2	5.3	5.1	5.5	4	1	W	M,t,C
9. Salvation (saved, eternal life)	5.1	3.6	5.2	3.0	7	5	B	—
10. Social recognition (respect, admiration)	5.2	4.9	5.2	5.1	5	5	B	—
11. True friendship (close companionship)	5.4	5.6	5.3	5.7	5	6	W	—
12. Wisdom (a mature understanding of life)	6.1	5.9	6.4	6.1	7	6	B	—
13. A world of beauty (beauty of nature and the arts)	5.6	5.6	5.8	5.8	7	6	Tie	—
14. Family security (taking care of loved ones)	6.7	5.8	6.9	6.1	7	7	B	M,t,C,K
15. Mature love (sexual and spiritual intimacy)	5.8	5.6	6.0	5.9	7	6	B	C
16. Self-respect (self-esteem)	6.6	6.5	6.9	6.8	7	6	B	—
17. A sense of accomplishment (lasting contribution)	6.4	5.3	6.7	5.7	7	6	B	M,t,C,K
18. Inner harmony (freedom from inner conflict)	6.4	5.9	6.7	6.4	7	7	B	M,t,C
19. Ambitious (aspiring, hard-working)	5.9	5.2	6.1	5.5	6	6	B	M,*C
20. Broad-minded (open-minded)	6.3	5.7	6.6	5.9	7	6	B	M,t,C,K
21. Capable (competent, effective)	6.5	6.2	6.6	6.2	7	6	B	—
22. Cheerful (lighthearted, joyful)	5.4	5.1	5.7	5.4	6/7	6	B	M,t,C,K
23. Clean (neat, tidy)	6.2	4.5	6.7	4.7	7	6	B	—
24. Courageous (brave, valiant)	4.9	4.6	5.1	4.5	5	4	B	—
25. Forgiving (willing to pardon others)	5.6	5.2	5.9	5.6	5	6	B	C*
26. Helpful (working for the welfare of others)	5.7	5.3	5.9	5.6	6	6	B	—
27. Honest (sincere, truthful)	6.4	6.5	6.7	6.8	6/7	7	W	—
28. Imaginative (creative)	5.8	5.6	5.9	5.7	6	6	B	M,t,*C
29. Independent (self-reliant, self-sufficient)	6.5	6.0	6.8	6.1	7	6	B	M,t,*C
30. Intellectual (intelligent, reflective)	6.3	5.7	6.5	5.9	7	6	B	M,t,C*
31. Logical (consistent, rational)	6.0	5.8	6.4	5.9	7	6	B	C
32. Loving (affectionate, tender)	5.7	5.5	6.5	5.8	7	6	B	—
33. Obedient (dutiful, respectful)	4.9	4.3	4.8	4.8	4	5	B	—
34. Polite (courteous, well-mannered)	5.7	5.5	6.1	5.8	7	6	B	C*
35. Responsible (dependable, reliable)	6.6	6.3	6.8	6.3	7	6	B	M*,t*
36. Self-controlled (restrained, self-disciplined)	5.9	5.5	6.0	5.5	7	5	B	—

[a]The tests are indicated for only items which had significant differences at the .05 level or better (no*) or .10 level (*) as follows:

M = Mann-Whitney U test
t = two-tailed t test
C = contingency table chi-square test
K = Kolmogorov-Smirnov two-sample test

The fact that blacks rated the vast majority of these value items to be of greater importance than whites prompted the summing of value ratings for each respondent on all items, as well as on the terminal and instrumental sub-groups, in order to test for overall differences. A two-tail *t* test was used. As noted in table 16–3, the difference between blacks and whites for instrumental values was significant at the .04 level, while the differences for terminal values and for the combined instrumental and terminal values were significant at the .06 and .07 levels, respectively.

Discussion

The respondents in this study were by design middle-class Americans—professionals with comfortable, but moderate, incomes. Given the high median and modal importance scores for both blacks and whites on all but a few of the value items measured, it can be concluded that the Rokeach values are basically American middle-class values.

The similarity of middle-class blacks and whites insofar as values are concerned is certainly one important finding that emerged from this exploratory study. Perhaps of even more significance is the consistency with which blacks rated items to be of even more importance than did whites. The fact that blacks rated 31 of the 36 items of greater importance than whites and that the summed scores were significantly higher, seem to support and extend the earlier findings of Darden (1977) and Frazier (1957) that middle-class blacks tend to embrace middle-class attributes to an even greater extent than do whites. Darden's (1977) study focused on life-style variables.

A discussion of differences between blacks and whites can begin with a consideration of the four items which were significantly different at the .05 level on all four tests. The two terminal values were family security (taking care of loved ones) and a sense of accomplishment (lasting contribution). The two instrumental values were broadminded (open-minded) and clean

Table 16–3
Comparison of Summed Value Ratings for Black and White Respondents

	Mean		
	B	*W*	*p*[a]
Sum of terminal value ratings	108.2	102.3	.06
Sum of instrumental value ratings	106.1	98.5	.04
Sum of terminal and instrumental value ratings	213.7[b]	201.3[b]	.07

[a]Significant on a two-tail *t* test of difference between group means.

[b]Mean combined sum not equal to sum of terminal and instrumental means because cases with a missing rating were omitted from the respective sums.

(neat, tidy). These items in many respects exhibit patterns similar to most other items. Blacks rated each of these items as being more important than whites. The distinguishing characteristic of each distribution is that blacks tended to rate the items as a 7 (great importance) more often than did whites.

The present findings exemplify Darden's (1977) contention that middle-class blacks, in an effort to be more accepted at this stage of social integration, will accentuate middle-class values to compensate for any prejudices that may exist among their white peers. A black respondent in Darden's study stated that he was conscious of keeping his home and himself cleaner and of being more considerate of his neighbors for this very reason.

This same response pattern essentially holds for the terminal value items which showed significant differences at the .05 level on three of the tests. They were equality (brotherhood, equal opportunity for all), freedom (independence, free choice), and salvation (saved, eternal life). Salvation exhibited relatively low average ratings and greater variation, as indicated by the modes for the two groups. The white group was bimodal (1 and 7), perhaps suggesting strong religious differences. Equality and, to some extent, freedom may well have more salience to blacks than whites.

Conclusions

The findings would seem to suggest that marketers indeed have a strong basis for attempting to reach middle-class blacks with special value appeals. Most of the dimensions probed in this study could be used effectively. Furthermore, the importance ratings for both groups are high enough to indicate that effective appeals can be made to middle-class members of either or both racial groups, depending on the product or service being offered, without offending the other.

Final judgments should await the extension of the methodology used in this exploratory study to a broader sample of middle-class black and white Americans.

References

Alexis, M. Some Negro-White Differences in Consumption. *The American Journal of Economics and Sociology* (January 1962).

Bauer, R.A. Negro Consumer Behavior. In *On Knowing the Consumer,* edited by J.M. Newman. New York: Wiley, 1966.

Bauer, R.A., and S.M. Cunningham. The Negro Market. *Journal of Advertising Research* (April 1970).

Bullock, H.A. Consumer Motivation in Black and White-I. *Harvard Business Review* (May–June 1961). (a)

Bullock, H.A. Consumer Motivation in Black and White-II. *Harvard Business Review* (July–August 1961). (b)

Bullock, H.A. Negro Family is Better Market for Luxuries than Whites with Same Income. *Advertising Age* (March 15, 1959).

Darden, D.K. The Black Bourgeoisie: "Super Americans?" *International Review of Modern Sociology,* 1977.

Fisk, G. *Leisure Spending Behavior.* Philadelphia: University of Pennsylvania Press, 1963.

Frazier, E.F. *Black Bourgeoisie.* New York: Free Press, 1957.

Ginzberg, E. *The Middle Class Negro in the White Man's World.* New York: Columbia University Press, 1967.

Henry, W.A. Cultural Values Do Correlate with Consumer Behavior. *Journal of Marketing Research* (May 1976).

Mock, W.L. *Negro and White Difference in the Purchase of an Automobile and Household Durables.* Unpublished doctoral dissertation, University of Michigan, 1964.

Moynihan, D.P. The President and the Negro: The Moment Lost. *Commentary,* 1967.

Rich, S.U. *Shopping Behavior of Department Store Customers.* Boston: Harvard University Graduate School of Business Administration, Division of Research, 1963.

Rokeach, M.S. *Beliefs, Attitudes and Values.* San Francisco: Jossey Bass, 1968.

Sexton, D.E., Jr. Black Buyer Behavior. *Journal of Marketing* (October 1972).

Siegel, S. *Nonparametric Statistics for the Behavioral Sciences.* New York: McGraw Hill, 1956.

Stith, M.T. Marketing and the Low Income Consumer: New Set of Organizational Goals. *Southwest Marketing Association Proceedings,* 1980.

Sturdivant, D., and W.T. Wilhelm. Poverty, Minorities and Consumer Exploitation. *Social Science Quarterly* (December 1968).

U.S. Bureau of the Census. *The Social and Economic Status of the Black Population in the United States,* 1974. Washington, D.C.: U.S. Government Printing Office, 1976.

U.S. Department of Commerce. *Minority Markets.* Washington, D.C.: U.S. Government Printing Office, 1975.

Vinson, D.E., J.E. Scott, and L.M. Lamont. The Role of Personal Values in Marketing and Consumer Behavior. *Journal of Marketing* (April 1977).

17 The Value of Higher Education and Its Impact on Value Formation

Hugh E. Kramer

College Education—An Exchange Issue

The question of how much we value a college education involves, in the final analysis, a value judgment. It is also an exchange issue involving trade-offs. How much are we willing to give up in time, effort, and money for the opportunity of being educated? A college education requires the payment of tuition and outlays for books and tools. Instead of spending days and nights studying, we could be earning a salary or wage or be spending those hours leisurely at the beach, at a football game, or in front of the television set. In addition, we are not even assured that these activities and expenses will result in the acquisition of an academic degree which will help us in our professional career.

The question "Is it worth it?" is, from the educators' and college administrators' viewpoint, a marketing issue when we define marketing as an exchange process directed at satisfying human needs and wants (Kotler 1980, p. 191). Thus, raising the issue of the value of a college education clearly touches not only the philosophical foundation and raison d'être of higher education, but also provides us with the necessary guidance for staying in touch with the needs and wants of students—our customers—in order to provide a relevant and rewarding college education for them.

Of course, much has been written over the years about virtually every aspect of higher education. Most of us, who had the good fortune of having received a college education, feel that this educational experience has indeed profoundly changed and enriched our lives and our ability to earn a good living.

Forces That Affect Human Development and Behavior

In what ways does a college education tend to affect people and their lives? The answer will obviously vary from person to person. It will depend on the unique experience of the individual in his unique set of personal and environmental circumstances, both fortunate and unfortunate. Each person experiences his life with varying degrees of satisfaction or dissatisfaction derived from interactions with family members, friends, peers, superiors and subordinates, or at home, on the job, at church, at school. Material success and mental happiness are products of positive attitudes from being born at the right time into the right family, the right community, and the right country. Good health, an attractive appearance, a healthy genetic psyche of minimal mental, emotional, and temperamental prerequisites are also important.

The Effect of a College Education

It is true that we have little or no control over the situational and biological factors mentioned above. We cannot choose our parents, our brothers and sisters, our country, our state of health, our sex, our race, and the environmental forces, opportunities, constraints, and prejudices around us.

Fortunately, there is another range of factors which we control in varying degrees. They are primarily of cultural and behavioral origin (figure 17-1). Cultural factors shape our personality and behavior from early childhood. Each member of a culture is not only distinguished from outsiders by a different language and different customs, but he also thinks differently, perceives his world differently, dreams differently, and has his emotions shaped by the norms of his culture. It is no wonder that a person's behavioral traits, which have been molded by cultural forces, are difficult to change in later years.

Education plays an important role in conditioning the individual's personality and attitudes to the norms and standards of his culture. Through education, all facets of human behavior—sensitivity, perception, motivation, learning skill, communicative skill, personality, and attitudes—are impacted.

Sensitivity refers to a person's ability to register slight differences in the attitudes or feelings of others. Although sensitivity usually is not listed as a component of human behavior, I feel it is important to recognize the crucial role sensitivity plays in person-to-person interaction. Even though some people are born with greater sensitivity than others, through education a higher level of sensitivity and awareness can be developed.

Perception is the process whereby stimuli detected by the five senses of sight, hearing, smell, touch, and taste are interpreted by the individual and translated into a response. Conscious perception is a selective process through which the individual attaches meaning to his experience. Selective perception clearly is influenced by education and the culture in which a person grows up.

Motivating is the act of stimulating to action. It involves an inner state that activates, directs, sustains, and, at times, stops specific behaviors. Mo-

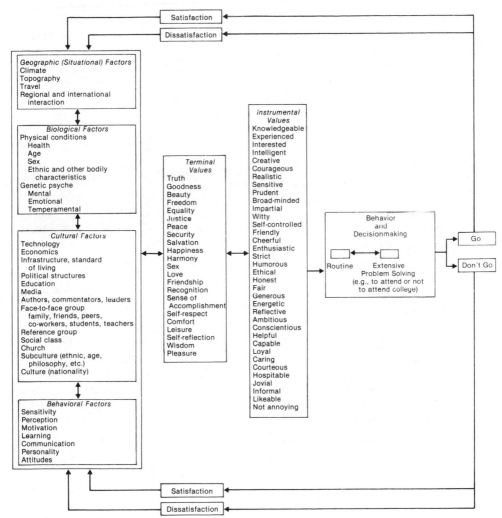

Figure 17-1. Framework for Understanding the Development and Interaction of Terminal and Instrumental Values

tivation is closely tied to personal values and the five basic needs on the physiological, safety, social, esteem, and self-actualization level, as well as to the two basic human desires to know (to get the facts, to satisfy curiosity) and to understand (to systematize and to look for relations and meanings) (Maslow 1954). Education affects both the direction, level, and intensity of motivation.

Learning refers to changes in response tendencies due to the effects of experience. It involves changes in behavior (overt actions, attitudes, and thinking) by means of discrimination and generalization. Learning is the object of education.

Communication involves the exchange of thoughts or feelings with the help of signals (symbols). Its essential ingredients are the transfer of meaning and understanding from an information source to an information receiver. It involves articulation (encoding), listening, and interpretation (decoding). Because of its crucial role in personal interaction, I think it is appropriate to list communication as a separate behavioral factor. Education assists in developing communication into a skill and tool for interpersonal relationships.

Personality denotes the state or quality of being a person, the pattern of collective character, behavioral, temperamental, emotional, and mental traits of an individual. A personality is shaped by numerous external and internal forces over a person's lifetime, including a college education.

Attitudes are internal states of a person concerned with their feelings about an object (affective sphere), their beliefs about the object (conative sphere), and their action tendency toward the object (conative sphere). Again, all three aspects of a person's attitudes are profoundly shaped by education.

A college education provides us with utility in a variety of ways: First, it prepares us for the requirements of a job or profession so that we can become a productive member of society and are able to earn a living for ourselves and our family. Second, it helps us acquire the knowledge necessary to discharge the duties and privileges of an intelligent citizen and active member of our political system. Third, an effective college education also contributes to higher moral standards and enhances our sensitivity and responsibility toward others. Fourth, subconsciously and gradually, our behavior and relationship with other people is molded through the educational process. Our motivation, the way we learn and communicate, our personality, and our attitudes improve.

A College Education Affects a Person's Values

How is this all brought about by a college education? To put it in terms of the learning experience, a college education provides us with general knowledge for life and specialized knowledge for earning a living. It enhances our intellectual abilities and skills, our emotional make-up, and our moral standards. Above all else, a college education affects our value system.

Is it possible to measure the effects of a college education? Yes, it certainly is. In fact, it is done every semester by issuing course grades and awarding academic degrees. We also evaluate students' performance and personality growth by letters of recommendations. However, in the long run, it becomes increasingly difficult to pinpoint the precise effect of a college education on a person's career development and his life-long pursuit of material and spiritual rewards. Such an evaluation, in turn, depends on a value judgment—on individual values and value systems (relationship of values to each other) which a person cherishes.

What are values and what purpose do they serve? Values are beliefs about what is good and what is bad. Values provide a general guidance system for a person's behavior. Also, as most of us have been witnessing with our own eyes, values change over time. In particular during the last few decades, major values, ideas of desirable behavior, lifestyles, social justice, patriotism, work, authority, racial relations, and views of marriage, family, and children have been shifting.

In addition to the societal values that determine the desirability and value of a college education, a college education itself frequently changes a person's value priorities and his perception of the value of a college education. Many other values also change during the growth process of a personality that takes place while attending college.

Many observers of societies' trends perceive two reasons for the recent shift in major values: First, the much larger share of a college-educated population in America, and second, more relevant and two-sided teaching and discussion of current issues at our colleges.

The following shifts can probably be discerned as a consequence of today's more widespread and improved college education:

Materialistic goals	leads to	Spiritual fulfillment
Waste of resources	leads to	Preservation of resources (ecology-minded)
The easy, hedonistic life	leads to	The exciting, meaningful life
Immediate gratification	leads to	Postponed gratification (the value of self-discipline)
Physical emphasis	leads to	Intellectual emphasis
Easy routine work	leads to	Challenging nonroutine work
Production orientation	leads to	Human orientation
Acceptance of authority	leads to	Participation
"Money talks"	leads to	Power of reasoning
"Caveat emptor" (buyer beware)	leads to	"Caveat venditor" (consumer protection)
Uniformity	leads to	Pluralism
Other-centeredness	leads to	Self-actualization
Majority rule	leads to	Consensus
Patriotism	leads to	Internationalism
Competition	leads to	Cooperation
Confrontation	leads to	Negotiation

To be sure, not all of these trends are part of society's recent shift in values. However, more of us agree that a college education tends to affect a person's outlook in the directions described above.

Terminal and Instrumental Values

In order to more fully comprehend the process of how values are formed and how they serve as a general guidance system throughout our life, it is useful to understand the formation and change process of values. Values can be perceived on two levels: a terminal level and an instrumental level. Terminal values, then, are the ultimate object or the end of an endeavor. As the preferred end-states of existence that people strive for, they give meaning to our life. Examples of terminal values include: truth, goodness, beauty, freedom, and equality. Instrumental values, on the other hand, are the means of achieving those ends. They are the instruments, standards, and norms by which a person's progress towards achieving life's final goals can be measured. In general, a person's behavior, knowledge, intellectual and temperamental characteristics, and moral stability are expressed on the instrumental value level. Examples of instrumental values include: knowledgeable, intelligent, creative, courageous, and sensitive. Figure 17–1 presents a framework for understanding the development and interaction of terminal and instrumental values.

Cultural factors strongly affect the development of terminal values. And terminal values, in turn, influence the degree to which instrumental values are held in esteem by society and individuals. Education exerts substantial influence on the direction and priority of terminal and instrumental values. Through careful observation of his own behavior and critical self-evaluation, a person can change his own behavior and personality.

A college education in particular affects cognitive and affective human behavior. The cognitive sphere is composed of the development of factual information, as well as the development of intellectual abilities and skill. Intellectual abilities are composed of the seven relatively independent factors: number facility, word fluency, visualizing ability, memory, perceptual speed, induction, and verbal reasoning (Bloom 1956). A skill is a physical or mental performance that the individual has learned to execute with ease and precision. The affective sphere is concerned with the progressive growth of feelings and emotions, and the formulation and change in terminal and instrumental values and attitudes. A good college education thus affects the full range of behavioral factors—sensitivity, perception, motivation, learning, communicative skill, personality, and attitudes.

According to the Paideia group (Adler 1982), three distinct modes of teaching and learning are essential to cover the full range of human behavior: (1) the acquisition of organized knowledge (language, literature, arts, mathematics, science, social studies) by means of didactic instruction, lectures, responses, and textbooks; (2) the development of intellectual skills—skills of learning (reading, writing, speaking, listening, calculating, problem solving, measuring exercising critical judgment) by means of coaching, exercises, and supervised practice; and (3) enlarged understanding of ideas and values (discussion and involvement) by means of Socratic questioning and active participation. An effective college education, then, should include all three teaching and learning approaches.

Instrumental values, in turn, are reflected in human behavior. An important part of human behavior involves the need to make decisions. Decisions fall on a continuum between routine decisions made with limited problem solving and those associated with extensive problem solving. The result of a decision is either to go ahead or not to go ahead (conative sphere). A decision to act or not to act leads to satisfaction or dissatisfaction in either case. In turn, this feedback influences the multiplicity of situational, biological, cultural, and behavioral forces and thereby closes the effects of mutual interaction in the model shown in figure 17-1.

Negative Effects of a College Education Are Also Possible

As with all complex forces interacting with the human psyche, a college education can also have negative results—*negative* in terms of disagreement with the traditional value system or in terms of creating unbalanced personality traits and attitudes. A disruption of traditional values by a new generation of college graduates frequently brings about new life styles, laws, customs, and a new economic and political order into a traditional society.

Creating an unbalanced personality, however, can have unsettling repercussions if the majority of college graduates are highly trained in their specialized field of study, but are lacking other components of education necessary to use their specialized knowledge for the benefits of society (see Freeman 1976). In addition, they may expect society to compensate them for their years of graduate studies and loss of income when they cannot find employment commensurate to their college education and expectation. The best protection against sterile results of higher education is a well-balanced education before specialization.

Factors that foster a balanced and healthy personality growth are environmentally related. An environment that focuses on cooperation rather than confrontation or competition, provides opportunities for employment or independent businesses, and offers friendly companionship and meaningful and warm human relationships can provide a buffer against negative effects of a misapplied or excessively specialized and fruitless college education.

Instrumental Values as a Mirror of Our Self-Image

In what way can the distinction between terminal and instrumental values provide utility to our own life? Figure 17–2 is an example of the Ideal Profile.

Figure 17-2
The Ideal Profile

Instructions:

Think about your own ideal personality traits and attitudes as exemplified by the instrumental values on this list.

1. Which of these are most important to you? Give them a weight on a scale from 1 (not important) through 5 (very important).

2. To what extent do you measure up to the ideal profile? Give yourself a grade from 1 (poor) through 5 (excellent) or ask your friend or spouse to do it.

3. Which instrumental values have decisively been enhanced by your college education? Give them a plus sign for yes, a minus sign for no, and a zero for undecided.

4. We can now multiply the weight in column 1 with the ranking of our personal profile scale in column 2 and thus receive an expression of the impact of college education in our life.

5. From time to time, repeat step 2 and compare any improvements.

Ranking / Item	(1) Weight 1–5 1 = Not important 5 = Very important	(2) Personal Profile Scale 1 2 3 4 5 poor excellent	(3) Role of College Education + = yes − = no 0 = undecided	(1) × (2) Weighted total (Multiply column 1 with column 2)
1. Knowledge, Experience, and Interest				
1.1 International knowledge and experience (a worldwide rather than parochial outlook; speaks foreign languages)	4	5	+	+20
1.2 General knowledge and experience (does well in a variety of tasks; sees the whole picture)				

1.3 Specialized knowledge and experience (in addition to, rather than in place of, general knowledge)

1.4 Updated knowledge (keeps up with all relevant, new developments)

1.5 Diversity of interest, hobbies (not directly related to job but enhances personality)

2. *Intellectual Abilities and Skill*

2.1 Intelligent (bright, rational, shows logical flow of thoughts)

2.2 Imaginative, creative, original mind (ability to think independently)

2.3 Courageous (is willing to take calculated risks and to assume responsibility)

2.4 Realistic (balanced, critical assessment ability; neither consistently optimistic, nor pessimistic in estimates; considers all factors that bear on a problem)

2.5 Perceptive (sensitive to all major or latent issues)

2.6 Prudent (shows mature judgment and, in particular, understands human nature)

2.7 Open-minded (broad-minded, adaptable, willing to learn and to change his/her mind; tolerant of other people's opinions; forgiving; no fanatic, but no *tabula rasa* either)

Figure 17-2 *(continued)*

Item / Ranking	(1) Weight 1–5 1 = Not important 5 = Very important	(2) Personal Profile Scale 1 2 3 4 5 poor excellent	(3) Role of College Education + = yes − = no 0 = undecided	(1) × (2) Weighted total (Multiply column 1 with column 2)
2.8 Impartial (displays social and cultural empathy independent of a person's race, creed, sex, or age; neither prejudiced nor opinionated; maintains objectivity; shows no evidence of favoritism)				
2.9 Witty (able to make clever and pointed statements, sometimes by using irony mockingly)				
3. Emotional Characteristics				
3.1 Even temperament (self-controlled)				
3.2 Friendly and cheerful				
3.3 Enthusiastic when appropriate				
3.4 Strict and stern when situation warrants				
3.5 Humorous (willing to laugh; funny)				
4. Moral Standards				
4.1 Integrity (has high moral standards)				
4.2 Honest and sincere (truthful; trustworthy; genuine; credible; reliable)				
4.3 Fair (just; being in accordance with a code of what is legally or ethically right and proper)				
4.4 Forgiving (not revengeful)				

5. *Behavior*
5.01 Energetic
5.02 Reflective and visionary
5.03 Ambitious and goal-oriented (but not overly ambitious or self-centered)
5.04 Conscientious (thorough, inquisitive mind and attitudes; not superficial)
5.05 Initiative and action-oriented (a doer rather than a talker; knows nothing happens unless action is taken)
5.06 Generous
5.07 Hospitable
5.08 Caring
5.09 Considerate (courteous and respectful) of other people's rights and feelings (tactful, polite)
5.10 Recognizes other people's strengths and accomplishments
5.11 Helpful (makes himself available when needed)
5.12 Confidence and loyalty inspiring (able to motivate others; dedicated to the organization and people; demonstrates that expecting and discharging confidence and loyalty is a two-way avenue)
5.13 Practices democratic rather than autocratic behavior (solicits and follows advice of his subordinates and peers; humble; is aware of his own limitations rather than being arrogant)

Figure 17-2 *(continued)*

Item / Ranking	(1) Weight 1–5 1 = Not important 5 = Very important	(2) Personal Profile Scale 1 2 3 4 5 poor excellent	(3) Role of College Education + = yes − = no 0 = undecided	(1) × (2) Weighted total (Multiply column 1 with column 2)
5.14 Communicates effectively both orally and in writing, verbally and nonverbally				
5.15 Good listener				
5.16 Informality (jovial) in personal relationships but amenable to complying with a more formal way, etiquette, or protocol when appropriate (informal interaction—the use of first names, etc.—is preferred by most Americans, but not necessarily acceptable in foreign cultures)				
5.17 Likeable and tender				
5.18 Religious (believes in God and salvation)				
5.19 Free from annoying manners (such as pipe smoking, taking snuff, heavy drinking, etc.)				

It may serve as a guideline for gradually improving behavior and relationships with others. The list in figure 17-2 is composed primarily of instrumental values. Should we value them differently we may weight them (for example, on a scale of 1 through 5, from "not important" to "very important").

As a next step we attempt to evaluate ourselves, by establishing our own profile as objectively as possible with all our strengths and weaknesses as we feel others probably perceive us (self-image). In column 2 we can now rank each factor by how closely our personality approximates the item's description on a scale from 1 (poor) through 5 (excellent).

Instead of doing the ranking ourselves, we can also ask our spouse or a good friend to rank us.

If we wish to isolate the role our college education has played in our personal growth we can introduce a third column into our chart. A plus sign may stand for "yes," a minus sign for "no" and a zero for "undecided." In a fourth column we then multiply the weight (column 1) with the score of our own personal profile component (column 2).

As a final and continuous step let us strive to improve our own behavior in accordance with the items in our Ideal Profile list. May I propose to display the list at a prominent location at our place of work or home in order to be continuously reminded of our struggle to improve ourselves and to monitor our progress?

To be sure, it is a cumbersome and painstaking process. But isn't it worth the efforts? We will not only improve our relationship to others and become more effective at home and at work, but we will gradually grow more perceptive, more open-minded, more reflective, more cheerful and happier. Our life is so short: why not make the most out of it as long as we still are on this planet?

References

Adler, M.J. *The Paideia Proposal: An Educational Manifesto.* New York: Macmillan, 1982.

Dewey, J. Theory of Valuation. In *International Encyclopedia of Unified Science,* 2/4. Chicago: The University of Chicago Press, 1939.

Freeman, R.B. *The Overeducated American.* New York: Academic Press, 1976.

Kotler, P. *Marketing Management: Analysis, Planning, and Control,* 4th ed. Englewood Cliffs, N.J.: Prentice-Hall, 1980.

Maslow, A.H. *Motivation and Personality.* New York: Harper & Row, 1954.

Nolan, C.A., C. Hayden, and D.R. Malsbary. *Principles and Problems of Business Education.* Cincinnati, Ohio: South-Western, 1967. Pp. 4–23.

Part V
Applications
in Consumer
Psychology and
Marketing

The last section presents four applications of values as tools for understanding individual behavior. Walter Henry traces the Japanese value system through two thousand years of cultural development in chapter 18. From this overview of the Japanese value orientation, the marketing distribution system that has developed is examined. In particular, consumer-merchant relations, wholesale-retail business practices, and store size factors are explored.

Veltri and Schiffman present us with a helpful analysis of AT&T's experience with lifestyle and value profiling of the residence telephone communication market. The authors use data collected during the past 15 years from AT&T's billing system, thus automatically capturing actual usage behavior.

Next, environmental values are emphasized in chapter 20. Fjeld, Schutz, and Sommer describe the values of cooperative versus supermarket shoppers and address the issues of values and voluntary simplicity.

Gutenburg and Kleist apply personal values to the study of volunteers in the not-for-profit organizations. Their research found that appeals need to be aimed at multiple values to be most effective. Appeals directed at individuals emphasizing either rewards or altruism exclusively were less effective than "dual value" approaches.

18 Impact of Cultural Value Systems on Japanese Distribution Systems

Walter A. Henry

Numerous students of management practice, consumer behavior, and distribution systems have pointed out the importance of understanding the dominant values of a society prior to understanding its practices. Bartels (1982) suggests that a nation's business is not primarily technological, but is an expression of the spirit of a people which is the product of their culture. It is readily observable that in Japan, distribution systems tend to be highly fragmented, retailing is dominated by small highly personalized shops, and mutual trust and long-standing interpersonal relationships are traditional trade practice (Shimaguchi and Lazer 1979; Shimaguchi and Rosenberg 1979). This rather simplistic statement of what is, presents numerous pitfalls for the unwary who attempts to enter the Japanese market without an understanding of the culture and tradition of Japan.

This chapter will briefly review the historic development of the Japanese culture. It will explore certain dominant values which may affect retailing and the distribution system for consumer goods and services; and it will suggest a model relating values, demographic and economic conditions, and the predominant system of retailing and distribution found within the society. The work is conceptual in nature and draws heavily from historians, anthropologists, and psychologists who have studied Japan and its people, various Japanese government statistics, and information provided by the Japan External Trade Organization.

Japanese Culture

An Evolution Through Time

The culture of any society is an evolution through the history of its people. In order to attempt to understand the dominant values that shape the way the Japanese people interact and handle their day-to-day activities today, it is necessary to trace briefly this documented evolution (Beasley 1981; Japanese National Commission for UNESCO 1958, Chap. 19; Lansom 1962; Shibusawa 1969, Chaps. 1–5, 10; Sumiya and Taira 1979). Figures 18–1, 18–2, and 18–3 provide a useful time line of the major political and religious

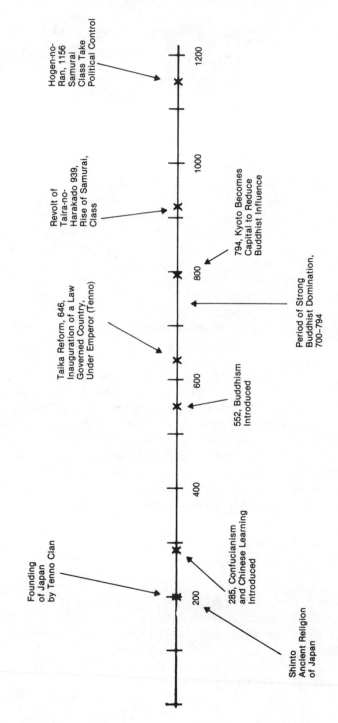

Figure 18-1. Japanese Time Line 0–1200 A.D.

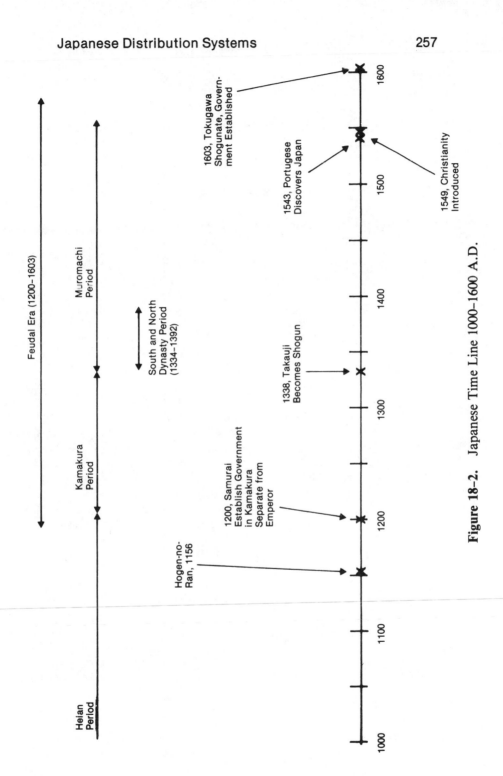

Figure 18–2. Japanese Time Line 1000–1600 A.D.

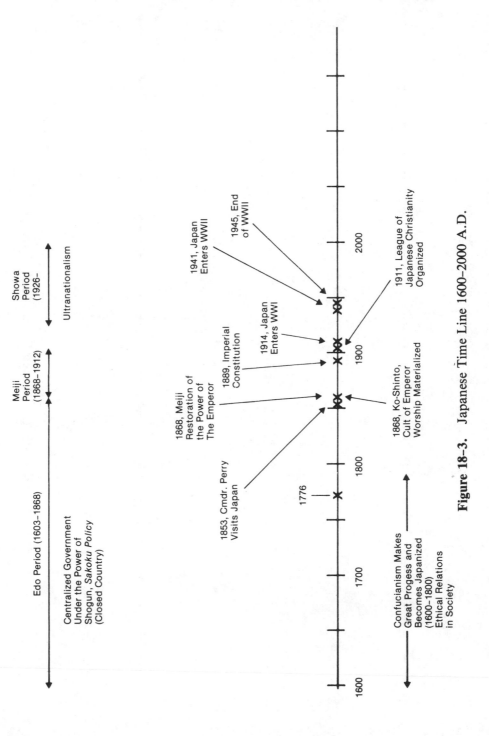

Figure 18–3. Japanese Time Line 1600–2000 A.D.

influences in the history of Japan. Japan is a very old island nation whose culture has been dominated by three principal religions and whose political system has been based until recent times on a sovereign with claimed divine lineage.

Establishment of a nation under a Tennō, or supreme divine leader, and the origin of the Shinto religion can be traced back to approximately 200 A.D. This ancient Japanese religion taught respect for clan leaders and their ancestors and established the claimed direct line of the Tennō (later the Emperor) to Amaterasu Ōmikami, the Shinto sun goddess. In the year 285 Confucianism was introduced from China, followed by Buddhism in 552. A permanent centralized government was established in the city Nara in 646 following the Taika Reform which legitimized the power of the Emperor. For the next 100 years, the Buddhist religion made great strides in the development of Japanese culture. Fearing the dominance of Buddhism, the central government moved the capital to Kyoto in 794 in order to separate civil authority from the center of Buddhist thought which had developed in Nara.

The revolt of Tairo-no-Harakado in 939 marked the start of the breakdown of centralized authority under the Tennō. The actual collapse was the consequence of a major civil war, the Hogen-no-Ran, which occurred in 1151. Although the Emperor remained in Kyoto, the Samurai class in 1200 established in Kamakura a separate government which became the actual seat of political power. Thus began a 400-year feudal period marked by continuing civil strife. Numerous Samurai rose to the level of Shogun during the period without lasting success. In 1543 Portugal discovered Japan and Christianity was introduced in 1549 by Jesuit missionaries.

Strong central government was restored in 1603 under the Tokugawa Shogunate based in Tokyo. This marked the beginning of the Edo Period which provided over two hundred years of peace and stability during which Confucianism had its strongest impact on the ethical values of Japan. Although the Emperor was still venerated within the Shinto religion, actual political control was maintained by the Samurai class under the leadership of the Shogun. A *Sakoku policy* (closed country) was maintained throughout the Edo Period, limiting until well after Commander Perry's opening of Japan in 1853 any role for Western culture or Christianity in the development of the Japanese society.

The Meiji Restoration in 1868 reestablished the civil and spiritual power of the Emperor. The Tennō was proclaimed to be both sacred and inviolable by the Great Japanese Imperial Constitution of 1889. Rapid economic and industrial growth marked the Meiji Period, which lasted to just prior to Japanese entry in World War I, at which time Japan was recognized as one of the five major powers of the world. Although Japan quickly accepted the processes of the industrial revolution, it also developed a highly protective nationalistic spirit. The resurgence of the Shinto religion with its Emperor worship cult supported these strong nationalistic feelings and continued to limit the impact of Western culture and Christianity until after World War II. Shintoism and ultranationalism received a severe set back with the advent of the U.S. occupation in 1945. The ideas of Western democracy replaced the ideas of a living god. The Tennō was reduced to a symbol of Japanese nationality. Although a democracy was established and Western values were introduced into Japan by mandate, acceptance is somewhat superficial. Considering the over seventeen hundred years during which the Japanese culture developed prior to 1945, this should not be surprising.

Dominant Values

Shotoku Taishi, the 7th century founder of Japanese culture, is credited with comparing Shinto, Confucianism, and Buddhism to the root, trunk, and fruit of a tree. "Shinto is the root planted deeply in the soil of the personality of the Japanese and their national tradition; Confucianism is the trunk and branches as the Ritsuryo system of Moral standards and Educational Ideas; while Buddhism produced flowers of religious sentiment, which bore fruit in the lives of the people" (Japanese National Commission for UNESCO, 1958, p. 492). An uncommon trait of the Japanese is their receptiveness to and coexistence of opposing values (Leaf 1961, pp. 62–71). It is quite natural for members of the same nuclear family to hold to Christian, Buddhist, and Shinto beliefs with complete acceptance by other family members.

Extensive studies of the Japanese cultural history (Japanese National Commission for UNESCO, 1958, Chap. 19; Lebra and Lebra 1974, pp. 3–145); point out that the Shinto religion stresses the values of preservation of family, community, and nation, as well as a deep respect of tradition, authority, and the placing of the greater good before oneself. Confucianism provides the ethical underpinning for society and interpersonal relations. Education is highly prized and is viewed as a way of repaying a debt to parents. Love in human relations and the pleasure of effort expended in doing good are stressed in Confucianism. There is a high value placed on self-esteem, reciprocity, and harmony. Rudeness is intolerable, even to the extent that polite lies will be used rather than the expression of contradictory opinions. Dishonesty, however, is not a characteristic of the culture. Mutual trust and harmony rather than formal contracts and advocacy are clearly preferred ways of dealing with others in personal and business matters. Buddhism brings to the Japanese culture a need for simplicity in life and a dominant aesthetic sense. Tranquility of the mind is continually strived for and there is a realization that life is temporary and changing. An overriding need to avoid the embarrassments of personal rebuff or the confession of failure is also strong in the culture. The use of multiple intermediaries is therefore common in interpersonal relations and business transactions.

Christianity and Western values, being recent events in the cultural development of the Japanese value system, do not hold the central position of Shintoism, Confucianism, and Buddhism. Western values were by and large compelled on an unenthusiastic people. The more formal and surface meanings of democracy and equal rights were accepted into the value structure. The interests of society and family are still predominant, however, over individual rights and responsibilities.

Human Relationships

What has emerged in the Japanese culture is a vigorous capitalistic economy with strong feudal overtones, mixed with the teachings of the three traditional religions of Japan. This intermingling of ancient Eastern and modern Western values and customs is particularly apparent in the area of human relationships, both in the business world and in everyday interpersonal activities. Of particular interest to this analysis are the concepts of *amae* and *giri* which are embedded in Japanese interpersonal relationships (Kitamura 1971; Lebra and Lebra 1974, pp. 145–154, 192–224; Minami 1971).

Amae is a word with no English equivalent. It's meaning is: to depend and presume on another's benevolence. It is an attitude expected to be found in a child's relationship with its parents. In the Japanese culture, it is also commonplace in most adult superior-subordinate relationships. An individual's behavior is predicated on an expectation that others will act toward him with kindness and good will.

Giri, on the other hand, has overtones of feudalistic obligation. It is the promise that controls many human relationships in Japan. Within the concept there is an implicit acceptance or satisfaction with one's position in the social hierarchy. Inherent in *giri* is the properness of loyalty and dedicated services by subordinates, and affection and paternalistic care on the part of superiors. These obligations are carried out without contractual requirements; they are simply expected and accepted as the correct thing to do.

Amae and *giri* appear to have strong impact on behavior not only at the level of interpersonal relations but also in the expectations between individuals and society or the nation state. The Japanese people are keenly aware of *on* (a kindness, an act of good will or favor from others) which is expected from others in various person-to-person, employee-employer, business-client, citizen-government relations. Having received *on*, an obligation (*giri*) or debt of gratitude is accepted which requires respect, justice, courtesy, and a desire to return *on* in some form appropriate for the individual having accepted *giri*. Western values favoring contractual relationships and individualistic attitudes obviously clash with these traditional Japanese ways of behavior. Although contractual agreements are entered into in Japan, there is often little or no detail to cover the specifics of a relationship, which will be left to *amae* or *giri*.

Distribution Systems

Physical Description

Understanding the distribution system and trade practices of Japan must be done through the perspective of its culture and heritage. As a first step, it is appropriate to compare the physical characteristics of the distribution system in Japan to that found in the United States. This will provide a base line of comparison reflecting a familiar culture and heritage.

Tables 18–1 and 18–2 illustrate several important differences in the area of retail and wholesale trade for the base year 1976. Although the gross national product and population of Japan are approximately one-half that of the United States, the population density is 13.5 times as great—785 people per square mile in Japan as compared to 58 in the United States. The total number of retail outlets are comparable in the two countries; however, the number of retail outlets on a GNP and per capita basis shows that Japan has approximately twice as many outlets as found in the United States. Productivity measured by sales per employee and sales per store is 68 percent and 43 percent below the average of U.S. retailers, respectively. This may be attributable to the relatively small size of Japanese stores. As seen in table 18–2, approximately 86 percent of all Japanese retail outlets have no more than four employees, and the vast majority of these have one or two person owner-operators. In the United States, only 55 percent have four or fewer employees. Many neighborhood stores have roots in their community which are generations old and have built up enormous amounts of good will and trust (Japan External Trade Organization, 1979).

In the area of wholesale establishments, again the total numbers are comparable, but when adjusted for GNP or population there are about twice as many wholesalers on a GNP or per capita basis. The productivity per employee and per wholesaler in the aggregate is slightly higher in Japan, 23 percent and 17 percent, respectively. These figures may not reflect, however, the productivity of the vast majority of small wholesalers (89 percent have less than 20 employees) due to the presence of ten very large general trading companies. These ten companies account for approximately $169 billion in sales or 22.5 percent of all wholesale sales. When their presence is removed from the data, the sales per wholesaler drops to $1.7 billion, which is below that of U.S. wholesalers.

Table 18–1

Comparative Japanese and U.S. Distribution System Data (base year 1976)

	Japan		U.S.	
General				
GNP	$563	billion	$1,171	billion
Population	113	million	208	million
Geographic area	0.144	million sq. miles	3.615	million sq. miles
Distribution				
Retail				
Number of retailers	1,615,000		1,553,000	
Number of employees	5,579,000		8,577,000	
Annual sales	$187	billion	$422	billion
Wholesale				
Number of wholesalers	341,000		370,000	
Number of employees	3,519,000		4,026,000	
Annual sales	$750	billion	$695	billion
Ratio Indicators				
Retail				
Number of retailers/GNP	2.9	/ $K	1.3	/ $K
Number of retailers per capita	14.3	/ K	7.5	/ K
Sales/Employee	$33.5	K	$49.2	K
Sales/Retailer	$115.9	K	$271.7	K
Wholesale				
Number of wholesalers/ GNP	0.6	/ $K	0.3	/ $K
Number of wholesalers per capita	3.0	/ K	1.8	/ K
Sales/Employee	$213	K	$172.6	K
Sales/Wholesaler	$2.20	billion	$1.88	billion
Wholesale sales/Retail sales	4.0		1.7	

Note: Data are from Ministry of International Trade and Industry, 1978, pp. 5–6.

The ratio of wholesale sales to retail sales in Japan is 4 to 1, and in the United States it is 1.7 to 1, providing additional evidence of the greater layering in the typical Japanese distribution system relative to that found in the United States. It is not unusual to observe the complex distribution system depicted in figure 18–4.

Manufacturers deal directly with primary wholesalers or the wholesaling arm of the general trading company with which they may be affiliated. The primary wholesaler in turn will serve a very limited number of major supermarket chains and the second tier of regional wholesalers. Secondary wholesalers supply directly to independent supermarkets in the region and to the numerous tertiary wholesalers who in turn make daily deliveries to small local retailers. The local retailers account for as much as 96 percent of all retail outlets in the industry.

Table 18-2
Comparative Japanese and U.S. Distribution System
(employment data, base year 1976)

	Japan	United States
Retail		
Number of Employees	Cumulative Percentage of Outlets	
1-2	61.9	n.a.
3-4	85.6	54.7
5-9	95.9	76.5
10-19	98.6	89.1
20-29	99.3	n.a.
30-49	99.7	97.0
50-99	99.9	99.1
100 or more	100.0	100.0
Wholesale		
Number of Employees	Cumulative Percentage of Outlets	
1-2	21.4	n.a.
3-4	46.0	45.9
5-9	74.4	68.8
10-19	89.0	85.9
20-29	93.7	n.a.
30-49	96.9	96.3
50-99	98.7	98.8
100 or more	100.0	100.0

Note: Japan data are from Japan External Trade Organization, 1982, p. 12. U.S. data are from U.S. Department of Commerce, 1976.

In addition to the fragmentation involved in the physical distribution of goods, there are also trade practices which are not common to the United States Consignment sales, the return of unsold goods, and extended terms up to 120 days are normal procedure. A high level of personal face-to-face involvement between the various wholesalers and retailers is also common practice. Agreements are entered into with a minimum of contractual arrangements and are more typically based on mutual trust formed through the extensive personal contacts which are traditional practice for Japanese business persons (Ministry of International Trade and Industry, 1978, pp. 13-21).

Model of Effects

As described above, there are both differences in the physical distribution and trade practice of Japanese and U.S. distribution systems. Some of these differences can be attributed to certain demographic and economic conditions (Dowd 1959). It is hypothesized, however, that a significant level of

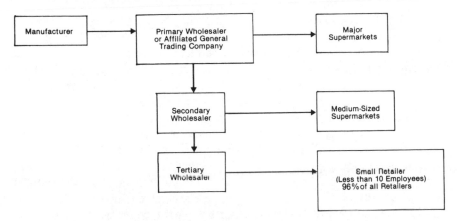

Figure 18-4. Distribution Routes in Retail Food and Household Products (Japan External Trade Organization, 1982, pp. 27-53)

variation can also be attributed to the differences of cultural and heritage symbolic of the two nations. With obvious oversimplification, the first order difference may be summarized as: the number of levels predominate in the distribution system, the ratio of small to large retailers, the level of personalization and trust in business relations, and the level of individualized service desired in purchase relationships.

Figure 18-5 illustrates the assumed first order causal paths. The number of levels present in the distribution is thought to be a function of both the predominate of small or large retailers and the form of business practices

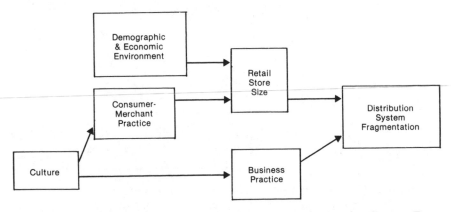

Figure 18-5. First Order Causal Paths Affecting Distribution System Fragmentation in Japan

determined by culture. Business practices may be roughly categorized into contractually oriented and trust oriented. The predominate form of business practice in turn can be assumed to reflect the values and heritage of the management. For convenience, these are labeled Japanese and Western. The Japanese title serves as a proxy for the values developed over Japan's almost seventeen-hundred-year history prior to 1945.

The distribution of small to large retailers is hypothesized to be a function of a number of demographic and economic variables, which are summarized under the title of population density, and the form of consumer-merchant relationship desired. At the extremes, this relationship would take on the form of a relatively impersonal, minimum cost goods transfer (Western culture) or a traditional Japanese exchange where the protocol in the act of shopping may be as important as the transfer of goods. This consumer-merchant relationship involves a high level of individual service, respect, credit, and home delivery of goods. Once again values and heritage are assumed to be causal; they affect what is desirable in the consumer-merchant interchange. The multivariate relationships predicted by the model controlling the number of distribution levels and the size of the retail outlets are more than likely interactive in nature.

Figure 18–6 illustrates the hypothesized interaction relating demographic and economic affects, consumer-merchant practice, and retail size. The Japanese consumer-merchant practices reflect the traditional value for love in human relations, the desire for self-esteem, harmony, and simplicity in one's life on both the consumer's and merchant's part. It also stems from the unique Japanese concepts of *amae* and *giri*. The small Japanese merchant depends and presumes on the benevolence of his customers, which he

Population Density

Culture		High	Low
	Japanese	small retailers	small retailers
	Western	small retailers	large retailers

Figure 18–6. Hypothesized First Order Effects of Culture and Demographic and Economic Environment on Retail Store Size

has nurtured over many years in a personal relationship which would be impossible in large retail operations (Japan External Trade Organization, 1979, pp. 32–35). Likewise, *giri* regularizes the relationship and places an accepted obligation on the merchant's customers for continued patronage to return *on* to the merchant for the *on* received. In our Western culture, more emphasis is placed on the contractual aspects of the exchange process involving return for service rendered on a per interchange basis. The main effect of the Japanese tradition will be to limit retail stores to small size. Western culture will put emphasis on efficient operation that stems from large scale operations.

High population density with respect to this analysis implies high levels of congestion, limited ability for personal transportation such as automobiles, and high land costs limiting the introduction of large scale supermarket retail outlets. All of the above would limit the ability of consumers to use remote large supermarkets and make such innovations prohibitive from an investment standpoint. Therefore, high population density is assumed to also limit the size of retail outlets. Where population density effects are more moderate, allowing investment in large scale retailing and customer access to remote locations, it is hypothesized that the strongly held Japanese cultural affects will continue to predominate. In high density situations where Western cultural values hold, it is assumed that the simple economics of the situation will favor small retail outlets.

The numbers of levels in the distribution system is assumed to be a function of the size of the retail outlets and the value orientation affecting business practice. The assumed interaction is shown in figure 18–7. The

Retail Store Size

		Small	Large
Culture	Japanese	highly fragmented	highly fragmented
	Western	moderate fragmentation	low fragmentation

Figure 18–7. Hypothesized First Order Effects of Retail Store Size and Culture on Distribution System Fragmentation

size of the retailers served by the distribution system will influence the number of levels in the system from an efficiency standpoint. All other things being equal, numerous small retail outlets will require a higher level of fragmentation in the distribution system. A Western cultural bias toward contractually oriented, impersonal relationships will tend to favor economic considerations above others. It can be assumed that this will act to reduce the level of fragmentation whenever this will bring about an increase in efficiency. Traditional Japanese values give the distribution system the role of sales agent for the manufacturer. Goods are received in trust from manufacturers and distributed to retailers. Wholesaler-to-wholesaler and wholesaler-to-retailer transactions operate in a highly personalized mode of business. Japanese businesses rely on the belief in benevolence and trust incorporated in *amae* and the feudalistic obligations based on debts of gratitude incorporated in the concept of *giri*. These values will favor high levels of fragmentation within the system, irrespective of economic impact.

Verification and Implications

The stated purpose of this chapter was to explore briefly the dominant values of the Japanese society, review their roots in religion and heritage, and explore the possible relationship between its traditional culture and its propensity for highly fragmented distribution systems. The model set forth in figure 18–5 as a result of this effort remains to be tested. It will be necessary to find sufficient variation in values extending from the traditional acceptance of *amae* and *giri* to the acceptance of Western traditions of business and interpersonal relations. A range of age and possibly education cohorts could provide the variation required. It would be hoped also that sufficient concentrations of people holding dissimilar values will allow testing the import on retail size. It would therefore be necessary to conduct empirical research in the high population density regions of Kinki, Tokai, and Kanto, as well as in the less populated regions of Hokkaida, Hokuriku, and Chugoku. With respect to values affecting business practice, again variation in the age and place of education of various management cohorts within the distribution system components could provide sufficient variation in values. Also within an industry such as food and related home products, those product lines originating subsequent to 1945 may not be as tradition bound as lines that extend further back in Japanese history.

Presupposing empirical support for the assumed causal relationships of the demographic and economic environment and the value characteristics affecting consumer-merchant relations and business practice within the distribution systems, the model suggests several areas of application. Of obvious interest will be the projection of value trends and their impact on retail trade trends. A movement toward a more Western value orientation brought about through greater exchange between Japan and the United States should increase the number of large retailers when economically feasible and reduce the fragmentation in the distribution system, whether servicing small or large retailers. The subsequent reduced fragmentation may also facilitate foreign imports. However, this will still depend greatly on the acceptance of foreign multinationals into a society with strong feelings of nationalism stemming from its Shinto heritage.

The model may also be useful in predicting dominant distribution tendencies in other Asian nations with shared religious beliefs and similar or different demographic and economic conditions.

References

Bartels, R. National Culture Business Relations: United States and Japan Contrasted. *Management International Review* 22 (1982):4–12.

Beasley, W.G. *The Modern History of Japan*. New York: St. Martin's Press, 1981.

Dowd, Lawrence P. Wholesale Marketing in Japan. *The Journal of Marketing* 23 (1959):257–262.

Japan External Trade Organization. *Planning for Distribution in Japan*. Tokyo: JETRO, 1982.

Japan External Trade Organization. *Retailing in the Japanese Consumer Market*. Tokyo: JETRO, 1979.

Japanese National Commission for UNESCO. *Japan: Its Land, People and Culture*. Tokyo: Printing Bureau, Ministry of Finance, 1958.

Kitamura, Hiroshi. *Psychological Dimensions of U.S.-Japanese Relations*. Boston: Center for International Affairs, Harvard University, 1971.

Lansom, G.B. *Japan: A Short Cultural History*. New York: Appleton Century-Crofts, Inc., 1962.

Leaf, Lawrence A. Japan's Unique Culture. In *Cultural Exchange Between Japan and North America*, edited by Kokusai Bunka Shinkokai. Tokyo: KBS, 1961.

Lebra, Taki Sugiyama, and William P. Lebra (Eds.) *Japanese Culture and Behavior*. Honolulu: The University Press of Hawaii, 1974.

Minami, Hiroshi. *Psychology of Japanese People*. Tokyo: University of Tokyo Press, 1971.

Ministry of International Trade and Industry. *Japan's Distribution System 1978*. Tokyo: Japan External Trade Organization, 1978.

Shibusawa, Keizo (Ed.) *Japanese Society in the Meji Era*. Tokyo: The Toyo Bunko, 1969.

Shimaguchi, Mitsuaki, and William Lazer. Japanese Distribution Channels: Invisible Barriers to Market Entry. *Msu Business Topics* (Winter 1979):49–62.

Shimaguchi, Mitsuaki, and Larry Rosenberg. Demystifying Japanese Distribution. *Columbia Journal of World Business* 14 (1979):32–41.

Sumiya, Mikio, and Koji Taira. *An Outline of Japanese Economic History 1603–1940.* Tokyo: University of Tokyo Press, 1979.

U.S. Department of Commerce. *County Business Patterns 1976.* Washington, D.C.: Bureau of the Census, 1976.

19

Fifteen Years of Consumer Lifestyle and Value Research at AT&T

John J. Veltri and
Leon G. Schiffman

This chapter focuses on AT&T's experience with lifestyle and value profiling of the residence telephone communication market during the past 15 years. Most of the developments in lifestyle research that will be considered here are derived from our experience with an internal AT&T consumer panel that presently consists of approximately 85,000 residence customers from across the United States. The data for this panel are transmitted to AT&T from the 19 operating company revenue accounting offices. Extensive demographic, attitudinal, and psychographic data are also collected from a self-administered mail questionnaire. A unique methodological advantage over other consumer panels is that the dependent variables are taken from the billing system, which automatically captures actual usage behavior. Therefore, AT&T does not have to rely on self-reported consumer usage data with their inherent potential for inaccuracy.

Overview of Lifestyle and Value Research at AT&T

Following a developmental framework, our approach will be to describe the progression of stages in lifestyle research which AT&T has passed from 1969 to the present. Figure 19-1 depicts these stages in a schematic fashion.

The initial data base consisted of a panel of about 30,000 customers. At that time, the overwhelming majority of AT&T's segmentation research featured demographic variables (stage 1). In 1974, AT&T began to experiment with attitudinal and lifestyle measures that ultimately provided an additional framework for segmenting the consumer marketplace (stage 2). Still further, in 1980, with increasing competition in the telephone product marketplace, AT&T expanded its focus to combine attitudinal data with values and lifestyle information (stage 3).

Beginning in 1982, in the midst of planning for the postdivestiture environment, AT&T redirected its research effort toward understanding consumer attitudes and preferences for its long distance services and those provided by its competitors (stage 4). As a further step in expanding its segmentation efforts,

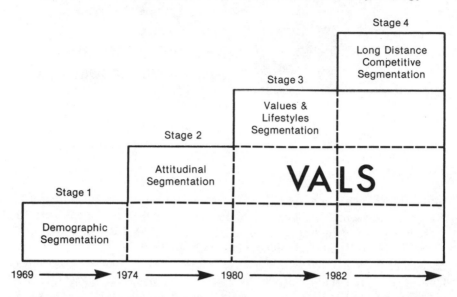

Figure 19-1. Developmental Stages of Lifestyle and Value Research at AT&T

AT&T joined the SRI Values and Lifestyles Program (VALS) in 1980. As illustrated in figure 19-1, the VALS Progrm has been used to augment the lifestyle information about the various segments of customers served by AT&T.

Stage One: Demographic Segmentation

As was commonplace in the early 1970s, AT&T concentrated on understanding and profiling its markets in terms of demographics. Table 19-1 identifies the specific demographic variables in use during this period. As this table reveals, the demographic variables were grouped into four categories reflecting similar attributes. Subscribers to each product and service offered by AT&T were profiled in terms of each of the demographic variables. As an example of how demographics were used, figure 19-2 graphically presents the relationship between several specific demographic variables and the subscription level to Touch-Tone® Service.

Demographic analyses such as this, when undertaken for specific geographic areas, proved particularly useful in providing the management of Bell Operating Companies with a profile of low and high potential markets. This represents a basic application of demographic analysis.

Table 19-1
Specific Demographic Variables by Category

Family/Housing
    Type of residence (e.g., 1 family, 2 family)
    Number of floors
    Number of rooms
    Own/Rent
    Family size
    Sex (Head of household)

Mobility
    Length of residence
    Number of moves in last 5 years

Socioeconomic
    Family income
    Education (Head of household)
    Occupation (Head of household)
    Socioeconomic status

Life Cycle
    Age (Head of household)
    Average age of family
    Family life-cycle category
    Employment status (Head of household)

Building on this demographic research, Richard B. Ellis (1974), Director, AT&T Advanced Information Systems, developed a composite demographic matrix based on socioeconomic stages and family life-cycle categories to create distinct *consumer cells,* each representing a segment of a particular size and market potential. His matrix is depticted in table 19-2. The percentage of the population in each cell reflects the intersection of family life-cycle and socioeconomic classes. This matrix represented AT&T's first movement from a single variable demographic segmentation to a matrix segmentation capturing the overlap of distinctly different demographic variables.

Although demographic segmentation had consistently provided actionable consumer insights, researchers at AT&T felt that the utilization of demographic variables had reached a point where it was time to explore variables that provided information about a different facet of consumer behavior. In particular, there was general agreement that attention should be given to understanding the attitudes and lifestyles of customers for particular telephone products and services.

Stage Two: Attitudinal Segmentation

By the mid-1970s, AT&T developed its initial battery of attitudinal-psychographic statements (Roscoe et al. 1977). After intensive exploratory research,

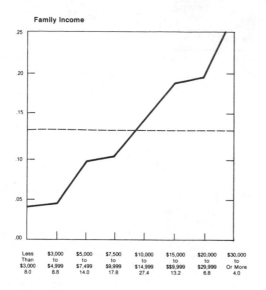

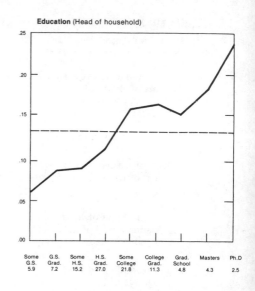

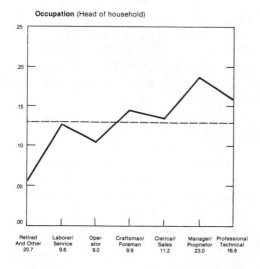

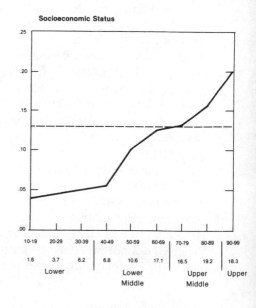

Figure 19–2. The Relationship Between Selected Demographic Variables and Touch-Tone Service Penetration

Table 19–2
The Socioeconomic/Family Life-Cycle Grid

		Socioeconomic Class				Life-Cycle Totals
		Lower	*Lower Middle*	*Upper Middle*	*Upper*	
L i f e - C y c l e C a t e g o r y	No Children	1.5	5.7	6.8	2.9	16.9
	Younger Children	0.9	6.2	8.1	4.3	19.5
	Older Children	1.4	8.7	10.8	4.8	25.7
	Older Households	12.5	13.5	8.8	3.1	37.9
	SES Class Totals	16.3	34.1	34.5	15.1	100.0

Source: Developed by Richard Ellis, AT&T.

the battery was reduced to 32 statements, a sample of which is presented in figure 19–3. (In later versions of the questionnaire, both the instructions and number of scale points were simplified.) From this battery of items, the following four attitudinal factors were derived: (1) thriftiness, (2) gadget-oriented, (3) fashion innovativeness, and (4) keeping-in-touch. The specific attitudinal-psychographic statements that comprise each of these four factors are presented in table 19–3.

Profiles that combined the new attitudinal data with the established demographic data were developed for the customers for each of AT&T's products and services. Table 19–4 summarizes the kind of information that was obtained from Touch-Tone Service customers. This led to the preparation of descriptively rich narrative profiles which were used in the development of promotional strategy.

Indeed, realizing that attitudinal-psychographic profiles are primarily useful for preparing advertising and promotional content, and that

Understanding what the telephone means to you, how you use it, and how it fits into your life is important to us in planning for your telephone needs. Each of the following statements is about telephones or how they fit into your life. Please read each statement and then put an X in the box which best indicates how strongly you agree or disagree with the statement in terms of your home phone. For example, if you strongly agree with a statement, you would put an X in the 3 box (⊠). If you somewhat disagree, you would put an X in the −2 box (⊠). If you neither agree or disagree, you would put an X in the "O" box (⊠).

	Completely Agree			Neither Agree nor Disagree			Completely Disagree
I spend a lot of time talking on the telephone	+3	+2	+1	0	−1	−2	−3
People who have stylish telephones are lucky because they can afford them	+3	+2	+1	0	−1	−2	−3
We live a long way from our friends and relatives	+3	+2	+1	0	−1	−2	−3
Those who know me would consider me to be thrifty	+3	+2	+1	0	−1	−2	−3
I need several telephones in my home because of my work/business	+3	+2	+1	0	−1	−2	−3
I am influential in my neighborhood	+3	+2	+1	0	−1	−2	−3
Pushbutton telephones probably break down a lot	+3	+2	+1	0	−1	−2	−3

Figure 19–3. Sample of Attitudinal-Psychographic Statements from an Early AT&T Study

demographic segmentation is principally useful for making media decisions, there was an ongoing effort to refine Ellis' (1974) original socioeconomic/ family life-cycle grid. This effort led to a new residence market segmentation model to guide aspects of AT&T's marketing strategy (see table 19–5). This new segmentation model was designed to reflect, as much as possible, the maximum differences in telephone buying behavior among groups of consumers.

It was necessary to determine which of these segments represented the greatest potential for specific products and services. This was accomplished

Table 19-3
Four Factors Derived from the Attitudinal-Psychographic Battery

Thriftiness

People who have stylish telephones are lucky because they can afford them.

Those who know me would consider me to be thrifty.

I usually look for the lowest possible prices when I shop.

I usually wait to learn how good a new product is before trying it.

Gadget-Oriented

A pushbutton phone is for people with more money than they know what to do with.

I find pushbutton telephones unattractive.

I prefer pushbutton phones even though they are more expensive.

A dial light on a telephone is an example of an unnecessary luxury.

The trimline phone is very stylish.

I prefer colored appliances.

I wouldn't pay extra for a decorator telephone.

Keeping-In-Touch

I prefer to have several telephones in my home as a convenience.

My home is small so I don't need more than one telephone.

I need several telephones in my home because of my work/business.

I spend a lot of time talking on the telephone.

I probably make more long distance calls than most people I know.

We frequently have someone in the family away from home.

My home is an open house, with friends and neighbors always visiting.

Fashion Innovator

If a new style of telephone were introduced, I would be more likely to get it than my friends.

We will probably move within the next three years.

I would enjoy moving to a different part of the country.

When I must choose between the two, I usually dress for fashion, not comfort.

I admit that I dress to please others.

I enjoy trying new products when they first come out.

Table 19–4
A Profile of Touch-Tone Customers in Terms of Four Attitudinal-Psychographic Factors

Demographics
Young head of household
Upscale
Large dwelling
Been more mobile

Gadget-Oriented	*Keeping-In-Touch*
Prefer expensive features	Several phones
Mechanical interests	Talk a lot on phone
Colorful appliances	Family on the go

Fashion Innovators	*Thriftiness*
More innovative	Not thrifty
New products	Risk-takers
Fashion conscious	
More mobile	

by developing a series of discriminant models in which each product/service (e.g., Custom Calling Services) was the dependent variable and a series of demographic and attitudinal variables were used as independent variables. The growth potential of each segment for these products and services amounted to millions of dollars in increased revenue for the Bell System.

Table 19–5
A Seven-Segment Model of the Residence Customer Market

	SES		
Children	High SES Young Singles/Couples	Low SES Singles/ Couples	Retired
	High SES Mature Singles/Couples		
	High SES Young Families	Low SES Families	
	High SES Mature Families		

Once this potential was established, the critical issue became the content of the message or "what to say" to the households comprising each high potential segment. To this end, table 19-6 illustrates the next step taken, which was to superimpose the data reflecting the four attitudinal factors onto each demographically derived segment. Table 19-6 shows the importance of each attitudinal factor in relation to each residence market segment. For instance, contrasting the High SES Young Family segment and the High SES Mature Family segment reveals that both were highly interested in keeping-in-touch; however, the young family segment is more fashion conscious and more concerned with thriftiness than the mature family segment. As an additional step, using the attitudinal statements that comprise each factor, narrative profiles were written for each residence market segment in order to develop a basis for creating promotional and advertising messages. This experience presses home the importance of values in distinguishing groups of customers.

About this same time, AT&T Long Lines was conducting a massive research study of consumers' attitudes pertaining to long distance calling and other modes of communication. Multivariate statistical analysis of the results revealed six distinct segments of the residence long distance market.

Six Long Distance Market Segments	Share of Population (%)
Routine communicators	18
Emotional communicators	17
Anxious worriers	16
Budgeters	18
Detached communictors	14
Functionalists	17

Further analysis revealed that the Routine Communicators, who constituted 18 percent of the population, could be characterized as follows:

Predominant attitude: Long distance is seen as an obligatory, everyday, necessary tool for frequent communication

Demographics: Younger, high socioeconomic status, high mobility

Lifestyle: Generally show stronger interest in most activity areas, especially cultural and social activities and prestige sports

Long distance usage: Highest monthly expenditures, most calls per month, longer than average calls

Community of interest: Largest number of communication contact among friends and relatives, highest telephone share

Reaction to long distance concepts: Stronger than average interest

Table 19–6

The Relationship Between the Seven-Segment Model and the Four Attitudinal-Psychographic Factors

Residence Market Segment	Keeping In Touch	Gadget-Oriented	Fashion Innovators	Thriftiness
Low SES Single Couple	1(−)	2(−)	4(−)	3(+)
Low SES Family	2(−)	3(+)	4(−)	1(+)
High SES Young Single Couple	4(−)	2(+)	1(+)	3(−)
High SES Young Family	1(+)	3(+)	2(+)	4(+)
High SES Mature Family	1(+)	2(+)	4(+)	3(−)
High SES Mature Single Couple	1(+)	4(+)	3(+)	2(−)
Retired	1(−)	3(−)	2(−)	4(+)

+ = Positive loading.
− = Negative loading.
Note: 1 = highest; 4 = lowest.

In contrast, the Budgeters, who were also 18 percent of the population, could be characterized as follows:

Predominant attitude: Are very conscious of the cost of long distance calls—feel they're a luxury

Demographics: Mostly females, higher incidence of widowed, divorced, or separated; lower socioeconomic status

Lifestyle: Stronger interest in handicrafts and social clubs

Long distance usage: Lower than average monthly expenditures, fewer calls per month, shorter than average calls

Community of interest: Average number of contacts, lowest telephone share

Reaction to long distance concepts: Average interest

This type of analysis led to the creation of two of AT&T Long Lines' most successful advertising campaigns—"Feelings" and "Reach Out and Touch Someone."

Stage Three: Values and Lifestyles Segmentation

In 1980, AT&T product management needed more detailed information on Design Line* Telephone customers; that is, customers of The Mickey Mouse

---

* Registered mark of American Telecommunications Corp.

Phone,* the Candlestick** phone, the Snoopy and Woodstock Phone,†
etc. Basically, they wanted to determine what personal value differences, if
any, existed among owners of the various Design Line Telephone models.

A questionnaire was developed to explore the interrelationship between
demographics, psychographics, media exposure, and value orientations of
customers owning various Design Line Telephones. Detailed analysis of the
results of this line of research again led to the creation of narrative profiles
of the customers for each Design Line Telephone model. An excerpt from
the Snoopy and Woodstock Phone customer profile follows:

> The Snoopy and Woodstock Phone customers can be characterized as
> basically 'at ease' and 'informal' people. Therefore, it is not surprising to
> find that they prefer home decorations that are both practical and relaxed
> in nature. Specifically, when it comes to home furnishings, they favor
> creating a 'homey' rather than an 'elegant' atmosphere. Similarly, they
> perceived their living rooms as being more casual than formal, and they
> seek durability over fashionability in their choice of furniture. Further-
> more, they seem somewhat unadventurous, being drawn to the safe and
> uniform rather than the unique and unusual (e.g., they tend to avoid mixing
> styles of furniture in a room). Nevertheless, they accept the idea that a phone
> does *not* have to match the decor of a room. Given their preference for in-
> formal and conventional furnishings, it is understandable that they are not
> particularly likely candidates for the services of an interior decorator.

As a further example of the type of information obtained, table 19–7
contrasts owners of The Mickey Mouse Phone and The Snoopy and Woodstock Phone. While it was assumed initially that the two phones would appeal to the same group of customers because they were both character
phones, in actuality there were some meaningful differences. Specifically,
The Mickey Mouse Phone appealed to all ages within the large $15,000–
$25,000 family income range; The Snoopy and Woodstock Phone appealed
to a younger, more affluent market segment. More significant in capturing
lifestyles and values, the results revealed that The Mickey Mouse Phone
customers' activities were centered around the home as a place to entertain
family and friends, and this character phone was more likely to be located
in a family room where it was readily observable. In contrast, purchasers of
The Snoopy and Woodstock Phone were outdoor people who embraced a
wide variety of physical and recreational activities. In keeping with their
generally more informal outlook, they located their character phone in the
child's room where it was less likely to be observed by adult visitors.

---

* ©Walt Disney Productions; Housing Produced by American Telecommunications Corp.
** Registered mark of American Telecommunications Corp.
† Housing manufactured by American Telecommunications Corp.; Peanuts Characters©
1958, 1965 United Feature Syndicate, Inc.

Table 19-7
A Lifestyle-Values Comparison of Owners of Two Character Telephones

Descriptor	The Mickey Mouse Phone	The Snoopy and Woodstock Phone
Dominant psychographic traits	Eclectic in home decorating outlook	At east/informal
Age	Broad age appeal	Under 35 years old
Family income	Between $15,000 and $25,000	Over $25,000
Room placement	Family room	Child's room
Total phone impact	Replacement of premium set	Additional set
Mass media	Low TV and magazine readers	Low media
Lifestyle activities	Home and family/friends oriented	Physically and recreationally active

These customer profiles were used by various Bell System operating telephone companies to position particular Design Line Telephones to particular lifestyle segments. For instance, one operating company developed a sales information guide to aid its retail sales personnel in identifying shoppers who would most likely find particular models appealing.

Stage Four: Long Distance
Competitive Segmentation

With the split-up of the Bell System, the orientation of the consumer panel has been refocused on long distance usage instead of a wider range of usage behavior (i.e., both long distance and local calling), telephone products, and related services. The thrust of these changes resulted in an expansion of the panel to enable AT&T to study the effects of competition in the long distance market.

VALS and AT&T

Superimposed onto AT&T's ongoing research efforts has been its involvement with the SRI VALS program (for a detailed discussion of VALS, see chapter 18). AT&T has approached the use of the VALS data in a number of different ways. Early experiences concentrated on tying in the VALS profile of various value segments with profiles of AT&T's products and services subscribers. This was largely an *intuitive matching process* and relied heavily on face validity.

A second effort was to develop a data base which contained information about telephone customers' equipment and long distance usage and their VALS classification. This resulted in the preparation of a purchasing index which portrayed product/service usage levels by VALS type. Figures 19-4 and 19-5 illustrate this application. In particular, figure 19-4 reveals

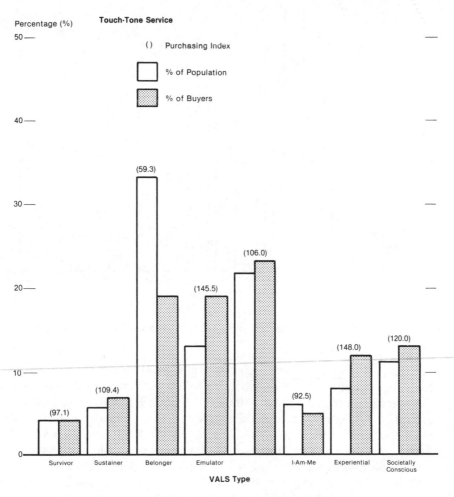

Figure 19-4.   Touch-Tone Service Penetration by VALS Types

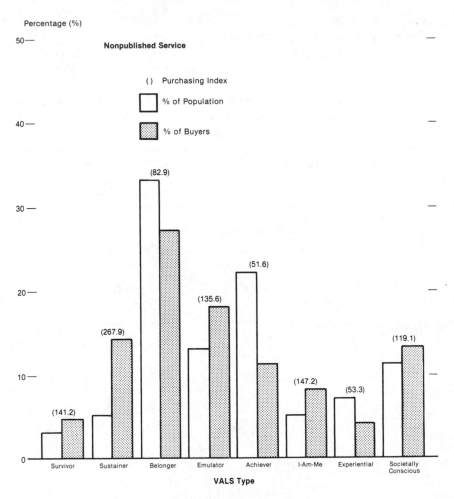

Figure 19-5. Nonpublished Service Penetration by VALS Types

that Emulators, Achievers, Experientials, and Societally Conscious customers are more likely to subscribe to Touch-Tone Service relative to their percent in the population. Similarly, figure 19-5 shows that "extreme groups of customers," composed of Survivors and Sustainers on the one hand and Emulators, I-Am-Me's, and Societally Conscious on the other hand, are more likely to have nonpublished telephone numbers than their relative percent in the population would indicate. It is interesting to note that the Achievers, the group after which the Emulators model themselves, tend to have published telephone numbers. In conjunction with the competitive segmentation of stage 4, AT&T's current efforts involve the exploration of the competitive long distance usage patterns by VALS types.

Conclusion

AT&T has matured over the past 15 years. It has progressed through different research developmental stages, from a purely demographic orientation to one where it is blending internal and syndicated values and lifestyles research. The corporate culture has changed dramatically, too. It has gone from an engineering/production oriented company to a simplistic marketing concern in a regulated environment to a growing marketing organization in a highly competitive environment. The future for AT&T is uncertain at this time, but very exciting.

References

Ellis, Richard B. Composite Population Descriptions: The Socio-Economic/ Life Cycle Grid. In *Advanced in Consumer Research,* II, edited by Mary Jane Schlinger. Ann Arbor: Association for Consumer Research, 1974, 481–493.

Roscoe, A. Marvin, Jr., Arthur LeClaire, Jr., and Leon G. Schiffman. Theory and Management Applications of Demographics in Buyer Behavior. In *Consumer and Industrial Buying Behavior,* edited by Arch Woodside et al. New York: North-Holland, 1977. Pp. 67–76.

20 Environmental Values of Food Cooperative Shoppers

Carla R. Fjeld,
Howard G. Schutz, and
Robert Sommer

The single event that served most to catalyze interest in the environment was the publication in 1962 of Rachel Carson's *Silent Spring,* which had an immediate and strong impact on the public, policymakers, and scientific community. The earlier conservation movement had been largely directed at the preservation of wilderness areas and endangered species. The environmental movement broadened the earlier goals to include quality of life issues, energy policy, pollution effects, and the reduction of demand for scarce, nonrenewable resources. More than the other social movements of its time, the environmental movement affected those values with a direct relationship to consumption. According to Rokeach (1973), values possess a hierarchical interconnected structure and are related to ways of living and behaving. A specific focus of the environmental movement was on reduction or redirection of demand toward products and services which are environmentally benign. Henion (1976) defined the ecologically concerned consumer as being one "whose values, attitudes, intentions, or behaviors exhibit and reflect a relatively consistent and conscious concern for the environmental consequences related to the purchase, ownership, use, or disposal of particular products or services." Such individuals tend to be of the higher strata with respect to education and socioeconomic standing and tend to make their purchases consistent with their attitudes regarding personal well-being, society, and ecology (Belch 1979).

The concept of trade-offs is critical to an understanding of how environmental consciousness affects behavior in the marketplace. Henion, Gregory, and Clee (1980) indicate that few customers will buy environmentally benign products on the basis of their ecological impact alone. Just as for other products, a bundle of attributes is sought, among which the consumer makes various trade-offs. These investigators found that while environmentally unconcerned consumers were willing to trade off environmental appropriateness for price and function, environmentally concerned consumers, as measured by previous purchase behavior and an index of environmental concern developed by Kinnear and Taylor (1973), were unwilling to subordinate price to ecology.

The term *voluntary simplicity* was used by Gregg (1977) to describe a way of life marked by a balance between inner and outer growth. The term implies frugal consumption, a strong sense of ecological urgency, and a dominant concern with personal growth. In 1976, the Stanford Research Institute (Elgin and Mitchell 1976) concluded that from 8 to 10 million adults in America were living, to varying degrees, lives of voluntary simplicity, and projected that by 1985, 36 million people in the United States, 16 years of age or over, would be living this way. Primary reasons for voluntarily choosing a simplified lifestyle are often highly personal. However, there are broader reasons for the choice which encompass philosophical or political reactions to perceived economic, technological, and moral issues.

Historically, voluntary simplicity has roots in the legendary frugality and self-reliance of the Puritans and in the teachings of spiritual leaders such as Mahatma Gandhi. The contemporary expression of these values is seen in the revival of small-scale technologies, in a preference for integration over specialization, for local control, and for an ecological perspective which emphasizes the interconnectedness of resources and peoples of the world. In terms of buying habits, today's adherents to a simpler style are likely to be characterized more by the consumer items they reject than by the items they purchase. Items which are likely to be avoided or used infrequently by this group are those whose ingredients, containers, or packages are energy-intensive or which seem superfluous.

The type of food cooperative that arose in the 1960s is an embodiment of the new interest in voluntary simplicity. An earlier depression-era wave of cooperatives had come out of the consumer movement and was largely concerned with consumer protection and product quality. The new wave cooperative, as it was sometimes called, was composed of young people primarily interested in ecology and nutrition. The emphasis of the cooperatives is on whole, unprocessed, and minimally processed foods and inducing members to "eat lower on the food chain"—both doctrines consistent with the ecological perspective of the membership. A further tenet of the new wave cooperative is support for local and organic agriculture. Coop stores often work to accomplish this objective by providing the names and addresses of growers and identifying items as organic or not organic. Local seasonal agriculture provides an alternative to more energy-intensive centralized farming procedures, which involve long distance transportation and thereby greater dependence on fossil fuels, excessive packaging dictated by the numerous handling operations and long transportation distances, standardization of food products which lead to the disappearance of local varieties, and excessive dependence on chemical fertilizers, pesticides, and additives. Critics maintain that these trends use excessive amounts of energy and have had an adverse effect on flavor and freshness of fruits and vegetables sold to the consumer (Handy and Pfaft 1975; Whiteside 1977). Supporters of the present marketing system maintain that it brings year-round availability of fresh fruits and vegetables that cannot be grown locally throughout the entire year.

The present study deals with several related questions involving some of the changes in values connected with the environmental movement. The first was to determine whether ecologically aware individuals would be more likely to patronize coops than chain supermarkets. The second was to determine whether coop shoppers and supermarket shoppers are alike in their attitudes toward having certain key produce items in the market throughout the entire year. This seemed an important question because it could be considered a practical outgrowth of a theoretical concern over environmental quality. The third was to determine whether there is a correlation between environmental attitude and the importance of a year-round supply of individually specified fresh fruit and vegetable items.

It was hypothesized that coop shoppers would score higher on proenvironmental attitudes, show a lower preference for out-of-season produce than would supermarket shoppers, and that there would be a negative correlation between proenvironmental attitudes and those toward year-round availability of fresh fruits and vegetables.

Procedures

Respondents were drawn from the shopping populations of five food coop stores in Oregon and California and five chain supermarkets in each of the same neighborhoods in which the cooperatives were located. The coops were all participatory, small-scale coops, with explicit commitments to member-education, bulk sales, and use of basic and minimally processed foods. The two in California were selected for study because of the geographic proximity to our research center; the three in Oregon were selected because they met the merchandising and member-participation criteria. Three trained interviewers approached shoppers and asked whether they would participate in a study of consumer attitudes. Those who agreed were given two scales. The first was concerned with year-round availability of fresh fruits and vegetables. The second was concerned with environmental issues. Respondents read and answered the survey while standing in the market. Interviewers remained close by, but provided no additional information. None of the respondents read the scale of environmental concern before completing the produce availability scale. The produce availability scale was preceded by the following statement:

> Some fruits and vegetables can be seen just about all year in the supermarket. Others are available only during local growing seasons. How important to you personally is it that each of the following foods is available throughout the whole year?

Numbers from 1 (low importance) to 4 (high importance) followed the name of each produce item. It was clearly stated that the questions referred to fresh rather than canned or frozen items. The items, listed in alphabetical order, were apples, asparagus, bananas, bell peppers, broccoli, cantaloupe, corn, green beans, Thompson grapes, lettuce, peaches, pears, pineapple, strawberries, tomatoes, and zucchini.

Also administered was the 16-item Environmental Concern scale which covers conservation and pollution issues (Weigel and Weigel 1978; Rozee-Koker and Dowell 1980). Respondents were asked to rate each statement along a five-point Likert-type scale ranging from strongly agree to strongly disagree. Seven of the statements are worded positively, so that a strong interest in ecology will be indicated by agreement with the statement. Nine are phrased negatively. The 16 items were selected by Weigel and Weigel (1978) from a pool of 31 conservation and pollution items used by Tognacci et al. (1972). The 16 were selected on the basis of their internal consistency (Cronbach's alpha coefficient = .88) and item-criteria correlations of 0.12 to 0.42 and a scale-criterion correlation of 0.58 ($p < .001$). Weigel et al. (1974) had previously conducted a study of the correlation of responses to each item on the scale with behavioral responsiveness to a request from a Sierra Club member for assistance. Each item correlated positively with the behavioral responsiveness which were: agreeing to work on environmental petition ($r = .50$, $p < .01$); litter pick-up campaign ($p < .05$, $r = .36$); and recycling behavior ($p < .01$, $r = .39$).

Results

The coop sample was composed of 94 females and 56 males. The average age of the sample calculated from ages recorded in deciles was 33.3 years. The supermarket sample was composed of 99 females and 68 males. The average age of the sample was 36.2 years. Table 20–1 shows the distribution of respondents within each educational level category.

Table 20–1
Distribution of Respondents According to Level of Education

	Cooperative		Supermarket	
	Frequency	*Percent*	*Frequency*	*Percent*
Some high school	1	0.7	11	6.6
High school graduate	15	10.2	24	14.4
Some college	57	38.8	67	40.4
College graduate	37	25.2	38	22.9
Postgraduate	37	25.2	26	15.7
Missing	3	—	1	—
Total	150	100.0	167	100.0

For scoring purposes, answers to the nine Environmental Concern statements which had been phrased in the negative were reversed. Thus, a higher score indicated a greater environmental concern. The average concern score of coop shoppers (N = 150) was 67.7 and for supermarket shoppers (N = 167) was 60.3 This gives item averages of 4.2 (± 0.45 SD) and 3.8 (± 0.61 SD), respectively.

Two analyses of covariance of the response data, one from the Environmental Concern scale and the other from the Produce Availability scale, were done using a fixed effects model, with state and market as factors and education as a covariate. The dependent variables were the attitudes toward the environment and produce availability. The state factor had two levels: Oregon and California. The market factor also had two levels: supermarket and cooperative. The analysis of covariance was done in order to reduce systematic bias in the response data which might be related to educational level. Table 20-2, which lists the average scores on each scale distributed according to educational level, shows that as educational level increases, environmental awareness follows suit. The results of the analysis of covariance of the environmental concern data are summarized in table 20-3. Since market was shown to be a statistically significant main effect, a two-tailed t test was done. The difference between the two types of markets (coops and supermarkets) on the environmental scale was found to be statistically significant. Coop shoppers had higher proenvironmental attitudes than supermarket shoppers (t = 7.49, df = 315, $p < .001$).

The importance respondents attached to the year-round availability of individual select produce items was indicated by choosing a value from 1 (low importance) to 4 (high importance). Responses to the 16-item scale were summed and the average for each respondent used in subsequent analyses. The average rating by the supermarket shoppers was 44.8 (N = 166) and by the coop shoppers, 38.4 (N = 150). This gives item averages of 2.8 (± 0.61 SD) and 2.4 (± 0.73 SD), respectively.

Table 20-2
Response to Environmental Concern Scale by Educational Level

Educational Level	Cooperative			Supermarket			Averages for Both Markets
	Mean	N	SD	Mean	N	SD	
Some high school	4.00	1	0.00	3.62	11	0.61	3.65
High school graduate	4.11	15	0.54	3.41	24	0.55	3.68
Some college	4.17	57	0.47	3.79	67	0.62	3.96
College graduate	4.43	37	0.28	3.86	38	0.62	4.14
Postgraduate	4.12	37	0.49	3.99	26	0.52	4.07

Table 20-3
Summary of Analysis of Covariance of Environmental Concern Data

| | Unmatched (i.e., total respondents) | | | |
	Sum of Squares	df	F	p
Total	108.010	312		
Main effects				
State	1.578	1	5.597	.02
Market	14.195	1	50.345	<.001
Covariate				
Educational level	5.861	1	20.786	<.001
Market × State	0.364	1	1.291	NS
Mean square error	86.842	308		

Table 20-4 shows the breakdown by educational level of the produce availability response data. As educational level increases, the average importance respondents give to the year-round availability of select individual produce items decreases.

The analysis of covariance with the 16-item average response data from the produce attitude scale as the dependent variable, market and state as main effects, and educational level as a covariate is summarized in table 20-5. This analysis shows that, with educational level held constant, the market (i.e., whether respondents were shoppers in the supermarket or cooperative) had a highly reliable impact on their interest in the year-round availability of the respective individual produce items ($p < .001$). Neither state (Oregon or California) nor the two-way interaction of state and market were found to be effects with statistically significant bearing on the Produce Availability score. The difference between the two types of markets (coop and supermarket) on the Produce Availability scale was found to be statistically significantly ($t = 5.25$, $df = 315$, $p < .001$). A consistent, year-round supply of select individual produce items is less important to the coop shopper than it is to the supermarket shopper.

Table 20-4
Attitude toward Produce Availability by Educational Level

| Educational Level | Cooperative | | | Supermarket | | | |
	Mean	N	SD	Mean	N	SD	Total
Some high school	3.81	1	0.00	2.87	11	0.56	2.95
High school graduate	2.70	15	0.73	2.74	24	0.59	2.72
Some college	2.40	57	0.71	2.86	67	0.64	2.65
College graduate	2.39	37	0.70	2.80	38	0.62	2.60
Postgraduate	2.30	37	0.74	2.62	26	0.54	2.43

Table 20–5
Summary of Analysis of Covariance of Produce Availability Data

	Sum of Squares	df	F	p
Total	148.107	312		
Main effects				
State	0.546	1	1.250	NS
Market	8.711	1	19.949	< .001
Covariate				
Educational level	3.750	1	8.586	.004
Mean square error	134.498	308		

To determine whether the relatively higher environmental concern and lower interest in the year-round availability of each of the seasonal produce items were correlated, a series of Pearson's correlation coefficients was calculated. None of the samples, whether treated as an aggregate of coops or supermarkets, or whether further distinguished by state and market type, showed a statistically significant correlation between the Environmental scale and the Produce Availability scale.

Discussion

Environmental concern is not an all-or-none phenomenon, but rather is felt to varying degrees by individuals and among individuals whether shoppers in the supermarket or cooperative market setting. However, given both interpersonal and intergroup variations in the degree of environmental concern expressed, the most important findings from this study are the greater concern for environmental quality and relatively less importance attached to year-round availability of respective produce items by shoppers in the food cooperative.

The average environmental concern response in both markets studied exceeded the scores of Sierra Club members in the 1978 study conducted by Weigel and Weigel. Several explanations for this can be suggested. One is that at least four years have elapsed since the previous study was done. During that time, environmental concern may have generally increased. However, Henion, Gregory, and Clee (1980) maintain that environmental concern has decreased during the past decades. When selecting products, consumers are giving greater importance to price than to ecological attributes. A more likely explanation is that the Weigel and Weigel study was done on the East Coast, whereas the current study was undertaken in California and Oregon, two states known for their environmental activism.

Knowledge of marketing priorities and of the simple physical setting of coops suggests cooperatives and their shoppers are distinguishable from the traditional market and from the society-at-large. They are distinguishable in part by virtue of a greater concern for the quality of the environment. This is evidenced by the results of the study of enviromental concern. The significant difference in the importance of having all 16 produce items available throughout the year suggests environmental concern is manifest in attitudes associated with produce availability. Coop shoppers consider a year-round supply of individual produce items to be less important than do supermarket shoppers. There are a multitude of factors which could play a role in this difference, such as flavor, color, etc. But among them must be a concern about the economies, both monetary and environmental, of mass production and long distance transport and storage.

Since the marketplace setting influences the demand for food items, it will be helpful to delineate features of the food market that will support an ecological perspective. First, there must be a recognition by the consumer that doing without is not excessively burdensome or tortuous, but instead can be practiced with only slight modification of existing consumption habits and modes of living. Relative to the present study, support for local seasonal agriculture can mean substituting some fresh fruit and vegetable items for others in the diet and increased use of canning, freezing, and other home preservation methods. A second requirement is that the physical setting and products available should uphold rather than detract from the values of material simplicity. Third, facts pertaining to the foods should be available. What are the ecological and financial costs associated with our present food production and distribution systems? In other words, why move toward small- and intermediate-scale technologies? Fourth, there should be opportunities for grower-consumer interactions. These could range from signs in the store transmitting information between growers and consumers to consumer-grower public forums. To varying degrees, each of these is being attempted in the cooperative and may partially explain why we found both a higher environmental concern and a higher regard for in-season produce than among the population-at-large.

References

Belch, M.A. Identifying the socially and ecologically concerned segment through life-style research: Initial findings. In *The Conserver Society,* edited by K.E. Henion, II and T.C. Kinnear. Chicago: American Marketing Association, 1979, 69–81.

Carson, Rachel Louise. *Silent Spring.* Boston: Houghton Mifflin, 1962.

Elgin, D., and A. Mitchell. Voluntary Simplicity. *Business Intelligence Program Guidelines,* 1976, p. 1004.

Esfandiary, F.M. Homo Sapiens, the Manna Maker. In *The Feeding Web: Issues in Nutritional Ecology*, edited by J.D. Gussow. Palo Alto, Calif.: Bull Publishing Company, 1978. Pp. 28–29.

Fjeld, C.R., and R. Sommer. Regional-Seasonal Patterns in Produce Consumption at Farmers' Markets and Supermarkets. *Ecology of Food and Nutrition* 12 (2) (1982):211–215.

Gregg, R. Voluntary Simplicity. *CoEvolution Quarterly* 14 (1977):20–27.

Handy, D.R. and M. Pfaft. Consumer Satisfaction with Food Products and Marketing Services. *U.S.D.A. Economic Research Service Agricultural Economics Report*, 1975, 281.

Henion, K.E. *Ecological Marketing*. Columbus, Ohio: Grid Inc., 1976.

Henion, K.E., R. Gregory, and M.A. Clee. Trade-Offs in Attribute Levels Made by Environmentally Concerned and Unconcerned Consumers when Buying Detergents. *Advances in Consumer Research* 8 (1980): 624–629.

Kinnear, T.C., and J.R. Taylor. The Effect of Ecological Concern on Brand Perceptions. *Journal of Marketing Research* 10 (1973):191–197.

Kreitner, P. Research: Who Shops Co-Op, and Why? *The New Harbinger* 3 (1976):11–17.

Mayer, J. Saving Energy in the Food System. *The Professional Nutritionist* 13 (1981):1–4.

Rokeach, M. *The Nature of Human Values*. New York: MacMillan, 1973.

Ronco, W. *Food Co-Ops: An Alternative to Shopping in Supermarkets*. Boston: Beacon Press, 1974. P. 23.

Rose, B. Proaction, Inc. *New Harbinger* 4 (1977):37–41.

Rozee-Koker, P., and D.A. Dowell. Environmental Concern and a Critical Belief System. Paper presented at the *Western Psychological Association Annual Convention*, Honolulu, Hawaii, 1980.

Tognacci, L.N., R.H. Weigel, M.F. Wideen, and D.T.A. Vernon. Environmental Quality: How Universal Is Public Concern? *Environment and Behavior* 4 (1972):73–86.

Weigel, R.H., D.T.A. Vernon, and L.N. Tognacci. The Specificity of Attitude as a Determinant of Attitude-Behavior Congruence. *Journal of Personality and Social Psychology* 30 (1974):724–729.

Weigel, R., and J. Weigel. Environmental Concern—The Development of a Measure. *Environment and Behavior* 10 (1) (1978):3–15.

Whiteside, T. Tomatoes. *New Yorker* (January 24, 1977):35–62.

21 Marketing to Volunteers: An Exploratory Study of Values and Other Characteristics of Contestant Fund-Raisers and Dropouts

Jeffrey S. Gutenberg and
Cheryl E. Kleist

A distinguishing feature of charitable nonprofit organizations is the need to establish appropriate exchange relationships with two customer publics: those who receive the benefits of the organizations' output and those who provide the financial resources (Shapiro 1973). In most common marketing exchanges (e.g., business-customer transactions), the consumers of the primary output provide financial resources in return. The nonprofit charitable organization must establish marketing programs which attract donors or other resource providers, as well as programs designed to attract resource consumers.

As poor economic conditions and planned reductions in government expenditures have resulted in increased competition in private donor markets, nonprofit charitable organizations have sought novel methods of increasing contributions from this sector. One such program is a touch-a-thon currently used by a private kidney disease foundation in the northeastern United States, as well as charitable organizations in other locations. This event offers a new car to the contestant who can touch the car in a required manner (e.g., with hand, elbow, etc.) without losing contact for a longer period of time than any other contestant. The required method of touching is changed every four hours. In 1982, the winner had to endure for over seventy hours before all of the other contestants had given in to fatigue. In order to become a contestant, however, applicants had to raise money for this kidney disease organization by soliciting funds from friends, neighbors, and relatives or by any other means they could devise. The top thirty fund-raisers qualify to win the car by participating in the actual touch-a-thon. Applicants (fund-raisers) are attracted initially by common promotional methods (newspaper and broadcast advertising, press releases, etc.).

There are many advantages to this fund-raising technique or to similarly structured fund-raising promotions. The charitable organization can enjoy the fund-raising services of many persons who, presumably, would otherwise not volunteer their efforts. Since the fund-raising period is of a relatively short duration (six weeks for this touch-a-thon), the long-run problems of managing a sales force (fund-raising staff) are avoided. A minimal budget is required because the main prize and minor consolation prizes are donated. Finally, given the diversity of contestants, market segments (sources of funds) which may otherwise not be targeted are utilized effectively.

The unusual structure of such an event poses many questions for one seeking to better understand the marketing dynamics of a contest or fund-raising promotion in order to improve its effectiveness. The first of these concerns the nature of those who enter the fund-raising promotion. What values do such persons hold and how do personal values relate to fund-raising behavior? Second, these programs have extremely high dropout rates. What differences in values and other characteristics distinguish those who continue competing in the fund-raising contest from those who start but do not continue? Third, how do these dropouts—those who have been marketed successfully up to the point of their dropping out—respond to attempts to re-ignite their interest?

These issues of values are important because values are considered to predispose individual behavior. Values may be thought of as enduring beliefs about behaviors or states of existence which are preferred to other behaviors or states of existence (Rokeach 1968). Thus, the values imbedded in promotional appeals for volunteers and in the incentive systems of volunteer programs would be likely to have an impact on the effectiveness of volunteer attraction. The attrition rate also may be related to values for volunteering. Organizational efforts to market to volunteers and to attract and maintain their services will be more productive if the correct values are addressed.

Voluntary behavior has been studied extensively by psychologists and, especially, sociologists for many years. Most studies concerned with the values of volunteers have examined members of voluntary associations rather than service volunteers, who may not perceive themselves to be members of the organization for which they are working. The results of one study of participation indicated that, in general, the values of voluntary association participants (members) were related to the values reflected in the association's incentives system (Houghland and Christenson 1979). For service volunteers, this would imply that a program designed to entice voluntary activity by offering an automobile as the primary appeal would tend to attract persons with materialistic values more than those who have stronger social, religious, or other orientations.

While there appear to be no published studies concerned specifically with the values of fund-raising volunteers or contestants in a fund-raising promotion, several have been concerned with the values and other characteristics of other volunteer workers, especially in social service contexts. Mahoney and Pechura (1980) compared the values of crisis center hotline telephone volunteers to a matched control group. Both groups were made up of college students. The results showed that volunteers were more altruistic, had more highly developed interests in social activity, and evidenced an increased need for inner direction. Begalla (1977) found that female volunteer workers valued work (paid employment), volunteer work, and homemaking behavior, in that order. These rankings were similar to those of groups of male and female supervisory employees. Nonsupervisory, nonvolunteer female employees also ranked work as most important, but they judged volunteer behavior as the least valued. Horn (1973) compared three matched groups on self-actualizing values and community-centered values. The two volunteer groups displayed a greater number of community-centered and self-actualizing values than the third, nonvolunteer group. Further, one of the volunteer groups was involved in high risk work (working with emotionally disturbed persons), while the other was performing low risk volunteer work (hospital receptionist). The high risk group expressed more self-actualizing values than the low risk group. These studies seem to show that service volunteers have different values than nonvolunteers, and that values affect the type of volunteer service chosen. Sager (1974) determined that the values of subjects who performed volunteer work with the retarded did not change after nine weeks of such service, thereby indicating the endurance of the values of volunteers. (This is to be expected, as values are conceived of as enduring orientations.)

Values are also reflected in expressed motives for providing volunteer service. MacDonald (1972) used three different enticements to attract student volunteers: pay, extra credit for course work, and love of science. (Of course, those working for pay are not volunteers.) The extra credit incentive was the most effective of the three. Chapman (1981) also examined the motives of student volunteers and found that of five factors, gaining work-related experience ranked ahead of academic reasons, which ranked second. However, gaining experience was not offered as an incentive in the MacDonald study. The motives of volunteers of Youthline, a telephone counseling service in New Zealand, reflected altruistic values (concern for others), self-actualizing values (personal growth), and social values (friendship, companionship) as the three most dominant (Drummond 1980). A study of adult 4-H leaders showed that rewards sought varied according to age and location of residence: young, urban dwellers preferred intrinsic rewards, while the older, rural volunteers favored extrinsic incentives (Burnette 1979).

Attrition has been studied much less frequently than volunteering. Mahoney and Pechura (1980) examined values differences between crisis center volunteers who completed volunteering and those who dropped out, and suggested that "value differences are critical in the volunteer selection process but are generally unimportant in retention'' (p. 1011). In a study by Fretz (1979), college student volunteers who dropped out (within one year of entering) of a social service program had tended to list understanding others as the reason for volunteering, while those who stayed had entered for personal rewards (understand myself or improve my interpersonal skills). In the touch-a-thon, this would imply that those who initially volunteer for materialistic reasons (winning the car) would be less likely to drop out than others who volunteer for altruistic values (helping those with kidney disease).

It became apparent that attrition is of major concern in promotions of this type. As marketing problems, the task of attracting participants is less difficult to deal with than the task of maintaining them. Given the relative lack of research findings applicable to this problem, especially in the context of fund-raising volunteers, it was decided that three important issues would be investigated:

1. How do continuing volunteer fund-raisers differ from dropouts in their value orientations regarding the fund raising event?
2. What other characteristics differentiate the two groups?
3. How effective are value-directed appeals in reactivating dropouts?

Method

Subjects

A total of sixty-three subjects participated in the study. All had enlisted as volunteer fund-raisers/contestants in the touch-a-thon and therefore had agreed to collect donations and to report their collections on a weekly basis, in return for the opportunity to win a new automobile if they were one of the top thirty fund-raisers. Of this total, thirty-three had reported their collections at least once during the first three weeks of the fund-raising period. The remaining thirty had attended the initial orientation meeting for contestants and had completed an application form, but they had not reported any money collected at any time.

Materials

Information about the subjects was obtained from a self-administered questionnaire completed prior to the beginning of the orientation meeting, which preceded the fund-raising period. Values were assessed by asking how important (on a scale of very important, somewhat important, or not important) the following were in their desire to enter the contest: to win a car; to win other prizes; to help the kidney disease foundation; to have fun with other people; to participate in an exciting public event. Other questions on the questionnaire were designed to obtain information about the subjects' self-confidence, organization, demographics, and media exposure.

Procedure

Volunteers classified as dropouts were contacted by telephone three weeks after the beginning of the fund-raising period and asked to start participating. After the appeal was made, the subjects were asked if they now planned to do so as a measure of behavioral intention, as well as their reason(s) for not participating thus far. Seven of the dropouts could not be contacted, reducing the size of this group to twenty-three. Two appeals were used. The first was a win the car message which emphasized that there was still a good chance to be one of the top fund-raisers and subsequently win the car. The second appeal focused on helping the kidney disease foundation; subjects were told that their efforts were needed to provide funds for kidney disease research and other programs of this organization. The win appeal was used with thirteen subjects who had expressed a materialistic orientation by either indicating that winning the car was the only most important reason for entering, or by indicating that all reasons were most important. The second response was interpreted as primarily a materialistic orientation, with other responses being given because they were seen as socially approved responses. The ten other subjects who chose helping the kidney organization as most important but had not indicated all other categories as such, were given the help appeal. Those subsequently collecting and submitting donations by the end of the collective period were considered reactivated by the appeals.

Results

Three types of analyses were undertaken: (1) the difference in value orientations between active fund-raisers and dropouts, (2) the differentiation of active fund-raisers and dropouts on other characteristics, and (3) the effects of two types of appeals (help or win) on dropouts to become active fund-raisers. These three concerns were of great interest to the kidney organization considering the high attrition rate that is typically experienced among its fund-raisers. Of the 210 individuals expressing initial interest, only 30 percent attended an orientation meeting that was mandatory for all fund-raisers. Further attrition occurred after this meeting and resulted in 33 active fund-raisers or only 16 percent of the original 210. To maximize the number of fund-raisers and to decrease attrition, it was important to determine differences between fund-raisers and dropouts and the effects of appeals on dropouts to become active fund-raisers.

Of those attending the orientation meeting, 30 or 48 percent dropped out and 33 or 52 percent became active fund-raisers. The difference in value orientations between dropouts and fund-raisers was the first type of analysis performed. While both groups most frequently reported a combination of values as the motive for fund-raising (help the kidney disease foundation and win the car), the fund-raisers had far fewer members (6%) compared to the dropouts (20%) with the sole value orientation of winning the car (see table 21-1). Another difference in value orientation between the two groups was the percentage expressing the desire to help the foundation as their most important value; 44 percent of the active fund-raisers expressed this motive, while only 20 percent of the dropouts did so. The value orientations of both groups were significantly different at the .10 level of significance with the likelihood ratio test ($X^2 \times 2$) = 5.45, $p < .10$). The likelihood ratio test was chosen because it is robust for small sample sizes (Hays 1963).

Various statistical tests were calculated to discriminate the active fund-raisers from the dropouts by other characteristics (see table 21-2). Neither sex, the availability of a car while fund-raising, nor previous involvement in the touch-a-thon indicated any significant differences between the two groups ($X^{2'}$ S(1) < 2.71, $p > .10$). However, significant differences between the two groups were evident for age, self-confidence, help received, amount of time devoted to fund-raising, and types of media sources advertising the fund-raising contest. Fund-raisers were significantly older than dropouts and were more varied in age ($t(61) = 6.44, p < .001$). The fund-raisers exhibited significantly greater self-confidence in both winning the car and being among the finalists than did the dropouts ($t(61) > 3.78$, $p < .001$). The fund-raisers also had significantly more people committed to help them than the dropouts ($t(51) = 6.77, p < .001$) and planned to spend significantly more hours a week raising the money ($t(56) = 2.10$,

Table 21-1
A Comparison of Value Orientations of Active Fund-Raisers and Dropouts

Value Orientations[a]	Fund-Raisers	Dropouts
Help others	44%	20%
Win car	6%	20%
Help others and win car	50%	60%

[a]X^2 (2) = 5.45, $p < .10$.

Table 21–2

A Comparison of the Characteristics of Active Fund-Raisers and Dropouts

Characteristics	Active Fund-Raisers	Dropouts	Significance
Age	$\overline{X}$ = 27.23 S = 6.44	$\overline{X}$ = 24.72 S = 5.79	***
Sex	48% Male 52% Female	50% Male 50% Female	NS[a]
Confidence among finalists	$\overline{X}$ = 3.78 S = .42	$\overline{X}$ = 3.35 S = .88	***
Confidence in winning car	$\overline{X}$ = 3.70 S = .68	$\overline{X}$ = 3.53 S = .73	***
Number of people helping	$\overline{X}$ = 13.16 S = 28.76	$\overline{X}$ = 4.23 S = 4.47	***
Hours per week	$\overline{X}$ = 22.43 S = 13.97	$\overline{X}$ = 20.6 S = 11.31	*
Use a car in fund-raising	91% Yes 9% No	83% Yes 17% No	NS
Previous year touch-a-thon involvement	9% Yes 91% No	0% Yes 100% No	NS
Media Print Display Broadcast-TV Broadcast-radio Personal	 20% 20% 19% 23% 18%	 15% 28% 23% 13% 21%	 *

*p < .05.

***p < .001.

[a]NS = nonsignificant.

p < .05) than did the dropouts. Finally, fund-raisers were significantly different from dropouts in the types of media they reported as sources of information about the touch-a-thon ($X^2(4)$ = 10.69, p < .05). The most noticeable differences between the two groups were (1) the most popular media source for fund-raisers (23%), the radio, was the least popular for dropouts (13%); and (2) the most popular media source for dropouts (28%) compared to fund-raisers (20%) was a large display with a sign-up table at a local shopping mall.

The third type of analyses performed was intended to evaluate the effect of a win the car appeal or help the kidney disease foundation appeal on dropouts of similar value orientations. Measures of behavioral intention,

Table 21–3
Reactivation of Dropouts
(in percent)

	Win Appeal	Help Appeal
Reactivated	38	40
Not reactivated	62	60
	100	100
	N = 13	N = 10

p = .69.

actual behavior, and reasons for dropping out were analyzed. Appeals to reactivate were successful with 38 percent of those receiving the win appeal and 40 percent of those given the help appeal, for an overall reactivation rate of 39 percent (see table 21–3). Using Fisher's Exact Test, the difference between the two groups was not statistically significant. Intentions to engage in fund-raising were compared with actual fund-raising. Seventy-seven percent of those given the win appeal and 60 percent of those who received the help appeal intended to begin collecting money. The difference between groups in reactivation after stating the intention to do so was not statistically significant using Fisher's Exact Test (see table 21–4).

A content analysis was used to analyze the reasons dropouts gave for their lack of fund-raising. The three most popular reasons given were illness, too busy, and no chance to win the car, which were represented by 30 percent, 26 percent, and 17 percent, respectively.

Discussion

The first concern of this study was the value differences of fund-raisers and dropouts. Active fund-raisers tended to get involved to help the kidney disease foundation as well as winning a car or just to help, whereas

Table 21–4
Actual Reactivation of Dropouts Who Intended to Raise Funds
(in percent)

	Win Appeal	Help Appeal
Reactivated	50	67
Not reactivated	50	33
	100	100
	N = 10	N = 6

p = .45.

dropouts tended to value the car. This would imply that appeals to contestants and reward systems should emphasize both values in order to attract those who will become active fund-raisers rather than dropouts. Since the marginal administrative costs of dropouts is not severe, the concern is more with the question of what appeals will attract a greater total of desirable contestants rather than the question of how the organization might avoid recruiting future dropouts. It may be that potential fund-raisers do not respond to appeals which only emphasize winning the car because they do not perceive the humanitarian consequences of their involvement. A dual-value appeal would therefore be more effective with this segment. It should be noted that while the statistical significance of the differences in values between the two groups was not especially high ($.05 > p > .1$), this was an exploratory study with a small sample size where probabilities of less than .1 are often considered statistically significant.

Higher levels of significance were found when using other characteristics to distinguish between groups. The finding that older volunteers were less likely to become dropouts implies that recruitment messages targeted specifically to younger audiences (e.g., posters on a junior college campus) would be less productive than those aimed at somewhat older persons. The findings that dropouts were less self-confident and were not as well organized as fund-raisers (planned to have fewer persons helping and to devote fewer hours to fund-raising) implies that organizational efforts to increase organizational skills in planning the fund-raising effort and in increasing self-confidence about such efforts would have a positive effect by reducing the dropout rate. Training sessions, for example, could be established as part of the orientation program. Perhaps the primary goal of these sessions could be to increase fund-raising skills, with the expectation that increased confidence will develop concurrently.

It appears that follow-up attempts to reactivate dropouts are moderately successful. Appeals selected to correspond to the value expressed by the dropout and delivered by telephone led to a positive behavioral response with many participants. The cost of such efforts is low; therefore, reactivation attempts should be made. Such attempts are likely to be as effective with those oriented to winning as to those oriented to helping, although the expressed intention of reactivation is likely to be higher with the win group. Most of the explanations given for dropping out initially (e.g., "I was ill for two weeks"; "My work schedule changed") seemed to be socially acceptable excuses covering a lack of confidence or other reasons.

A final tentative conclusion is that recruitment approaches which require some initial extra effort on the part of the participant will yield higher rates of actual fund-raisers than methods which require no such effort. While the display and information table (with volunteers to explain the contest) in the shopping mall attracted many potential fund-raisers, the dropout rates for participants recruited in this manner was higher than for approaches such as radio announcements or newspaper ads. These methods required that a phone number be called to learn more about the event.

In conclusion, volunteer associations that are dependent on fund-raising and volunteer recruitment for continued existence are likely to try similar contests. As federal and state supported activities decrease and economic hardships make more traditional fund-raising techniques less productive, the fund-raising contest in which the fund-raiser volunteer may win an award of great value is likely to become more popular.

This is especially true for target markets which have been exposed to an increasing number of similar, repetitive fund-raising approaches. These approaches lose their effectiveness as saturation takes place. The present study is rather unique and could not rely on past research for much direction, since these studies were primarily concerned with volunteer work rather than fund-raising behavior, were typically of much longer duration, and did not attempt to reactivate those who had dropped out. The present study, although exploratory, provides valuable insight for other volunteer organizations that may wish to try a similar fund-raising procedure.

References

Begalla, M. The Comparison of the Performance and Achievement Value of Work, Volunteer, and Homemaking Behaviors of Supervisory Male and Female Employees, Non-supervisory Female Employees, and Female Volunteers. *Dissertation Abstracts International* 37 (1977): 7029A–7030A.

Burnette, D. Evaluation of a Learning Module on Incentives in 4-H. *Dissertation Abstracts International* 39 (1979):5457A.

Chapman, T.H. University Students' Reasons for Volunteering. *Dissertation Abstracts International* 41 (1981):4576A.

Drummond, W. Profiles of Youthliners and Issues Relating to a Telephone Counseling Service in a New Zealand City. *Adolescence* 15 (1980): 159–170.

Fretz, B. College Students as Paraprofessionals with Children and the Aged. *American Journal of Community Psychology* 7 (3) (1979):357–360.

Hays, W.L. *Statistics*. New York: Holt, Rinehart & Winston, 1963.

Horn, J. Personal Characteristics of Direct Service Volunteers. *Dissertation Abstracts International* 34 (1973):1725B–1726B.

Houghland, J., and J. Christenson. Voluntary Organizations and Dominant American Values (abstract). *Sociological Abstracts*, 1979, S11413.

MacDonald, A.P., Jr. Characteristics of Volunteer Subjects Under Three Recruiting Methods: Pay, Extra Credit, Love of Science. *Journal of Consulting and Clinical Psychology* 39 (2) (1972):222–234.

Mahoney, J. and C.M. Pechura. Values and Volunteers: Axiology of Altruism in a Crisis Center. *Psychological Reports* 47 (3) (1980):1007–1012.

Rokeach, M. *Beliefs, Attitudes, and Values*. San Francisco: Jossey-Bass, 1968.

Sager, W.A Study of Changes in Attitudes, Values, and Self Concepts of Senior High Youth While Working as Full Time Volunteers with Institutionalized Mentally Retarded People. *Dissertation Abstracts International* 34 (1974):4760A.

Shapiro, B. Marketing for Nonprofit Organizations. *Harvard Business Review* 51 (September-October 1973):123-132.

AUTHOR INDEX

SUBJECT INDEX

Absolution method, 140
Accomplishment, sense of, 81, 82, 149, 235
Achievers, 38, 45, 46–47, 49, 51, 81, 284
Advertising, 7, 111–135, 169–183
"Advertising: Attacks and Counters" (Greyser), 116
Aesthetic values, 149, 151, 220
Affective sphere, 242, 245
Agatha Crum, 93
Age, 15, 17, 18, 83, 145, 174, 220, 268; and prediction of values, 202–204, 206–215; and VALS typology, 41, 43, 45, 49, 51
Alexander the Great, 14
Amae, 261, 262, 266–267
Ambition, 149
American Indians, 94, 95
Americans View Their Mental Health (Gurin et al.), 78
Andy Capp, 87, 91–92, 93, 94
Anglo–Americans, 93, 94, 220
Aristotle, 14
Arm and Hammer deodorant, 57, 60
Arm in Arm deodorant, 57, 60
Arrid deodorant, 57, 60
Ashe, Arthur, 42
Aspirin, 174
AT&T, 271–285
Attitudes: and behavior prediction, 187–198; and consumer choice, 170, 172, 273–280; and education, 242, 244; research techniques, 140–144, 273–280; unconsequential, 220; and values, 7, 8, 9, 17, 77, 85, 139–144
Attribution theory of values, 214
Audience involvement, 169–183
Audubon Club, 73
Authoritarianism, 14
Automobiles: brand identification, 7–8; choice criteria, 10, 15, 55, 57, 60, 61, 64, 220, 232; market segmentation, 171
Axiology, 220

Ban deodorant, 57, 60, 61
Baptists, 82

Beauty, 149
Beer, 11
Beetle Bailey, 93
Being values. *See* Terminal values
Beliefs, 7–9, 157
Bell Operating Companies, 272
Belongers, 38, 43–45
Belonging, 83–84
Benefits, 157–163
Big business, attitude toward, 190–192
Blacks, 80, 231–236; and funnies, 93, 95; income, 231; and middle-class values, 231–236; product expectations, 147–153; and VALS typology, 42
Blondie, 93, 94, 97
Body All deodorant, 57, 60
Born Loser, 93
Brands, 3–12, 22–25, 191–192; comprehension, 170; and Hispanics, 228; identification, 7–8; segmentation, 56–65
Bricoleur, 113
Bringing Up Father, 87
Broad-mindedness, 235
Broom Hilda, 92
Buddhism, 259, 260–261
Budweiser beer, 11
Buster Brown, 87
Buyer behavior: and attitudes, 187–198; research needs, 21, 22–25, 88, 214–215

Cadillac Seville, 57, 60
California, 207, 289, 291–293
Capability, 149
Career counseling, 13, 27, 28–29
Catholics, 83
Cathy, 87
Causal modeling, 21
CB radios, 189, 196
Charitable donations, 15
Charm, 100, 101, 102
Cheerfulness, 61
Chevrolet Chevette, 7–8, 10
Chevrolet Corvette, 57, 60, 61
Chevrolet Impala, 57, 60
Chevrolet Monza, 57, 60

Contributors

Robert P. Bush, Louisiana State University

Lawrence A. Crosby, Arizona State University

Ernest Dichter, Ernest Dichter Motivations, Inc.

Carla R. Fjeld, University of California, Davis

James D. Gill, Arizona State University

Jeffrey S. Gutenberg, State University of New York

Jonathan Gutman, University of Southern California

Joseph F. Hair, Jr., Louisiana State University

Walter A. Henry, University of California, Riverside

Rebecca H. Holman, Young and Rubicam, New York

John A. Howard, Columbia University

Martin I. Horn, Needham, Harper & Stevens

Lynn R. Kahle, University of Oregon

Harold H. Kassarjian, University of California, Los Angeles

Cheryl E. Kleist, State University of New York

Hugh E. Kramer, University of Hawaii

Robert E. Lee, Ford Motor Company

J. Michael Munson, The University of Santa Clara

Thomas E. Ness, University of South Florida

Robert E. Pitts, University of Mississippi

Richard W. Pollay, University of British Columbia

Terry E. Powell, Georgia State University

Ved Prakash, Florida International University

Thomas J. Reynolds, University of Texas, Dallas

Donald P. Robin, Mississippi State University

Leon G. Schiffman, Baruch College, CUNY

Howard G. Schutz, University of California, Davis

Daniel L. Sherrell, Louisiana State University

Robert Sommer, University of California, Davis

Melvin T. Stith, Florida A & M University

Humberto Valencia, Texas Tech University

John J. Veltri, Market Information Systems, AT&T

William D. Wells, Needham, Harper & Stevens

Arch G. Woodside, University of South Carolina

About the Editors

Robert E. Pitts is director of the Bureau of Business and Economic Research and associate professor of marketing at the University of Mississippi. He is a frequent contributor to academic literature, with articles appearing in the *Journal of Marketing,* the *Journal of Advertising,* the *Journal of Consumer Research,* the *Journal of Social Psychology,* the *Journal of Business Research* and the *Southern Economic Review.*

Arch G. Woodside is professor of marketing, University of South Carolina. He is the editor of the *Journal of Business Research,* and coeditor of *Advertising and Consumer Psychology* with Larry Percy (Lexington Books, 1983). He completed his Ph.D. in business administration at Pennsylvania State University in 1968. He is President of Division 23 (Consumer Psychology) of the American Psychological Association for 1983/84.